From the Kitchen to the Parlor

STUDIES IN LANGUAGE AND GENDER
Mary Bucholtz, *General Editor*

Advisory Board
Penelope Eckert, Stanford University
Kira Hall, University of Colorado
Janet Holmes, Victoria University of Wellington, New Zealand
Miyako Inoue, Stanford University
Sally McConnell-Ginet, Cornell University
Marcyliena Morgan, Stanford University
Deborah Tannen, Georgetown University
Ana Celia Zentella, University of California, San Diego

Reinventing Identities: The Gendered Self in Discourse
Edited by Mary Bucholtz, A. C. Liang, and Laurel A. Sutton

Pronoun Envy: Literacy Uses of Linguistic Gender
Anna Livia

Japanese Language, Gender and Ideology: Cultural Models and Real People
Edited by Shigeko Okamoto and Janet S. Shibamoto Smith

Language and Women's Place: Text and Commentaries
Revised and Expanded Edition
By Robin Tolmach Lakoff
Edited by Mary Bucholtz

From the Kitchen to the Parlor: Language and Becoming in African American Women's Hair Care
Lanita Jacobs-Huey

From the Kitchen to the Parlor

Language and Becoming in African American Women's Hair Care

Lanita Jacobs-Huey

OXFORD
UNIVERSITY PRESS

2006

OXFORD

UNIVERSITY PRESS

Oxford University Press, Inc., publishes works that further
Oxford University's objective of excellence
in research, scholarship, and education.

Oxford   New York
Auckland   Cape Town   Dar es Salaam   Hong Kong   Karachi
Kuala Lumpur   Madrid   Melbourne   Mexico City   Nairobi
New Delhi   Shanghai   Taipei   Toronto

With offices in
Argentina   Austria   Brazil   Chile   Czech Republic   France   Greece
Guatemala   Hungary   Italy   Japan   Poland   Portugal   Singapore
South Korea   Switzerland   Thailand   Turkey   Ukraine   Vietnam

Library of Congress Cataloging-in-Publication Data
Jacobs-Huey, Lanita, 1971–
From the kitchen to the parlor : language and becoming in African American women's
hair care / Lanita Jacobs-Huey.
p. cm. — (Studies in language and gender)
Includes bibliographical references and index.
ISBN-13 978-0-19-530415-2; 978-0-19-530416-9 (pbk.)

1. Hairdressing of African Americans.   2. Hair—Social aspects—United States.
3. Hair—Care and hygiene—United States.   4. African American women—History.
5. African American women—Race identity.   6. African American women—Social life and customs.
I. Title.   II. Series.
TT972.J33 2006
391.5'089'96073—dc22   2005050858

Printed in the United States of America
on acid-free paper

for Gwendolyn Stewart,
my first and most cherished hairstylist

FOREWORD

Research on language and gender in African American speech communities dates back at least as far as the notional beginning of the field of language and gender studies in the early 1970s. Yet formany years the intellectual contributions of much of the pioneering scholarship in this area was not fully recognized. This oversight can partly be attributed to a general scholarly inattention to racial and ethnic diversity in the majority of feminist linguistic research, a problem that has hindered the development of other academic disciplines as well. As critics have pointed out, throughout much of its history language and gender research in the United States was primarily focused on the speech of women of the white middle class. Despite the existence of a few influential early studies of black women and girls, only in recent years have language and gender scholars begun to fully acknowledge the theoretical and methodological importance of incorporating a wider range of language users, linguistic varieties, and social contexts into research.

Moreover, a number of early investigators of African American female and male speech—most of them African American themselves—did not receive the attention their work merited from other language and gender researchers because their theoretical, methodological, and political commitments did not conform to then-central trends in the field. This was not simply a matter of being out of step with mainstream concerns, but rather of purposefully developing an alternative perspective that more adequately captured the complex realities of racialized gender and gendered racialization than had yet been offered by dominant feminist linguistic approaches. In part this was a problem shared by feminism more generally: as articulated by European American women, its most visible proponents, feminism often represented the relationship between women and men as inevitably oppositional, with men necessarily seeking and holding power over women. For African American women, this situation seemed to offer an untenable choice between a gender-based alliance with white women or racial solidarity with black men. The explicit focus on comparing women's and men's speech, which long predominated in language and gender research, further reinforced this division by highlighting cross-gender differences in language use rather than points of similarity and commonality.

By contrast, research on language and gender among African Americans was often innovative in taking a deliberately noncomparative approach, in which gender was not foregrounded as the primary explanatory parameter. Speakers' linguistic interactions were analyzed on their own cultural terms, and the resulting findings provided an important counterpoint to widespread scholarly and lay misrepresentations of African American women. At the same time, the tendency of much early feminist linguistic research to position women as subordinate to male power was overwhelmingly rejected by researchers of language and gender in African American communities. Perhaps the most consistent finding of such researchers was the clear evidence of African American women's social agency, often in the face of significant structural constraints. In this regard, the study of African American speech communities is of particular importance in the continued progress of the field of language and gender studies, by offering a representation of women that neither diminishes their abilities nor romanticizes their struggles.

Into this theoretically and politically fraught history, Lanita Jacobs-Huey makes an intellectual intervention that is as groundbreaking as it is vital. In *From the Kitchen to the Parlor: Language and Becoming in African American Women's Hair Care*, Jacobs-Huey draws inspiration from early scholarship on both black and white women's language use while laying out a wholly new direction of inquiry grounded in multisited ethnography, discourse analysis, and the investigation of embodied social practice. Recognizing that, next to language itself, hair is the most complex signifier that African American women and girls use to display their identities, Jacobs-Huey examines how hair and hair care take on situated social meanings among African American women in varied linguistic interactions—whether with one another, with African American men, or with European American women. Based on years of ethnographic fieldwork in a range of sites, from cosmetology schools in South Carolina to hair care seminars in Beverly Hills, from standup comedy clubs in Los Angeles to online debates about black hair, Jacobs-Huey's multifaceted approach comprehensively documents exactly how and why hair comes to matter so much in African American women's construction of their identities, and how language both mediates and produces these social meanings. Along the way, the author takes seriously her commitment to ethnography as an intersubjective relationship between self and other by reflecting on her own role in the research process, her own racialized and gendered identity, and her own understandings of black hair and its meaning.

From the Kitchen to the Parlor thus represents a new stage in language and gender research, one that creatively brings together the most powerful tools and acute insights of a variety of disciplines to examine an issue that has never been studied through a linguistic lens: the practices and discourses surrounding black hair. Jacobs-Huey compellingly demonstrates the symbolic and social significance of hair among African Americans in constructing race, gender, and other dimensions of identity. In its multisited analyses, this volume forges numerous new directions for language and gender studies. As a study of language and gendered political economy, it offers a rare study of African American women's discourse in the workplace, examining stylists' tenuous position as service providers in a cultural context in which "kitchen beauticians" frequently win out over hair professionals, and documenting stylists' appropriation and interweaving of culturally valued discourses of science and religion to legitimate their professional status. As a contribution to the emerging field of language and the body, it provides a rich portrait of the politics of beauty in African American women's lives, one that closely attends to the role of embodiment, gesture, and the material world in the linguistic navigation of beauty work—even in the "bodiless" world of cyberspace. As an addition to our knowledge of African American discourse practices, it demonstrates the nuanced and subtle ways in which speakers employ the tools of indirectness to achieve such diverse interactional goals as humor, negotiation, and critique. And as an ethnography that sensitively and skillfully portrays ordinary people's ordinary lives, it is rich in methodological creativity and theoretical insights gleaned from the ethnographic dialogue.

Thus *From the Kitchen to the Parlor*, like many of the studies of African American language and gender that preceded it, speaks to a number of different audiences, but it has special importance for language and gender research. This most recent contribution to Oxford University Press's series Studies in Language and Gender asks fresh questions and offers insightful answers. Most important, in offering the field an exceptionally rich representation of African American women in diverse cultural contexts, *From the Kitchen to the Parlor* promises to change what we know and how we think about the intricate relationships among language, gender, and race, and the theories, methods, and politics that underlie them.

Mary Bucholtz
Series Editor

ACKNOWLEDGMENTS

This "hair story" began during my graduate training in linguistic anthropology at UCLA and, as such, my gratitude begins there. I owe Marcyliena Morgan a special "thanks" for inspiring me as an undergraduate and graduate student to look at language and ethnography as windows into the study of culture, gender, class, and race/ethnicity. I also want to thank Asif Agha, Roger Andersen, Alessandro Duranti, Candy Goodwin, Chuck Goodwin, Paul Kroskrity, Emanuel Schegloff, and especially Elinor Ochs—whose impassioned and varied approaches to teaching and research affirm my appreciation for the theoretical promise and methodological rigors of language analysis still today. I must thank another important cohort at UCLA: the Discourse, Identity, and Representation Collective (DIRE), which included Marcyliena Morgan and my then student colleagues Patricia Baquedano-López, Dionne Bennett, Kesha Fikes, Soyoun Kim, Adrienne Lo, Sepa Seté, and Steve Ropp. To them I owe endless gratitude for critical and collegial dialogues around race and discourse that ultimately helped me navigate my place in the academy.

Other colleagues and friends provided critical comments on this manuscript at various stages: they include Niko Besnier, Marvin Sterling, and John Rashford. I especially thank Nancy Tuan and Sandi Morgan, Fran Mascia-Lees, and Susan Herring for their respective contributions to several publications that inform chapters 5, 6, and 7 of this book. I also thank Darnell Hunt and John L. Jackson for assisting me with the more pragmatic details of bookwriting.

I am indebted to my senior colleagues in the USC Anthropology Department, whose collective passion for ethnography and individual scholarship provides a steady source of inspiration for me in my own attempts to tell stories that are Geertzian "thick." My colleagues in the USC Program in American Studies and Ethnicity also afforded ongoing opportunities for intellectual exchange (and priceless fellowship) that helped me to chart new interdisciplinary pathways in this and ongoing research. I must also thank another invaluable and supportive cohort, WHAM (Women Helping and Motivating), which includes Andriette Ward, Donna Washington, Arleen F. Brown, and Carolyn Brown, each of whom saw me through the arduous process of writing this book.

Other friends, students, and colleagues who unwittingly inspired me to keep the faith when the life-stories surrounding this story's telling seemed overwhelming include Patricia Baquendano-López, Brandon Bowlin, Nathaniel Dumas, Chip and Jeanne Gaines, Imani Johnson, Rita Jones, Katrina Jones, Mary Lawlor, Tené Lewis, Cheryl Mattingly, Kimberly Moore, Sadie Moore, Courtney Mykytyn, Viet Nguyen, Kim Parchman, and Monique Ward.

The fieldwork on which this book is based has been generously supported by various organizations, including the UCLA Eugene Cota Robles Fellowship, National Science Foundation Doctoral Enhancement Grant, Wenner-Gren Foundation Pre-Doctoral Grant, Ford Dissertation Fellowship for Minorities, College of Charleston Research Starter Grant, USC Faculty Development Award, and the USC Anthropology Department's Visual Anthropology Endowment Fund.

Peter Ohlin at Oxford University Press, as well as two anonymous reviewers, helped to refine and extend this work in important ways. I am especially grateful to Mary Bucholtz, a dear friend and amazing editor, who believed in this book even when I could not see past the politics of representation and envision a larger story worth telling. Their partnership undoubtedly made for a stronger book, though I must accept sole responsibility for any shortcomings in the pages to come.

I extend my deepest gratitude to the women and men who gave me permission to listen to and observe their conversations and engagements around hair. If ethnography, at its best, is a reciprocal exchange, then I most certainly have emerged with the greater blessings. To all who inspired this telling, I say thank you, thank you, thank you. I extend my final thank-you to my husband and colleague, Stan Huey, Jr., who has nurtured both my heart and intellectual passions over the long haul and inspired me to seek and tell the best of stories.

CONTENTS

From the Kitchen to the Parlor

Introduction

From the Kitchen to the Parlor

HAIR. It may seem like a mundane subject, but it has profound implications for how African American women experience the world. Historically, Black women's tightly curled hair textures have pre sented an array of challenges, epitomized in debates concerning Black hairstyles as indicators of racial consciousness, the suitability of Afrocentric hairstyles (e.g., braids, Afros, dreadlocks) at work, and the extent to which cultural notions of "good" versus "bad" hair continue to privilege Eurocentric standards of beauty. One important implication of such debates is that Black women's hairstyle choices are seldom just about aesthetics or personal choice, but are instead ever complicated by such issues as mate desire, mainstream standards of beauty, workplace standards of presentation, and ethnic/cultural pride.

Over the past decade, a proliferation of academic books, anthologies, novels, and biographies have been published that explain why hair remains a highly symbolic and, at times, controversial medium for African Americans, particularly women (e.g., Bonner 1991; Bundles 2001; Byrd and Tharps 2001; Due 2000; Harris and Johnson 2001; Lake 2003). Recent work by Noliwe Rooks (1996), Ingrid Banks (2000), Kimberly Battle-Walters (2004), and Yolanda Majors (2001, 2003, 2004) are especially relevant testaments to the central role of hair in Black women's lived experiences and conceptions of self. Rooks's book, *Hair Raising: Beauty, Culture, and African American Women*, examines how historical and contemporary Black hair advertisements inflect the politics of Black women's self-concepts and bodily and business practices. Banks's text, *Hair Matters: Beauty, Power, and Black Women's Conscious-*

3

ness, employs interview and focus-group methods to explore how Black women and girls of diverse ages and socioeconomic backgrounds discuss hair in relation to their identity, cultural authenticity, gender, and sexuality, among other factors. Battle-Walters's book, *Sheila's Shop: Working-class African American Women Talk About Life, Love, Race, and Hair,* shares insights gleaned from a 16-month study of a southern beauty-salon show to describe how working-class African American women—who are underrepresented in sociological studies—come to see themselves as victors rather than as victims during salon conversations. Majors's articles similarly employ ethnography to explore constructions of self among African American women in a midwestern hair salon; however, she carefully examines women's conversations—or "shoptalk"—to illuminate how women learn, construct, and transmit their understandings of the world through such verbal strategies as participation, collaboration, and negotiation. While the aforementioned work is complementary to this book, these authors leave room for a broader analysis of the vital yet undiscussed role of language in negotiating the social meaning of hair for African American women.

This book breaks new ground as an ethnographic and multisited account of how Black women use language to negotiate the significance of hair in their everyday lives. As a linguistic anthropologist, I am interested in how African American women use both hair itself and language about hair as cultural resources to shape the way they see themselves and are seen by others. By exploring how women make sense of hair in the everyday and across the many places where the subject of hair is routinely taken up (e.g., beauty salons, hair educational seminars, stylists' Bible study meetings, hair fashion shows, comedy clubs, Internet discussions, cosmetology schools), I aim to present situated and lived accounts of the role of hair and language in the formation of Black women's identities. In essence, I want readers to understand how, when, and why hair matters in African American women's day-to-day experiences and how it is they work out, either by themselves or with others, when exactly "hair is just hair" and when, alternatively, "hair is not just hair."

Why study hair?

Hair appeals to anthropologists as a highly symbolic part of the body that offers insights into individual and collective culture. Hair also provides individuals with a means of representing themselves and negotiating their place in the world (Furman 1997; Ilyin 2000; McCracken 1995; Obeyesekere 1981; Peiss 1998; Scranton 2000; Severn 1971; Simon 2000). Further, what people do and say through hair care can shed light on how members of a cultural group use hair more broadly as a signifier of status, and hair care as a site of routine cultural practice. In this book, I examine Black hair as a window into African American women's ethnic and gender identities, and Black hair care as a linguistic and cultural engagement with these identities. I argue that each site presents opportunities for learning and change, thus offering insights into the discursive and corporeal dynamics of African American women's being and becoming. The terms *being* and *becoming*, which are used throughout this text, refer to Black women's self-perceptions as individuals and members of a collective *(being)*, as well as their transition into different dispositions, ideological stances (or positions), professional statuses, and phases of life *(becoming)*. In other words, I take women's being and becoming to be dynamic accomplishments and processes, and look primarily to language to see how this gets done.

My work builds upon an established body of research on African American women's hair by anthropologists, historians, visual artists, performers, biographers, and novelists. Through a cross-section of methods, including narrative, focus groups, interviews, surveys, observation, photography, memoir, performance, and visual/textual analyses, these authors document the many ways in which hair is culturally and politically meaningful across cultures, time, and place (e.g., Bonner 1996, 1997a, 1997b; Cunningham and Marberry 2000; Ebong 2001; Gaskins 1997; Gibson 1995; Mastalia, Pagano, and Walker 1999). My contribution to this body of work is to incorporate language as well as the role of gender and professional socialization (Garrett and Baquedano-López 2002) into current understandings of how African Americans, particularly women, make sense of the role of hair in their daily lives.

Language, gender, and multisited ethnography

My approach to hair is a decidedly anthropological pursuit, born of ethnographic observations and a quest to understand how cultural significance is nested in the mundane realities of everyday life. My focus, at its heart, is also language-centered and mines ordinary conversations and more specialized performances for insights into the role of hair, language, and culture in the constitution of African American women's being and becoming. This linguistic-anthropological approach foregrounds talk and discourse as integral to the construction of cultural identity and political ideology. By analyzing women's everyday conversations about hair care, I aim to delineate the dynamics of Black women's becomings: that is, how their socialization into new roles and sensibilities is negotiated in actual dialogues and hair-care practice.

This book's focus on women's language, embodiment, and beauty work marks both its relation and its contribution to language and gender research. To date, language and gender studies have paid limited attention to embodiment, which various scholars have shown to be a vital aspect of gender (Butler 1990; Camaroff 1985; Lock 1993; Young 1993). This book reveals language as an integral, albeit missing, link in this work by showing how the embodied social action of Black women's hair care remains deeply indebted to language for its accomplishment. This book also seeks to augment existing research exploring the role of language in girls' and women's cosmetic practices (e.g., Eckert 1996; Mendoza-Denton 1996; Talbot 1995) by describing the processes through which language mediates African American women's beauty work on themselves and others.

Further, by examining Black women's hair-related talk and practice on their own terms rather than in comparison to either Black men (Anderson 2003; Gilbert 1994; Marberry 2005) or White women (McCracken 1995), this book pushes the boundaries of language and gender work well beyond its earlier preoccupations with theoretical paradigms of *difference* (i.e., how the monolithic category of "women's speech" differs from equally homogeneous conceptions of "men's speech") and *dominance* (i.e., the extent to which "women's speech" reflects and re-inscribes male dominance; for discussion see Hall and Bucholtz 1995; Henley 1995; Holmes 1995; Morgan 1999; Stanback 1985). Situated within the contexts of Black women's hair-related talk and practice, this study partakes in a very conscious shift within language and gender studies to focus more on context, ethnography, and women's talk in their own terms and communities of practice (Bucholtz 1999a; Coates and Cameron 1988; Crawford 1995; Eckert and McConnell-Ginet 1992a, 1992b, 1995, 2003; Uchida 1992). The present study contributes to this shift through its focus on Black women's talk in the contexts of their cultural and professional communities and workplaces.

This book draws upon a growing body of literature on African American women's speech practices and discourse styles (e.g., Etter-Lewis 1991; Foster 1995; Goodwin 1980, 1988, 1990; Hudson 2001; Johnstone 1997; Lanehart 2002; Mitchell-Kernan 1971, 1972, 1973; Nelson 1990; Nichols 1978, 1980, 1983; Morgan 1994a, 1996a, 2004; Stanback 1985; Troutman 1999, 2001, forthcoming). Collectively, these works highlight the sociocultural pragmatics of Black women's discourse and thus broaden current understanding of how Black women speak and use language to mediate their complex identities. I build upon this work through a multisited examination of how Black women use language to negotiate their everyday lives and construct professional identities with respect to hair. This study purposely moves beyond the conventional single-site location of most ethnography to multiple sites of observation and participation that crosscut dichotomies such as the local and the global, real life and performance, and everyday talk and professional discourse (Marcus 1995). As multisited ethnographers track metaphors, conflicts, thematic plots, and people (who themselves are often in transit; see Clifford 1997b), they expose the relational and provisional nature of their findings. The insights gleaned from my own multisited ethnography bear out this claim.

From the kitchen to the parlor: a study in/of transformations

My observations of African American hair engagements over the course of this study entailed all sorts of transformations: Young girls and adolescents were socialized into womanhood through informal hair-care sessions in their kitchens; clients collaborated with hairstylists in their aesthetic refashioning vis-à-vis new hairstyles; cosmetology students transformed themselves from "kitchen beauticians" to "hair experts" by trading cultural ways of talking about hair for cosmetological jargon; licensed cosmetologists were apprenticed into higher levels of authority and expertise through hair-care seminars designed to make them talk and act like "hair doctors." In many ways, these women's socialization into new ways of seeing and representing themselves mirrored my own transitions while conducting this study.

My attempts to become a different sort of Black hair-care expert, for example, required that I move beyond my own personal convictions about Black hair to consider how African Americans discuss hair in relation to their gender and lived experiences. Toward this end, I immersed myself in the many sites where Black hair care is regularly discussed and practiced. I also employed such methods as ethnographic observation, interviews, and the transcription and analysis of naturally occurring talk in order to unpack Black women's multiple and seemingly contradictory stances toward hair. Most important, I began to ask what were, for me, essentially new questions about African American hair. Those questions included: How does hair get discussed, by whom, and in what contexts? How do conversations about hair reflect or construct political, racial, spiritual, and other identities, ideologies, and stances? How does hair itself "speak" as a malleable medium and important aspect of the racial, political, gendered, and symbolic body? What might intra- and intercultural dialogues about Black hair reveal about the political dimensions of Black hair and identity? How do hair and hair care afford opportunities for gendered talk and interaction? Pursuing answers to these questions moved me beyond the deeply personal lens through which I initially framed Black hair and into the heart of how women themselves arrive at complicated understandings of hair over the course of their lives. My shift in this regard was but one of many important transformations to come.

My socialization into new ways of knowing African American women's hair care was itself a pivotal journey—one that would consume six years of my life and provide an array of epiphanies and analytic challenges. My experiences of rediscovering African American women's hair captivated me and sent me dashing in pursuit of other hair-care sites to explore. But the challenges I faced while learning to observe and ultimately translate my discoveries were akin to combing through my "kitchen" with a fine-toothed comb.

Culturally astute readers will likely wince at my use of such a graphic metaphor. In African American hair care, *kitchen* has two denotations, the first being an intimate space where girls' informal hair grooming and socialization often begins, and the second being the nape of the neck where Black hair is typically more curly (Gates 1994; Smitherman 1994). I intend to invoke both meanings. For me, conducting research on African American hair care has been tantamount to combing, in a literal and figurative sense, through each of these delicate spaces with various degrees of success.

Before I dared even to imagine this book, many Black women weighed in on what my work could and, most importantly, *should* say about African American hairstyling (see also Banks 2000). Some African American women encouraged me to use my research to critique Black women's hair-straightening practices as indicative of self-hatred or, at best, as an unwitting reification of Eurocentric standards of beauty. Other African American respondents cautioned me against "outing" Black women's private hair conversations for the presumed scrutiny of predominantly White academic audiences. Still, others were concerned about additional matters of representation, specifically whether transcribed excerpts of their speech would become fodder for derogatory assessments of African American Vernacular English (AAVE) and of themselves as AAVE speakers.

My admonishers generally held strong beliefs about Black hair and wanted me to tell stories inspired by their personal convictions and experiences. Considering all they perceived to be at stake in my study—I could expose African American women's hair secrets or "dirty laundry" to outsiders; alternatively, I could ignore problems such as Black business owners' slipping foothold on a multibillion-dollar Black hair-care industry, or the fact that "kiddie perms" and cultural notions of "good" and "bad" hair were warping young Black girls' concepts of beauty—most women desperately wanted me to "get it right" (see also Zentella 1997).

"Getting it right" from such a vast array of vantage points, however, was difficult, if not impossible, to reconcile with my observations of the complex ways in which Black women practiced and discussed hair. Thus I took another lesson from the sum of these diverse opinions. Instead of focusing solely on African Americans' multiple and competing stances on hair, I fixed my attention on what their opinions say about the politics of conducting and translating ethnographic research so that it resonates with both lay/communal and academic audiences.

I write this book at a time when ethnography as a *process* and a *product* are considered to be mutually constitutive. Anthropologists increasingly recognize that ethnographic fieldwork and writing up one's findings are codependent endeavors, since what happens in the field ends up shaping the stories that anthropologists eventually tell. We are also aware that the role of research participants in shaping the story should not be underestimated. As feminist ethnographers have shown (Behar 1995, 1996; Rooks 1996; Visweswaran 1994), research participants are not passive entities awaiting discovery or description; rather, they are individuals with specific motivations who control access to informative people, significant places, and cultural "secrets." In more ways than one they influence the kinds of interpretations scholars can make of their data during and after their fieldwork. Ethnography is inherently intersubjective in this way, and my attempts to untangle the linguistic and cultural intricacies of Black women's hair care have demanded such a reckoning.

This reckoning reflects another irrefutable fact about anthropological subjects in the present: A group once called the "natives," whom anthropologists now rightly refer to as *research participants*, are vigorously gazing and talking back as researchers, students, and lay critics of academic presentations and published scholarship. Their vocal presence has compelled me throughout this project to consider how my own positionality as a "native" researcher and my ways of asking, seeing/interpreting, and speaking have influenced my engagements in and beyond the field.

As the child of a cosmetologist and an African American woman, I was intimately familiar with the dilemmas of hair care, the politics of hairstyles, and the major debates surrounding Black hair before initiating this study. I also shared plights experienced by many of the Black women I followed in my research, including the challenge of finding a competent and efficient stylist who could create both manageable and attractive hairstyles, products that work well on Black hair textures, and a romantic partner who appreciated my hair in a range of styles. But this intimacy, as subjectivities go, was surface-level and subject to my own visceral reactions and personal hair dramas. It wasn't until I began observing and later analyzing how women talked about hair that I gained a deeper appreciation for their expectations of my work and the role of hair in shaping their lived experiences.

In writing this book, I have had to reconcile my accountability to multiple constituencies, including African American women, anthropologists, linguists, feminists, hairstylists, and my very first research participant: my mother, "Joyce," a cosmetologist. This reconciliation proved to be one of my most formidable challenges (indeed, a source of long-term writer's block) since each constituency has multiple and often-contradictory opinions about how this story should be told.

This book, then, is about the different ways in which hair and talk about it feature in African American women's being and becoming, and an attempt to critically account for the dilemmas of representation that affect most researchers, especially "native" scholars who conduct research in their own communities. Its telling owes to one of my most inspiring epiphanies yet: When I look back on this multisited journey, I realize that my perceived successes and failures, in and beyond the field, also managed to get me into the heart of anthropology and the essence of what this science demands of its practitioners.

Getting to the heart of anthropology also managed to align my work more squarely within the objectives of language and gender studies—in ways that I least expected. Language and gender studies emerged in the 1970s as a critical response to concerns about the relative powerlessness of "women's speech" in relation to men (Cameron 1990, 1992; Lakoff 1975). This agenda set the stage for decades of interventionist research that sought to compare and contrast (often White and middle-class) women's speech in same-sex and mixed-sex conversations (Thorne and Henley 1975; Crawford 1995). As this agenda evolved, so too did my understanding of how my own work fit within established research paradigms concerning language and gender. I realized that my focus on Black women's richly situated talk and hair-care practice actually heeds a longstanding call among language and gender scholars to explore women's talk within their own communities of practice (Coates and Cameron 1988; Eckert and McConnell-Ginet 1992a, 1992b, 1995, 2003). Additionally, my interest in how Black women "do" being professional hair-care experts and powerful business women intersects with a broad array of literature concerning gender and expertise as something that is enacted or accomplished through talk (Borker and Maltz 1989; Gal 1991, 1995; West and Zimmerman 1987).

These encouraging realizations typify some of the conceptual shifts that shaped "when and where I enter" (Giddings 1994) as a budding theoretician of African American women's language and culture. Other equally important shifts came by way of practice or, more precisely, from entering the field as a "native" anthropologist.

When and where I enter

There are many groups for whom a sojourn or liminal state is necessary for induction into a community of practice (Lave and Wenger 1991). For boxers, it involves considerable time spent training for bouts in the ring (Rotella 2003; Wacquant 2004); for hairstylists, it is hours of professional training in cosmetology school. For anthropologists, ethnography is both a rite of passage and the modus operandi—it is the way we seek answers to questions about humanity and culture as well as a means of representing those findings.

My ethnographic study of African American women's hair care entailed participant-observations of hair-care settings throughout the English-speaking African diaspora, particularly the United States and London, England. The work began as a pilot study in my mother's beauty salon, where my "native" status as an African American woman and daughter afforded entry but did not absolve me from the need to negotiate legitimacy and trust with people both familiar and unfamiliar to me.

My audio- and videotaped observations of Black women's hair-care activities required our mutual willingness to be vulnerable and exposed. For example, my work required me to be a persistent voyeur of clients in various states of aesthetic disrepair. I also witnessed stylists' mixed fates in their negotiations with clients; when patrons openly challenged cosmetologists' expertise or, worse, requested another stylist, my spectatorship was complicit in affronts to their social face as professionals.

I in turn experienced my own share of verbal blunders that were witnessed and occasionally made public by the women and men I observed. Early in my fieldwork, I wrote an unpublished essay describing the dilemmas I faced observing and later writing about Black women's hair-care practices. I shared the essay with my mother, who immediately took issue with the fact that I had described her and other stylists as "hairdressers" in the introduction. She rebuked me: "I am not a hairdresser—I don't dress the hair. I cultivate the hair!" I had committed the ultimate breach: calling my mother out of her name. In doing so, I had also insulted the community of practice to which she and other hairstylists belonged. This wouldn't be the first time I unwittingly breached the linguistic protocols governing hairstylists' representations of themselves and their practice.

A second time I managed to get in trouble over language occurred during my 18-month study of a cosmetology school in South Carolina. As is often the case with long-term fieldwork, my proclivity for observation encountered the obligatory expectations of my research participants, who thought it best that I both observe and participate in school activities should the need arise. When the school experienced a heavy volume of walk-in clients, I therefore shifted from observer to receptionist. I learned even more about the importance of language among cosmetologists by serving in this capacity. While assisting a client one afternoon, I asked an instructor, Mrs. Collins, the price of a "wash-and-set" and received an unconventional reply.[1] Rather than answer my question, she challenged it: "Do you mean *shampoo*? Because you wash dogs, not hair." I had received from Mrs. Collins yet another lesson in proper language use, only this time before an impressionable audience of clients and students. But there was much more going on in this public shaming than my subsequent loss of face. Mrs. Collins's correction, much like my mother's reprimand, intensified my awareness of the potential minefield of language and demonstrated the work of language socialization that I would see time after time across multiple hair-care settings. These reproofs also socialized me into proper language use befitting our respective roles as "hair expert" versus "hair novice." My linguistic mishaps were advantageous insofar as they helped to illuminate what was particularly at stake for stylists in these interactions.

For many hairstylists, language is a primary means through which they construct themselves as "hair experts" and distinguish themselves from a bounty of unlicensed "kitchen beauticians." Their use of specialized hair jargon, as opposed to cultural hair terms, can serve to validate their hard-won roles by obscuring hair-care knowledge primarily born of lay experience. In this sense, language serves as a mediator of professional identity and as a pivotal resource in Black women's being and becoming.

As I continued my observations of hair-related talk and interaction, I realized that explicit and implicit language instruction constituted a central means through which stylists socialized hair-care apprentices (and novices like me) to recognize their identities as established stylists or hair experts in the making. In beauty salons and classroom instruction, Black stylists employed verbal strategies of correction and specialized hair terminology as a rhetorical display of their expertise. Further, their lexical choices and other tactical framings of professional hair care had important consequences for the discursive roles and types of knowledge and authority presumed by themselves, their clients, and other hair-care participants.

Revelations such as these also fostered my own professional becoming as a linguistic anthropologist by helping me to think as one. Linguistic anthropologists presume a theory of language as a principal mediator of cultural identity, beliefs, and social action. We employ various methods—ethnographic interviews, participant-observation, and the careful transcription and analysis of everyday talk—to illuminate how people accomplish embodied social actions such as gender through linguistic practice (Bucholtz and Hall 2004, Gumperz and Gumperz 1982, Kroskrity 2000a, 2000b). Moreover, we assume that while speakers' identities and statuses are fluid and can shift from moment to moment, they can be constructed and mediated by the indexical relation of language to stances, social acts, ideologies, and beliefs (Ochs 1992). My observations repeatedly bore out these assumptions, offering insights pertinent not merely to the meanings attached to Black hair but also to the place of language, gender, and hair-care practice in Black women's being and becoming.

Overview of the book

This book represents what I learned about the linguistic construction of identity, ideology, and expertise in Black women's engagements from the kitchen to the beauty parlor and beyond. The chapters that follow form an assemblage of hair-care scenes that present women's identity and ideologies about hair as linguistic achievements, assertions, and actualizations that are negotiated in and through talk. Collectively, they contribute a complex portrait of the role of hair in the discursive formation of women's identity and lived experiences.

Chapter 1 begins this endeavor by focusing on a routine type of interaction between clients and stylists in hair salons: client-stylist negotiation. In particular, I draw from observations in salons in Oakland, Los Angeles, and Beverly Hills, California, and in Charleston, South Carolina, to explore the verbal and nonverbal strategies used by clients and stylists to mediate their respective identities as hair-care novices and experts while negotiating hair care. Since African American female clients often came to the salon with significant prior experience in caring for their own and other women's hair, they seldom behaved as hair-care novices. For both the client and stylist, then, this situation introduced the challenge of establishing which of them would act as the hair-care authority at any given point. To negotiate their expertise, clients and stylists employed indirect and direct discourse styles that are characteristic of African American speech communities. For example, clients used cultural discourse styles such as indirectness to temper the directness of their hair-care requests and recommendations and to judiciously discern hair-care costs. Stylists in turn employed similar strategies to convince clients to accept their aesthetic and "scientific" recommendations. I analyze these varied stances and discursive positions to draw attention to women's situated talk at work, a topic of growing interest among language and gender scholars (e.g., Goldstein 1995; Holmes 1995; Kendall and Tannen 1997; McElhinny 1995; Sunaoshi 1994; Tannen 1994, 1995).

My observations in hair salons piqued my interest in cosmetologists as members of a community of practice with their own standards regarding language as a means of socialization and a basis for membership (Bergant 1993). Chapter 2 presents findings from my subsequent observations of hair educational seminars and hair shows in cities throughout the United States and in London, England. As an observer in these sites, I found that stylists were intensely aware of their clients' lay hair-care expertise. In fact, during discussions that underscored the technical skill necessary to provide hair service, many African American cosmetologists problematized Black female clients' knowledge and freedom to choose other stylists or do their own hair. Notably, across all of the Black hair-care communities I observed, stylists framed their work and professional identity as analogous to that of medical doctors. One stylist stated, "We are like doctors; we diagnose and treat sick hair. . . . Therefore we must use our terminology as a verbal skill that gains respect from people . . . around us." Given the risks imposed by African American women's considerable hair-care knowledge and experience, stylists' constructions of themselves as doctors constitute attempts to minimize the relevance of clients' lay knowledge and thus to resolve the challenges posed by clients' lay hair expertise. At a communal level, the positioning of themselves as doctors and of professional hair care as science serves to legitimize cosmetology as a science-based industry on par with the medical profession. Here we see another instance wherein language is employed by Black women (and men) to construct provisional stances of authority and relations of power with clients and other hair-care practitioners. Moreover, this and other forms of hair discourse are inherently heteroglossic (Bakhtin 1968, 1981), drawing meaning and legitimacy from the use of multiple genres and intertextual ways of knowing and speaking (Hanks 1990, 2000).

In chapter 3, I present findings from a two-year study of a nonprofit organization I call Cosmetologists for Christ (CFC). In monthly Bible study meetings held in an affluent Beverly Hills salon, African American stylists and others affiliated with the beauty industry described prayer and testimony as a way to "frame their work with their words." In particular, CFC members advocated the laying on of hands and the use of spoken prayer in their workplaces to minimize conflict between themselves, their clients, and their colleagues. They also used testimony to construct their individual salons as "houses of God" and their collective identities as "ministers of the body and spirit." Some stylists also blended spiritual and scientific genres to socialize clients and stylists alike into a greater appreciation of the "truth" about salon hair care. Such intertextual narratives illustrate how African American Christian cosmetologists use religious (and scientific) discourse in their everyday lives to craft moral selves, spiritual practices, and sacred and professional workplaces. Their testimonials, prayers, and fellowship provide explicit examples of the beauty salon as a gendered site of moral and professional socialization, and spirituality as one of many lenses through which Black hair care is framed.

Chapter 4 looks beyond the contexts of Black women's hair-care practice to consider narrative performances about hair in Black comedy clubs. Black stand-up comedy, the site of my current longitudinal ethnographic study (Jacobs-Huey 2003a), is an especially fitting stage for examining the cultural and gendered significance of Black hair, for the subject routinely emerges in Black humor. Jokes about hair often rely on the audience's shared cultural knowledge and experiences with Black hair textures, styles, procedures, and terminology. African American comics exploit this in-group knowledge through embodied and highly gendered humor that plays on cultural discourse styles, innuendo, and comedic strategy. In doing so, they expand current understandings of how and why hair matters in African American women's and men's everyday lives and provide a broader context for the chapters that follow.

In chapter 5, I share insights gleaned from a two-month Internet debate about Black hair and identity politics. As a "lurker" turned participant observer in this forum, I noticed that contributors who identified themselves as Black women used communicative strategies similar to those used by both clients and hairstylists in face-to-face interaction to make political claims about hair. For example, many African American women employed cultural discourse styles to communicate their own hair care ideologies while critiquing those of others. They also utilized cultural hair terms to establish their cultural knowledge and extensive Black hair-care experience, and hence their right to speak on such issues as whether or not hair straightening is indicative of self-hatred among Black women. In cyberspace, participants' references to hairstyle and texture became an explicit means of constructing racial identity and authenticity. The question "BTW [By the way], how do you wear your hair?" was an indirect way of assessing a speaker's ethnic identity and presumed racial consciousness vis-à-vis their hairstyle choices. Further, those perceived to lack cultural knowledge of Black hair and hair-care practice were ultimately silenced in the discussion; those silenced included self-identified African American men and European American women who otherwise empathized with Black women via Afrocentric and feminist stances, respectively.

Chapter 6 explores conversations involving Black and White women across multiple settings (e.g., cosmetology schools, hair educational seminars, Internet discussions) that further elucidate what is at stake for Black women in discussions about hair. African American women's hair narratives were, in many ways, filtered through their experiences of marginalization as a collective of women whose ethnic features were long considered unattractive. Their shared experiences as children with access to few Black dolls and, for some, as cosmetology students with a limited supply of Black mannequins socialized them into similar ways of knowing and experiencing their hair; their comments also show Black women's ideas about hair to be intricately connected to cultural identity, gendered experiences, and racial consciousness. In three separate hair discussions, White women unwittingly ran into trouble despite their attempts to align with Black women. I explore the nature of their linguistic missteps and Black women's (mis) readings to illuminate what went wrong and what contributed to these women's conversational alignments and misalignments.

In chapter 7, I reflect on my own and other scholars' engagements as a "native" anthropologist and offer, in the way of a postscript, insights into issues of positionality, voice, and accountability. I analyze other pivotal behind-the-scenes engagements between my research participants and me that ultimately shaped the nature of my observations and findings. I explicitly mark my "native" status not as a means of privileging my "insider" status or to bolster any assumptions about the authenticity of my claims. Rather, I endeavor to critically examine the professional and personal implications of what conducting this research has entailed for me as an African American female anthropologist (with curly hair) who rediscovers the unfamiliar in the familiar and ultimately wrestles with what it all means.

In doing so, I hope to link this study to major shifts in the study of culture and language and gender. As a discipline whose history is entrenched in colonialism and the emergence of scientific racism, anthropology is reckoning with its past and considering, in theory and practice, how its engagement with the world affects the world. This critical reflexivity is abetted by the palpable presence of "natives" who are intently gazing and talking back, and the waning of what Renato Rosaldo (1989: 30) calls the classic tradition of the "Lone Ethnographer who rode off in the sunset in search of the native." Anthropologists conduct fieldwork in distant villages, as well as cyberspace, boxing rings, bars, academia, and places called "home." This multisited study is one such example of emerging "native" scholarship that proposes language as a mediator of cultural identity, and ethnography as a holistic way of seeing and being in the world.

This study also attests to related transitions within language and gender studies. As Bucholtz (1999a) explains, current work in this arena is "transgressive" insofar as it sidesteps stagnant theories concerning "difference" and "dominance" in order to focus more productively on gender and identity as constructs that are mediated in and through talk. This recognition of gender as socially constructed and further nuanced by race, class, and sexuality among other qualifiers resounds throughout the social sciences such that what we mean by gender, culture, or identity, for that matter, can no longer be understood as rigid, fixed, timeless, or coherent (Abu-Lughod 1991; Geertz 1971). Rather, we must recognize these concepts as notions that are situated, emergent, and inextricably shaped by relations of power. This book privileges these insights and seeks to broaden them through a multisited examination of Black women's everyday talk and hair-care practices. I want to show women's talk and hair-care practice to be linguistic and corporeal achievements that reveal the constitutive relationships between women's language, hair, and their very being and becoming.

1

Negotiating Expert
and Novice Identities
through Client-stylist Interactions

I n this chapter, I return to the place where this multisited study began—a small beauty salon in northern California. It was my mother's salon, a place I knew intimately in my youth. Throughout my adolescence I visited my mother's salon after school to do homework, run errands for clients, and occasionally get my own hair styled. I was also an attentive bystander in lively conversations about hair, spirituality, Black entertainers, and women's notions about life as it should be lived. As youth are wont to do, I often took many of these conversations for granted.

While honing my skills as an ethnographer in graduate school in anthropology, I returned to this salon and gazed anew at women's everyday talk and interaction. With an ethnographer's eye, I came to see this and other beauty salons as quintessential Black women's—sites of regularized interaction not around simply the giving and receiving of hair care, but cultural exchanges about life. I also realized that clients' and stylists' routine conversations about hair entailed highly symbolic collaborations concerning expertise, identity, and hair aesthetics. For example, in many of the hair-care negotiations I observed, women judiciously decided who among them would be the "expert" or "novice" on matters of hair treatment and style. In doing so, they implicated the significance of hair as a reflection of the stylist's skill and as a mediator of the client's identity or "presentation of self" (Goffman 1959).

These initial insights provided the impetus for a six-month investigation of my mother's beauty salon. In audio- and videotaped participant-observations, I focused on the micro-level dynamics of client-stylist negotiations and learned even more about the way hair-care decisions were made. I found that Black women's hairstyle decisions seldom conformed to the exclusive whims of stylists, nor did they always adhere to the "client is always right" principle. Rather, client-stylist negotiations mediated clients' economic investment and aesthetic preferences, and stylists' creative agency, expertise, and ability to advertise their skills as cosmetologists.

Such dynamics are not unique to African American stylists and clients. Debra Gimlin (1996) and Frida Kerner Furman (1997) observed similar dynamics in their respective studies of salon encounters involving European American and Jewish American women. However, I found distinguishable aspects of Black women's hair care that generalized across salons I later observed in Los Angeles and Beverly Hills, California, and Charleston, South Carolina. These differences are rooted in the particular experiences many African American women have with hair care from an early age.

Hair expertise from the kitchen to the parlor

As with most women, hair care among Black females often begins at home. Prior to the advent of electric hair-grooming aids, many Black women congregated in their kitchens to receive and provide hair care. With a stove and a sink, the kitchen presented an ideal site for washing, braiding/plaiting, "relaxing" (chemically straightening), and "pressing" (thermally straightening) Black women's wavy to curly hair textures. Now with the wider availability of professional-quality, hair-care products and appliances (e.g., hair dryers, small electrical stoves) among consumers, Black women and girls practice hair care not only in their kitchens but also in bathrooms, bedrooms, or other spaces featuring power outlets (see fig 1.1). Home-based hair care is a pivotal part of many Black women's childhood and adolescent socialization. As recipients and providers of home-centered hair care, Black females learn important cultural ideals about womanhood and the presentation of self (Gates 1994). Some more enterprising adolescents and women earn capital or other bartered rewards as informal "kitchen beauticians" to their friends, relatives, and acquaintances. Through their engagements as kitchen beauticians, hair care recipients, or mere bystanders in hair care at home, Black girls and women acquire considerable experience with chemical products and hairstyling tools that can both beautify and occasionally damage their hair (Bonner 1991; Powlis 1988).

Thus by the time most African American female clients seek routine professional hair care as adolescents or young adults, their basic knowledge about hair care is often quite advanced. Many know a great deal about their hair as well as the chemical and thermal treatments used to manipulate Black hair textures. Also, very few patrons enter the salon without having experienced (or caused) the notorious burning associated with chemical or thermal hair straightening. Clients' prior experiences with scalp abrasions and hair breakage as recipients or providers of hair care at home means that clients seldom qualify as hair-care novices when these treatments are being applied to their hair in salons. In fact, most clients are aware that remaining silent about the

Figure 1.1. Monique and Renee style their hair at home.

idiosyncrasies of their hair or whether a chemical treatment is producing a burning sensation could result in severe hair damage or loss.

Black women's prior knowledge and experience inform their selection of hairstylists who are able to recognize and handle a range of hair types without causing damage. Black female clients exert agency any time they seek stylists or "kitchen beauticians," as well as when they literally take hair care into their own hands. (Clients' ability to do their own hairstyling is actually a major concern among many Black cosmetologists. In chapter 2, I explore how stylists attempt to mitigate this risk through specialized language and hairstyling techniques designed to increase clients' allegiance to and respect for salon services.)

Blurring expert/novice distinctions in hair-care negotiations

Because many African American clients assess professional hairstylists according to a wide variety of personal experiences, including mishaps, the role of clients as service recipients and that of stylists as service providers are identities that are constantly mediated and reaffirmed over the duration of hair-care negotiations. So, too, are the novice/expert distinctions (Jacoby and Gonzales 1991) implicitly governing client-stylist negotiations. In the hierarchy of knowledge and skill, clients are presumed to be hair-care novices, and licensed hairstylists are recognized as certified hair experts. Yet these assumptions are routinely unsettled by stylists and clients alike.

For example, in my observations of salons in northern and southern California and in South Carolina, clients and hairstylists displayed an awareness of their respective roles; but rather than be constrained by these role expectations, they strategically weaved in and out of expert and novice stances with varying degrees of strategy and success. Taking a novice stance involves yielding diagnostic power to the other party, while expert stances involve assuming some degree of authority, either directly or indirectly, about how the client's hair should be treated and/or styled.

Both parties, for example, enact authoritative stances by raising questions, making suggestions, and ratifying or objecting to hair-care recommendations. Sometimes clients and stylists also employ hedges to mitigate their relative authority or agency for strategic ends. In addition, clients and hairstylists employ other verbal and nonverbal stance markers, including "smile voice" intonation, direct or averted eye gaze, affect-laden facial expressions, gestures, and silence.

Black female clients also use direct and indirect verbal strategies to mitigate the emphatic force of their requests. For instance, I have observed several clients qualify their hair-care recommendations with comments such as, "Excuse me. I'm trying to run things, huh," or "Let me be quiet and let you decide; you're the professional!" Such statements acknowledge the presumed knowledge and skill hierarchy implicitly governing client-stylist relations. Clients' deferential and self-effacing commentaries, however, may also be perfunctory since they serve the dual function of preserving the professional face of the hairstylist while also making the client's hair-care preferences known.

I have also observed clients lobby aggressively for the privileges afforded by the "client is always right" dictum. One client, "Janette," did so after her stylist mulled too long over the hairstyle photographs Janette had given her. When Joyce, her stylist, began to describe aspects of the styles that she did and didn't like, Janette—whom I had mistakenly assumed to be shy—asked bluntly, "Can you do it?" Janette's question contests the assumptions underlying her stylist's behavior that privileges her artistic license as a stylist. In particular, Janette suggests that her own preferences as a paying customer trump the aesthetic preferences of her stylist and thus leave only one question worth considering: Can her stylist create the style depicted in the photographs?

In my pilot study, I analyzed how clients and stylists use language to weave in and out of expert and novice stances in order to judiciously discern hair-care costs (1996a) and negotiate hairstyles that conflict with their stylists' preferences (Jacobs-Huey 1996b; see also Gimlin 1996). In this chapter, I revisit a negotiation I analyzed previously (Jacobs-Huey 1996b). My earlier analysis focused on the strategic maneuverings of a client, Nana G, to abandon the plan to grow her hair longer, which had already been established between her and her stylist, Joyce. Upon more nuanced inspection, however, the negotiation illuminates much more. Nana G and Joyce's interaction also reveals the stakes entailed in hair-care negotiations for both clients and stylists. Understanding the various motives at play helps us appreciate the discourse strategies both women employ to make their preferences known. Nana G, for example, variously enacts novice and expert stances through an array of verbal and nonverbal discourse styles. However, her strategies fail to convince Joyce, her stylist for over ten years as well as her relative.

Renegotiating a pre-established hair-care plan

Nana G and Joyce's conversation took place in the spring of 1995 in Joyce's beauty salon in Oakland, California. Situated in a working-class and predominantly African American community, the salon catered largely to Black women of various ages and class backgrounds. During the time I conducted observations there, the salon had two operators: Joyce, who ran the salon, and Tonya, a younger and highly spirited stylist who rented the salon's second booth in 1993 after obtaining her cosmetology license.

I learned a lot from watching the two of them at work. Joyce, who serviced mainly middle-aged professional women, specialized in traditional straightened styles, while Tonya created more trendy hairstyles requiring the application of gel, weaves, and color treatments for her predominantly young clientele. Their work in different aesthetic genres inspired all sorts of diplomatic collaboration; they freely consulted with one another about procedural matters, but always deferred to the other's aesthetic preferences and expertise with regard to their own clients' hair.

Joyce and Tonya's conversations also yielded insights into clients' presumed role during hair-care negotiations. Both often complained of clients who "expect to look like models presented in hair magazines" but don't fully appreciate the time and energy required, both at home and in salons, to achieve and maintain specific hairstyles. Their shared sentiments in this regard become relevant to Joyce and Nana G's service encounter. In this interaction, Nana G, who has faced repeated difficulty maintaining her hair at home, appeals to Joyce for a haircut. This deviates from Nana G and Joyce's prior agreement for Nana G to "grow her hair."

Additional aspects of Nana G's hair-care history are pertinent to understanding the episode I will discuss. Several months prior to this negotiation, Nana G experienced severe hair breakage caused in part by irregular salon visits and a poor hair-care regimen at home. To improve the condition of her hair, she and Joyce coalesced around the goal of restoring Nana G's hair to its healthy, longer state. To reach this goal, they agreed that Nana G should be consistent in timely salon visits and home hair-care maintenance. (Clients' hair care at home remains integral to the success of salon hair care.) As in the past, at the time of her interaction with Joyce, Nana G again faces difficulty meeting these goals, given the hectic demands of her life and work. She has also grown increasingly intolerant of her hair because it is in the middle stages of growth: neither short enough nor long enough to constitute a viable style. Unhappy with her look, she appeals to her stylist, Joyce, for a shorter (and presumably more manageable) hairstyle.

Anyone who has weathered the middle stages of hair growth will likely empathize with Nana G's proposal. Joyce, however, is less sympathetic to Nana G's hairstyle rut, especially since Nana G's proposed solution breaches the terms of their pre-established hair-care plan. The conflict between Joyce's investment in restoring Nana G's hair to its former glory and Nana G's desire for a haircut presents a dilemma. They must decide whose preferences, desires, and expertise will ultimately determine Nana G's hairstyle. I should note that this is an interesting challenge, since both women are especially adept at indirect and direct strategies of persuasion. I have seen them both use their respective skills to get formerly reluctant folk (including their children) to do all manner of volunteer service within their families, church, and wider community.

Like most hair-care negotiations I observed, their attempt to reach a consensus spans various phases of Nana G's hair appointment. Strikingly, however, Nana G's bid for a haircut is far from straightforward. She initiates her request with an indirect complaint while attempting to catch Joyce's eye in the mirror. When Joyce, who is preoccupied with other tasks, fails to acknowledge Nana G's glance and hairstyle complaint, Nana G begins to speak in such a manner as to be overheard by Joyce and others in the salon. Specifically, she speaks at a louder volume and directs her comments to other clients in the salon. Nana G's manner of speaking is atypical, since client-stylist negotiations are usually two-party engagements. Nana G's turn begets another atypical response: Joyce does not acknowledge Nana G's request until her hair appointment is almost over. In the analysis below, I consider the probable reasons for both of these strategies (see appendix for transcription conventions).

(1) Co-constructing Hair Treatment and Style

```
     1    Nana G:   POPPA GE::NE says I need to do something with my hea:d
     2              (1.5)
     3              [It needs to be cut because >you know it grow so fast uh<
     4              [((looks briefly in the mirror at Joyce, who is preoccupied
     5                  with other tasks and does not return her gaze))
     6              I don't have no uh
     7              (1.0)
     8              no sty:le or nothi:n
     9    Nana G:   (1.0)
    10              I'm just [THERE!
    11                       [((throws hands up in exasperation, looks outside
    12                          salon door))
    13              (1.0)
    14              I know I work ha:rd [hmmph heh hh
    15                                  [((leans to side of chair, with head in hand))
    16              (1.0)
```

17		HA HA:::
18		[Joyce fix my hair so pretty and tomorrow (.)
19		[((*looks toward another client who is sitting under dryer*))
20		[*I'm gon' look like King Kong that just came out of Japa:n*
21		[<You WATCH
22		[((*looks at mirror while pointing at client under dryer*))
23		(1.0)
24		*ARRRGGH*
		((About 50 minutes later))
25	Joyce:	[((*looks briefly at Nana G and then pours hair moisturizer onto*
26		*hand*))
27		[°I sort of wanted to see your hair <u>grow</u>°
28	Nana G:	(0.5)
29		[Hmmmm?
30		[((*leans head to side while observing Joyce in mirror*))
31	Joyce:	(1.0)
32		(I want)/(I hhh hh) I sort (.) of (.) wanted to see it grow
33		[((*Joyce applies moisturizer to Nana G's hair, then looks at*
34		*Nana G in mirror*))
35	Nana G:	[We:::ll then let it grow
36		[((*Nana G rubs chin, while looking pensively at Joyce in*
37		*mirror*))
38	Joyce:	[((*nods head vertically*))
39	Nana G:	[Leave it alone
40		(0.5)
41		Leave it alone
42	Joyce:	((*sing-song voice*)) [>'Member how it used to *be*?<
43		[((*smiles at Nana G through mirror*))
44	Nana G:	Mm [hmmmph
45		[((*Joyce nods vertically while massaging Nana G's hair*))
46		(1.0)
47		Leave it alone
48		(0.5)
49		We(h)'ll see what ha(h)ppe(h)ns (.) hmmph heh heh
50		(1.5)
51		[<u>LE</u>::ave it °alone°
52	Joyce:	[You can always (.) <you know like comb the sides ba:ck or
53		somethin'
54		[((*illustrates by pulling back the sides of Nana G's hair*))
55	Nana G:	(1.0)
56	Nana G:	[Mm hmmm
57		[((*nods head vertically*))
58		(1.0)
59		((*sing-song voice*)) LE:ave it °alone°

Assessing the fate of Nana G's hair-care request

When we consider the fact that Nana G's haircut request violates her and Joyce's preestablished hair-growth plan, Nana G's invocation of her husband (Poppa Gene) in line 1 makes strategic sense. Nana G reports her husband's assessment of her hair: "POPPA GE::NE says I need to do something with my hea:d." She marks Poppa Gene's reported comment in the accusatory he-said-she-said format discussed at length in Goodwin's (1980, 1990) study of African American girls' allegations of gossip. Nana G's use of he-said-she-said differs from Black girls' use since it is not meant to provoke confrontation between Joyce and Poppa Gene (see also Morgan 2002). Rather, it serves to deflect the emphatic force of Nana G's ensuing request for a haircut. Nana G's report of Poppa Gene's recommendation accomplishes several strategic ends. Poppa Gene's statement is both a negative appraisal and a prescriptive complaint about Nana G's hair. His reported use of the modal *need* leaves little doubt that she should improve the condition of her hair. Rather than request the haircut on her own account, Nana G constructs Poppa Gene as an authority—indeed, a relevant one—who prescribed her need for a new hairstyle. As Joyce is quite familiar with *Poppa Gene* as an endearment term for Nana G's spouse, Nana G's reporting of his complaint illustrates her strategic use of indirectness. Specifically, she positions Poppa Gene as an important and extremely salient intermediary (Morgan 1996a) and uses his complaint as a launch pad for her own "expert" hair recommendation.

Nana G next validates her husband's reported stance when she states, "It *needs to* be cut because >you know it grow so fast uh< I don't have no uh (1.0) no sty:le or nothi:n" (lines 3–8). She accomplishes this validation through a series of referential transitions: She segues from what "Poppa GE::NE says" to making her own authoritative pronouncement about the idiosyncrasies of her hair and strongly recommending that it be cut. Her diagnosis, "It *needs to* be cut because >you know it grows so fast<," is delivered rapidly, and the modal *needs (to)* is stressed to underscore the necessity of a new haircut. Her use of the pronoun *it* serves to animate her hair as the instigator of her styleless dilemma, on the grounds that "it grow so fast." Her switch here from first person to third person to convey what is, arguably, her own "expert" knowledge about her hair is telling (i.e., Nana G doesn't say "*I* need it cut" or "*I* don't like it this way."). While her use of the third person may seem to mitigate her stance as "expert" and even downplay her own very deep investment in the outcome of this negotiation, it is equally plausible that her use of the "third person" is a bid for a more expert stance, free of personal subjectivity and cloaked in the "objective" language of expertise.

Nana G's bid apparently falls on deaf ears. She tries to solicit Joyce's attention through the mirror when making her "expert" diagnosis; however, although Joyce is standing nearby, she is preoccupied with taking two pills and fails to return Nana G's gaze (lines 4–5). Joyce's failure to respond even during the 50 minutes in which she chemically treats and shampoos Nana G's hair further suggests that her silence was deliberate.

What happens immediately following Joyce's initial failure to respond is a complicated attempt on Nana G's part to weather Joyce's rather pregnant pause and save face. Her labor is diplomatic; that is, she seeks to save not only her own face but also that of her stylist. Her subsequent complaint in lines 6–10, "I don't have no uh (1.0) no sty:le or nothi:n (1.0) I'm just THERE!," goes public. Her pitch, eye gaze, and gestures suggest that she is speaking to everyone but Joyce. In fact, in the lines that follow, Nana G's gaze is seldom, if at all, directed toward Joyce, arguably the primary player in her appeal for a new hairstyle. Instead, Nana G looks outside (line 11), toward another client who is under the dryer (line 19), and finally at the mirror in front of her (line 22). Still, despite her efforts to engage others, Nana G cannot seem to find a witness.

Nana G finally references her stylist directly when she acknowledges, "I know I work ha:rd hmmph heh hh (1.0) HA HA::: Joyce fix my hair so pretty and tomorrow (.) *I'm gon' look like King Kong that just came out of Japa:n* <You WATCH" (lines 14–21). After a pause, she groans (line 24), reinforcing the extent of her frustration.

Nana G is doing a lot of careful and thoughtful work in this excerpt. Her self-effacing commentary underscores the importance of a proper presentation of self, a value that is presumably shared by the women in the salon. Specifically, her self-critique allows her to save face by acknowledging the poor shape of her hair and thereby forestalling criticism of her hair by others. It also acts as a distancing maneuver from her prior expert stance by establishing Joyce as a competent hairstylist—indeed, an expert capable of making her hair look "pretty." Nana G's statement thus reduces the possibility that her complaints might be interpreted as an indictment of Joyce. Instead, she blames the poor shape of her hair not simply on the fact that "it grow so fast," but also on her busy schedule (line 14).

Strikingly, Joyce does not respond to Nana G's distress call until her hair appointment is almost over. As suggested earlier, her silence may reflect the fact that Nana G's appeal breached (Garfinkel 1967; Goffman 1974) the dyadic nature of client-stylist negotiations and violated the terms of her and Joyce's hair-care plan. These breaches of the client-stylist dyad occurred when Nana G invoked her spouse, Poppa Gene, as a non-present intermediary to underwrite her bid for a cut, and when she addressed her preferences and complaints to nearly everyone in the salon but Joyce.

When Joyce finally responds to Nana G's request for a haircut, she too employs an array of expert and novice stances. As she applies moisturizer to Nana G's hair, Joyce says in a low volume, "°I sort of wanted to see your hair *grow*°" (line 32). Her hedged statement seems to convey a novice stance by framing her hair-care preference as a desire versus an expert recommendation.

Nana G requests clarification, and Joyce reiterates her hedged recommendation in line 32: "(I want)/(I hhh hh) I sort (.) of wanted to see it grow." (It is also possible that here Joyce weakens an upgraded, more assertive stance about her hairstyle preference by shifting from *I want* to *sort of wanted*, but the beginning of her utterance is difficult to hear.) Nana G's response is reluctant, as

Figure 1.2. Nana G. and Joyce negotiate Nana G's hair-care plan.

foreshadowed by her elongated *Well*, a discourse marker that conversation analysts have shown to preface dispreferred talk in which a speaker conveys reluctance (Pomerantz 1975): "We:::ll then let it grow Leave it alone (0.5) Leave it alone" (lines 35–41). Her accompanying nonverbal cues further communicate her reluctance. She rubs her chin while looking pensively at Joyce in the mirror. Joyce agrees by nodding emphatically and (finally) meeting Nana G's gaze in the mirror (see fig. 1.2).

Joyce strengthens her appeal by stopping work momentarily and challenging Nana G to fondly recall how her hair "used to be." Her query in line 38, "'Member how it used to *be*?" is conveyed in sing-song cadence that serves to soften its illocutionary force. Yet Joyce means to wait until she hears from Nana G; she does not resume work on Nana G's hair until she consents. Nana G acquiesces and laughingly suggests a more collaborative coda in lines 44–51: "Mm hmmmph (1.0) Leave it alone (0.5) We(h)'ll see what ha(h)ppe(h)ns (.) hmmph heh heh (1.5) *LE*::ave it °alone°."

It is only at this point that Joyce conveys empathy for Nana G's hairstyle dilemma. She suggests, "You can always (.) <you know like comb the sides ba:ck or somethin'" (lines 52–53). With a nod, Nana G replies, "Mm hmmm ... LE:ave it °alone°" (lines 56, 59), this time with audibly less reluctance; she consents in sing-song intonation. Nana G's consensual reply resituates her as an authority. Essentially, she, the client, gives Joyce permission to proceed in accord with their preestablished hair-care plan.

Expert and novice as negotiated roles

Client-hairstylist negotiations would seem to dichotomize clients as novices and hairstylists as experts. However, a close examination of Nana G and Joyce's interaction demonstrates how their presumed roles as novices and experts become blurred, challenged, and skillfully contested during negotiations about hair. Both adopt stances in talk to construct themselves and each other at various moments as hair experts and as novices. Nana G relies on he-said-she-said and indirectness to request a style that violates the terms of her and Joyce's original agreement. In turn, Joyce employs silence, hedging, and a gentle challenge, among other authoritative and mitigated stances, to strategically oppose Nana G's request. As both women skillfully maneuver between expert and novice stances, they effectively mediate their respective domains of authority and their conflicting desires. Their interaction exemplifies how clients and stylists employ language strategically to construct expert and novice stances and identities, as well as to sustain professional, personal, and even kin relationships within the high-stakes process of negotiating hair care.

There is more to consider about this exchange, especially given the degree of strategy presumed to be at play. After Nana G's hair appointment, I asked Joyce to explain what had happened during her visit. Joyce replied, slightly agitated, "Well, she was trying to get me to cut her hair even though we agreed we were going to grow her hair. That's why I didn't say anything to her when she was complaining. Plus, I think longer hair is more becoming on her." Joyce's reply suggests that her earlier novice stances were specifically designed to socialize Nana G's compliance to Joyce's own aesthetic hair-care preferences.

Joyce's skillful use of language, along with her underlying beliefs about the "best" style for Nana G, raises questions about the ideologies and verbal strategies governing other stylists' interactions with clients, and particularly the extent to which Joyce's beliefs and verbal tactics are representative of a larger community of hairstylists. Answering these questions necessitates looking beyond the symbolic space of the kitchen and hair-care negotiations in the salon to the places where Black stylists learn to speak and act as hair experts, such as hair shows, seminars, and cosmetology schools.

Notably, in my observations across all these sites, stylists described themselves as "hair doctors." This analogy was frequently used as a communal rallying cry that celebrated cosmetology as a science-based practice and instantiated key differences thought to exist between themselves and ill-reputed kitchen beauticians. Stylists' metaphorical alignment with doctors also provided an important means of socializing Black hair-care specialists into collective ways of thinking and speaking about themselves and their work. There was more at stake for stylists in the "hair doctor" analogy, to be sure. In the next chapter, I discuss other complex meanings and entailments of this metaphor for Black cosmetologists.

2

"We Are Like Doctors"

Socializing Cosmetologists into the Discourse of Science

Nana G and Joyce's negotiation in chapter 1 exemplifies the various postures clients and stylists enact to construct themselves as hair novices and/or experts. As we saw, both women weaved in and out of novice and expert stances in their attempt to decide the best hairstyle for Nana G. Their shifting stances expose the slipperiness of these binary roles in salon negotiations. In my ongoing observations, I realized that this slipperiness constitutes one of Black stylists' most significant dilemmas and informs their socialization practices throughout the African diaspora.

In hair-care seminars throughout California, Georgia, and the Carolinas, as well as in London, England, and in a South Carolina cosmetology school, licensed hairstylists diligently worked to shore up the presumed boundaries between hair novices and hair experts. To accomplish this work, many relied on language as a strategy of representation and socialization. Specifically, cosmetologists actively socialized new and established stylists through and to expert discourse and hence expert identity. Black stylists also described themselves as "hair doctors" and encouraged novice stylists to do the same. Stylists frequently invoked this metaphor to frame their interactions with clients in order to legitimize their work as science-based. For example, hairstylists stressed the use of specialized hair terminology versus lay terms as a rhetorical means of displaying their expertise among each other and especially clients. Stylists likewise encouraged novice hairstylists to use the terms *curly hair* versus *nappy hair, wavy* or *fine hair* versus *good hair, shampoo* versus *wash, curling iron* versus *curler,* and, as Joyce so clearly taught me, *hairstylist* versus *hairdresser.*

Stylists also emphasized their preference for salon-use-only versus over-the-counter hair products to further distinguish themselves from "kitchen beauticians." Collectively, these strategies allowed stylists to position themselves within a discourse of science that lent them expert status and hence authority in interactions with clients.

At the same time, however, cosmetologists also recognized the agency of clients as potential producers of negative publicity and as consumers who could always decide to go elsewhere or do their hair at home. Stylists privately acknowledged that if they failed to please their clients, their patrons could complain to family, friends, and acquaintances. Additionally, stylists realized that if they did not demonstrate professional knowledge and skill beyond the level of their most competent clients, these women might be persuaded to take matters of personal hair care into their own hands.

Becoming a hair doctor thus entails authoritative positioning through language as well as an admission that stylists, unlike the physicians to whom they liken themselves, are particularly vulnerable practitioners (Jacobs-Huey 1998). Not only can clients use the services of kitchen beauticians (or become one themselves), they also can contest stylists' expert recommendations on the basis of knowledge gleaned from doing their own or others' hair at home. For many stylists, learning to talk and think like "hair doctors" is a tactical response to such risks. By using specialized language, hair products, and hairstyling procedures, stylists attempt to restrict participation in their profession to the specially trained in order to ensure their continued role in Black women's beauty work.

In this chapter I explore language socialization practices among cosmetologists across various educational contexts that further elucidate what it means to be a hair doctor. These contexts span cities in the United States and London, England, and include a cosmetology school; advanced hair educational seminars; regional, national, and international hair shows; and continuing education classes, which are required for all state-certified cosmetologists. This diverse array of sites reflects the fact that many cosmetologists extend their professional training beyond the 1,600 hours of instruction and annual continuing education courses required for state certification. To gain more elite status and keep abreast of new hairstyles and products in their field, many African American cosmetologists also participate in hair-care seminars and hair shows sponsored by such multimillion-dollar Black-owned companies as Bronner Brothers Enterprises and Dudley's Cosmetology University. For example, student stylists regularly compete in the Bronner Brothers Student Woman "Trend Total Look" Competition and the Master Barbering Competition for cash prizes ranging from $100 to $300. The nation's top Black hair-care specialists—many of whom are male and not all of whom are African American—also showcase their skills in an annual Hair Battle for cash prizes of up to $5,000 and sometimes even a car. These battles are elaborate productions involving multimedia presentations, choreographed dance routines, live models, and the creative maneuverings of a master stylist who conjures up highly embellished hairstyles within a span of minutes. For many Black stylists, the prestige of winning and even participating in such contests far out-weighs the prizes; these resourceful entrepreneurs exploit the symbolic currency (Bourdieu 1977) of their wins by marketing their awards at work, launching their own product lines and educational seminars, and, as I will explain in greater detail, describing themselves as hair doctors.

This analysis builds upon my earlier examination of the use of the "hair doctor" metaphor by a male stylist, Khalif, who was facilitating an educational seminar entitled "The Science of Hair Care" (Jacobs-Huey 1998; see also Majors 2004). In my previous work, I showed how Khalif encouraged his audience of 20-plus licensed stylists and cosmetology students to emulate doctors by using their language, as he put it, "as a verbal skill that gains respect from people." Language, he argued, is one of stylists' most important resources in constructing their expertise. As a participant-observer in other hair-care seminars, I realized that Khalif's instruction reflected a larger rallying cry among cosmetologists. Hairstylists throughout the English-speaking African diaspora use this trope to socialize other stylists into more professional ways of being and representing themselves. Their alignments with doctors offer a glimpse of Black women's professional becoming vis-à-vis language and hair-care practice, and broaden our understandings of how women (and men) construct and negotiate competencies at work.

Socializing hair doctors

Cosmetologists learn what it means to be a hair expert in large measure through language. Hair shows, cosmetology schools, and required continuing education courses are rife with such prescriptions and models of appropriate professional language, as well as personal narratives of successful and failed expert language use. In talking about what it means to be a hair doctor, stylists reveal implicit and explicit linguistic ideologies (Schieffelin et al. 1998) about language use as a mediator of professional expertise.

Candid in-group conversations between cosmetologists also exemplify what Goffman (1967:112) calls "backstage" talk. Their discussions occur behind the professional curtain of salon encounters and are restricted to bona fide members of their field (i.e., licensed and student cosmetologists, instructors, and hair product manufacturers). These interactions divulge the representational strategies adopted by stylists to structure their "front-stage" encounters with clients. More poignantly, these backstage discussions socialize their recipients, shaping the way hairstylists, whether newcomers to their field or experienced practitioners seeking additional training, view themselves and their work.

[They] depend on us to be hair doctors

I first heard the "hair doctor" metaphor during a $50 Los Angeles hair-care seminar for licensed and student cosmetologists. This description of stylists as scientific experts was one of many surprises at the seminar. To begin with, as

I set up my camera, I was privy to whispered conversations between the seminar coordinators. Apparently, the scheduled facilitator had failed to show and they needed to find an alternate speaker—fast! After several desperate phone calls, they located Khalif, a cosmetologist, salon owner, and renowned competitor in national hairstyling competitions and shows. Using his business partner as a live on-stage model, Khalif led a compelling all-day session that simultaneously advertised a line of hair products and heralded the legitimating power of language in the field of cosmetology.

In example 1, Khalif expounds on the "hair doctor" metaphor, while engaging in a live demonstration of chemical hair relaxing.

(1) Constructing Stylists as Physicians and Hair as an Organ

1	Khalif:	Now we can look at it like this: You have a problem. They
2		don't know what it is. They wanna do exploratory surgery,
3		right? But you know once hhh the body is open then it's
4		vulnerable to any bacteria although it's supposed to be in
5		this sterile atmosphere. Even when you get closed up and
6		you go to your room you're exposed, okay? Same relative
7		thought . . . with hair, you know? . . . I make reference to
8		the physicians because that's what I feel that we are, you
9		know, because . . . we manipulate the cosmetic . . . you
10		know, uh manipulating the elements and moving around
11		uh organs, you know, I mean, hair is like a organ. Let
12		somebody burn you . . . or it fall outta the bowl =
13	Audience:	[Hmmm hmmm
14	Khalif:	[= or give you a bad cut and you'll know what I mean!
15		(0.5)
16	Audience:	[Heh heh heh
17	Khalif:	[You'll feel real bad until it comes back, until it gets better,
18		so we, they [clients] depend on us to be hair doctors, to
19		know what we're doing in order to . . . assure them
17		positive results every time. No one wants to see the
18		failures. No one wants to, they don't accept failures—you
19		know what I mean—and they're not gonna leave smiling
20		if you failed at what you, you know, wanted to do to
21		their hair. They respect you saying that "No, you can't
22		*get* this" >you know what I mean< 'cause that's your
23		. . . physician's viewpoint of their condition and they
24		can appreciate that as a professional, but they don't
25		want you to attempt and fail because you were lacking
26		in technology

Khalif's lesson features several references to medical practice that underwrite stylists' positionality as hair doctors. He describes hair as an "organ" (line 11) and asserts that cosmetology involves "exploratory surgery" (line 2) and advanced knowledge of chemical "technology" (line 26). Conversely, Khalif frames clients as patients who "depend" on their doctors to properly diagnose (line 18) and perform chemical "surgery" on their hair (line 2). As he explains in lines 18 to 21, "[Clients] don't accept failures . . . and they're not gonna leave smiling if you failed at what you . . . wanted to do to their hair." Khalif's conceptualization privileges a hierarchical view of the client-stylist relationship in which clients depend on stylists to be hair doctors, and stylists take responsibility for properly diagnosing and treating clients' hair.

You're a doctor

Khalif's framing of stylists as doctors reverberated across other educational settings, including a retailing/marketing seminar for salon owners in South Carolina. The facilitators, Carol and Gwen, advised audience members to publicly display their licensed certification and awards in their salons, much in the manner of physicians. They argued that mirroring doctors in this way enables stylists to impress their clients and thus offset challenges to their authority and pricing.

(2) Representing Stylists as Competent Doctors

1	Gwen:	And uh just take that with you . . . that's something that's very
2		important for you to make money, your clients [need] to see
3		what you're doing. The class that you take, everything that
4		you do, have certificates, put your certificates and then you
5		can take it to a trophy shop and have them put it on a . . .
6		wooden board with a clear cover on it and put it on the wall.
7		Those are your accolades and that's how you are able to
8		charge your clients more and I think it is so important 'cause
9		when you're in it, you are all about money
10	Carol:	Right
11	Gwen:	You're in this to make money, so you have to do things to keep
12		yourself—it's just like a doctor. You're a doctor. You got your
13		dermatologist, your gynecologist, you're a cosmetologist. So
14		that, when you go into a doctor's office and you sit down and
15		talk to him and he has plaques and trophies and everything in
16		there, and you're like, "Oh I have a good doctor" =
17	Carol:	[All my stuff is up in the shop
18	Gwen:	[= and it builds trust. It's just like when I talk to my client and
19		I'm giving you a consultation, you can't tell me anything
20		because "I know that I know that I know." You know? So
21		you have to know, you have to be like that, and . . . those
22		clients that's gonna challenge you and when clients—you, you
23		have to *((slaps hands on every word))* have (.) to (.) know what
24		you're talking about You gotta know your product, you gotta

25   know your hair, you gotta to know what you're touching and
26   ' know what you're feeling. Because you have to shut a person
27   up sometimes. And you shut a person up with knowledge.
28   You know what I'm saying? So you have to let them *see* what
29   you're doing and if you decided one day you wanted to
30   charge fifty dollars for a hairstyle, you been to Paris to the
31   hair show, you know you been to every Bronner Brothers
32   show, you know you been to the International Business
33   Show you have taken classes, you got trophies, you got this,
34   you got that, you competed in competition, your person
35   is going to think twice before the question you about
36   the price

Gwen's didactic discourse bears interesting parallels with Khalif's exhortations. In lines 12 to 13, she, like Khalif, aligns hairstylists' identity and practice with that of medical doctors. Her comment, "It's just like a doctor. You're a doctor. You got your dermatologist, your gynecologist, you're a cosmetologist" takes full advantage of phonological and semantic parallelisms (*dermatologist, gynecologist, cosmetologist*) to inscribe this association. However, Gwen understands that cosmetologists' expertise must be constructed and recommends several strategies for stylists to accomplish this "face-work" (Goffman 1967: 12). For example, she urges hairstylists to publicly display their credentials (e.g., trophies, awards, certificates) and to rhetorically perform their expertise when talking to clients. Such material and verbal displays of knowledge will presumably build trust.

Gwen also invokes the term *consultation* (line 19) to referentially link client-stylist negotiations to a common medical practice. Diagnostic consultations are speech events that entail knowledge requests and exchanges between novices and experts, respectively (Cicourel 1995; Todd and Fisher 1993). These encounters presume the novice's willingness to solicit expert advice, and the expert's obligation to provide an informed response or solution. Gwen's description of hair-care consultations privileges such conventions, while also implicating the dilemma of client expertise, a problem rarely faced by medical doctors. She argues in favor of "know[ing] what you're talking about" during consultations to prevent clients from haggling over prices, hair treatment, and products (lines 22–24). Crucially, stylists' linguistic displays of expertise can short-circuit clients' own speech: "You have to shut a person up sometimes. And you shut a person up with knowledge" (lines 26–27).

That's my head!

In example 2 above, Gwen and Carol urge stylists to act like doctors by displaying their official certification and professional accolades in their salons. They also encourage stylists to convey an unassailable level of expertise when conversing with clients. In example 3, they propose additional stances to substantiate the classification of themselves and other stylists as hair doctors. Hairstylists, they argue, must act as though they "own" their clients' hair.

(3) Enacting Stances of Ownership over Clients' Hair

1	Carol:	I always tell my clients, "First of all, you need to come to
2		me to get your hair conditioned the right way because I'm
3		never gonna tell you [that] you can do it the way I'm doing
4		it. 'Cause you can't. . . . The safest way to do it, if you
5		can't come to me, is to use the product . . . But you can't
6		do what I do 'cause I'm licensed. That's what I do. I'm a
7		hairstylist. You're the client." You have to keep them in . . .
8		[their spot
9	Gwen:	[in their proper place
10	Carol:	They're the client, right. You know, and you're the stylist.
11		Let them know, "I'm running this. That's my head!" heh
12	Audience:	Heh heh
13	Carol:	So *that's my head* =
14	Gwen:	You're in charge of that
15	Carol:	= and that's what they pay you for. You have to really take
16		charge and show them you know that "this is my head" but
17		they'll respect you for it and they'll appreciate it when
18		you're keeping their hair healthy and keeping their hair
19		looking good and they have no breakage. They may say their
20		little smart remarks every once in a while, but really they
21		appreciate it when they come every week, that's showing
22		you they appreciate it.

Carol and Gwen's claim of ownership is a bold one that reflects a hierarchical approach to hair care. For stylists, hair care is not just an intimate social interaction, but also a commercial and artistic exchange. Many stylists therefore view the hairstyles they create both as commodities and as expressions of their creativity. However, stylists cannot always actualize these dual interests. As the case of Nana G and Joyce in chapter 1 exemplifies, clients' desires occasionally conflict with their stylist's wishes. When faced with such dilemmas, stylists can either comply with their clients' requests in accord with the "client is always right" principle, or suggest a compromise since, as stylists often remark, their work "walks the street"—that is, clients publicly display stylists' work on their hair wherever they go. Cosmetologists may also adopt Joyce's strategy and lobby in favor of their own hair-care preferences. Carol and Gwen's co-constructed stance (Goodwin and Duranti 1992; Jacoby and Gonzales 1991) concerning taking ownership over clients' hair seeks to maximize stylists' agency as simultaneously creative artists and successful businesswomen. Carol's comments in particular model for salon owners the proper way to socialize clients' dependency on salon hair care. As she reportedly tells her clients in lines 4 to 6, "The safest way to do it, if you can't come to me, is to use the product . . . But you can't do what I do 'cause I'm licensed." Here, Carol makes allowances for clients' use of salon products but poses limits aimed at ensuring that they return to her salon. Her stance teaches stylists to maximize their revenue by nurturing clients' dependency on products that are sold in their salons. Presumably, this strategy has further benefits by teaching clients to sustain a consistent hair-care regimen at home that makes salon work easier. However, stylists must also remind clients of the need to consult a licensed stylist, lest they falsely assume that they too can be "hair doctors" by using these products at home.

Well, why do you need to go to him?!

The "hair doctor" trope resonated far and wide among the Black hair-care professionals I observed. In a continuing education class in South Carolina, the instructor, Mr. Park, developed this theme to bolster stylists' appreciation for the serious nature of their work. Moments before example 4 below, Mr. Park described his predominantly Black female audience as hair doctors and charged them to make a habit of consulting with clients before providing chemical services. Then, using role reversal and other incongruous scenarios, he revealed some of the key assumptions of the "hair doctor" trope:

(4) Socializing Stylists to Diagnose and Prescribe Proper Hair-care Treatments

1	Mr. Park:	But *please* with the chemicals, and I know I just *ba::rely*
2		touched the surface on chemical but take some ti:me ... ...
3		Lear::n about the *chemical.* -Chemical is a very important
4		u:h uh that's one of the most important things . . . in the
5		field when it comes to product -- the chemical because the
6		chemical is what's causing people hair to drop off. And if
7		you don't know how to use that chemical, you're gonna
8		mess up a lot of people too. And get into doing hair
9		consultations. You know, you don't walk into a doctor's
10		office and say, "Doc, I got this stomachache and even at
11		night, I feel cold with two blankets on the bed. Give me
12		some Pepto-Bismol - uh uh some potnum," and he say,
13		"Okay, I'll write this up." *Well, why do you need to go to*
14		*him?!*
15	Audience:	Mm hmmm
16	Mr. Park:	You Are The Same Way When It Comes To *Hair*! When
17		a person come into your salon and you give a hair
18		consultation, when you get ready to use that chemical, you
19		better *know* what kind of chemical to use, or what *strength*
20		of chemical to use because if you ain't got yourself together,
21		you don't know. A person can come into your salon with
22		*coarse* hair and you go put some some *mi:::ld* relaxer on it!

23	Audience:	Mm hmm:::
24		Heh heh
25	Mr. Park:	You know what you gon' do?
26	Audience:	That's right heh heh
27	Mr. Park:	You gon' lose that customer! You gon' lose the customer
28		because . . . the mild relaxer is not gonna do the hair no
29		justice
30	Audience:	Yeah you right
31	Mr. Park:	-- And even if it look like it did it some justice then, by the
32		next *day,* the hair done revert *right back!* Then the person
33		come in there with with maybe thin hair or not so thin hair
34		and then you go slap a *super!*
35	Audience:	Heh heh
36		HEH HEH HAA::::::
37	Mr. Park:	You don't know what's going on. And what happened? The
38		person hair don't fall off right that minute. But I tell you it's
39		on the way. It's on the way . . .

Mr. Park, an impassioned educator, enacts a humorous role reversal to socialize stylists to be judicious when engaging their clients and applying chemical hair treatments. Role reversals exploit the notion of the *breach* (Garfinkel 1967; Goffman 1974), and all of its instructive connotations. As Schieffelin (1990:151–154) explains, breaches—disagreements in interpretations of language, instruction, arguments, and so on—may expose the implicit cultural expectations and assumptions underlying a social practice. Mr. Park deliberately breaches the presumed organization of doctor-patient consultations to delineate the proper roles expected of stylists and clients. In Mr. Park's verbal enactment, the patient tells the doctor what ails her and suggests an unconventional prescription, which the doctor eagerly supplies. Skillful orator that he is, Mr. Park enacts not one but multiple breaches in this dramatic play; he requests Pepto-Bismol and a folk remedy known as "potnum." The patient's request for a popular over-the-counter medicine and an at-home concoction within the formal space of the doctor's office confound what he, his audience, and most others have experienced within medical encounters. Namely, even though the Internet and heavy advertising by pharmaceutical companies have made it increasingly plausible for medical patients to proffer their own diagnoses to doctors, a relatively small number of patients exploit this privilege; further, it is safe to assume that even fewer do so by requesting over-the-counter products that they can just as easily purchase themselves, or folk remedies that they can concoct at home. In fact, doing so would be akin to asking a salon stylist how much they would charge to wash one's hair in the kitchen sink and press it beside the stove. Likewise, Mr. Park's audience appreciates the humor of his implausible scenario and acknowledges in line 15 the strictly rhetorical nature of his query, *"Well, why do you need to go to him?!"*(lines 13 and 14).

To state the lesson of this role reversal even more plainly: Patients seldom tell doctors what they need or want (especially if they make or buy it themselves), nor do doctors comply willy-nilly with patients' wishes. Rather, patients describe their symptoms and await diagnoses from medical experts. These are crude notions of the doctor-patient relationship, to be sure, but the implications for stylists and clients are readily apparent (see Todd and Fisher 1993 for a more complicated analysis of doctor-patient consultations). It follows, then, that clients should not tell their stylists what to do. Instead, they should act in accord with their role expectations as novices during hair-care consultations and accept the professional assessments of their stylist.

Mr. Park's ensuing talk plays on shared cultural understandings of yet another incongruous scenario. In this lesson, he stresses the importance of learning about chemical hair treatments and conducting consultations with clients before chemically treating their hair (see lines 2–9). He localizes this point by discussing a chemically straightened hairstyle familiar to stylists as a "relaxer" and to clients, more colloquially, as a "perm." (The term *relaxer* is also used to describe a chemical hair-straightening treatment, as in, "She got/wears a relaxer.") Since the relaxer is a popular hairstyle among Black women, most, if not all, of the seminar participants are intimately familiar with this term. In fact, many stylists' knowledge of relaxers has come the hard way, that is, through failures—typically in their household kitchens, in their "floorwork" as cosmetology students (Jacobs-Huey 2003b), and (God forbid) in their salons. Here is how the process of relaxing hair most assuredly begets failure: When a super-strength relaxer is applied to fine, straight hair, the hair will be overprocessed, become weak, and break off. Alternatively, should a mild-strength relaxer be used on coarse, thick hair, the hair will be underprocessed and revert back to its natural curly texture. Again, each outcome represents failure, especially the irrevocable pairing of super-strength relaxer and fine hair. Many in Mr. Park's audience are intimately familiar with the fateful consequences of these scenarios and convey their empathy through a series of anticipatory completions (Lerner 1996). For example, their laughter and agreement tokens in lines 23 to 24, 26, 30, 35–36 corroborate the subtext of Mr. Park's lesson even before he makes explicit his pedagogical point.

This point is, in many ways, similar to the principles conveyed by Khalif, Carol, and Gwen in the previous examples. Mr. Park and Khalif share an interest in promoting stylists' knowledge of chemical hair treatments. In fact, they both situate this knowledge as an important qualification of bona fide "hair doctors." Mr. Park also shares Carol and Gwen's presumption that cosmetologists have exclusive knowledge and diagnostic skills that should be gladly solicited by their clients. Collectively, these stylists' educational discourse presents crucial models for being and becoming professional in a vulnerable field of practice.

Academic and lay responses to "hair doctors"

When I present this data to academic and lay audiences, I often get varied reactions. For many scholars, stylists' framings of themselves as "hair doctors" is but one of many examples of how the use of medical jargon imbues speakers with power and authority (see Litt 2000; Sinclair 1997). Academics with a special interest in language socialization also view the data as illustrative of how apprentices are linguistically socialized both through and to professional discourse and identity (see Garrett and Baquedano-López 2002; Lave and Wenger 1991; Ochs and Schieffelin 1984). Scholars of narrative appreciate these discursive representations of stylists as interactions through which Black women and men represent and constitute their professional identities and lives (see Briggs 1996; Bruner 1996; Ochs and Taylor 1995; Ochs and Capps 1996). As evidenced in my earlier work (e.g., Jacobs-Huey 1998, 1999), I appreciate the relevance of each of these theoretical perspectives.

However, this data often resonates in an intensely personal and negative way among Black women, irrespective of their professional backgrounds. Many are cynical of the "hair doctor" metaphor and resent its connotations; in particular, they do not appreciate being relegated to the role of "patients" in the minds of cosmetologists. Other women lodge similar complaints by recounting salon experiences that corroborate the subtext of the "hair doctor" metaphor; that is, their reported encounters seem to be governed less by the "client is always right" motto than by stylists' preferential regard for the belief that their work "walks the street." I empathize with women who are skeptical of the "hair doctor" trope, and of stylists who employ it as a means of representation and socialization. Yet, as an ethnographer who received liberal access to stylists' "backstage" conversations, I feel an obligation to say a few words in their defense. The representational strategies employed by stylists to actively construct their expertise are not unlike the specialized discourse practices of doctors, lawyers, professors, and other professionals (e.g., Drew and Heritage 1992; Meehan 1981; Mertz 1992; Waitzkin 1985). These "experts" also use jargon, albeit with relatively fewer social sanctions, to construct their professional identity and exclusive membership in their respective fields (see also Biber 1995; Biber and Finegan 1994; Drew 1992; Gunnarsson et al. 1997; Jacoby 1998; Myers-Scotton 1998). That said, it is also important to properly contextualize the "hair doctor" trope in light of cosmetologists' lived experiences. Stylists actually do this work themselves by exposing the tenuousness of the metaphor in actual practice. Their disclosures present a sobering coda to discourse that instantiates stylists in hierarchical roles relative to clients.

Sobering Codas

Despite stylists' statements like "[They] depend on us to be hair doctors," and their claims to ownership of clients' hair, stylists are painfully aware of clients' preexisting hair-care knowledge and experience. Cosmetologists also know that their Black female clients enjoy a range of hair-care options that weaken their dependence on any individual stylist. Under these circumstances, cosmetologists' metaphorical alignments with doctors are best seen as idealized mantras meant to inspire their everyday practice rather than as ideological framings that reflect the realities of their profession. Accordingly, cosmetology trainers as far afield as London, England; Atlanta, Georgia; and Raleigh, North Carolina, frequently remind stylists, "Clients are only *your* clients as long as they're sitting in your chair" (stylist in Raleigh, North Carolina). Similarly, African American cosmetology personnel in South Carolina chide their students as follows: "Some of you walk around talking [and] thinking, 'That's *my* client!' That's *not* your client. You don't *own* her!" Such cautionary remarks certainly qualify the hierarchical client-stylist distinctions implicit in the "hair doctor" trope.

But some of the most insightful admonitions are voiced by the very hair doctors we have considered thus far, such as Khalif, who underscored the importance of speaking and acting in ways that build clients' respect for stylists. As the seminar he was conducting became more relaxed and the discourse more informal, Khalif revealed that the prevalence of kitchen beauticians was a chief motivation for his advice. He lamented, "That . . . makes us STARVE! That'll make us starve to death. We'll starve to death . . . with people doing their hair at home. That's why we have to keep the technology at a high plane where they [clients] know they can't deal with us." Khalif's comment reveals with unusual honesty the financial advantages of professional expertise.

One strategy Khalif proposed to "keep the technology at a high plane" involved the creation of new words to overwrite lay hair terms and thus obscure clients' knowledge of salon procedures. He likewise encouraged stylists to use the verb *silken* versus *press* to describe a thermal hair straightening procedure in which a hot metal comb is used to straighten "virgin" (non-chemically treated) hair textures. Most Black women refer to this procedure as *pressing hair* and have practiced it for years in their household kitchens (Banks 2000; Bonner 1997a; Rooks 1996). Khalif expounded upon his preference for the term *silken* after mistakenly using the phrase *pressing hair* during an on-stage demonstration (fig. 2.1). When one of his pupils good-naturedly reminded him that the proper term was *silken,* Khalif conceded, "Right, I'm 'silkening' it. I've just been reminded that I'm 'silkening' it. We all know it's still a press, but in order to get the clientele to cooperate and . . . feel like they don't know what they're . . . talking about, you be like, 'I'm about to *silk[en]* your hair.' "[1]

Khalif's candid remarks about using new hair terms to befuddle clients raises the ire of many women. However, when such remarks are understood in context—that is, in relation to his lamentation of loss of income ("We'll starve to death . . . with people doing their hair at home")—the realities compelling (though not necessarily excusing) this practice become readily apparent. "Kitchen beauticians" pose a very real and constant threat to licensed African diasporan cosmetologists. Given this reality, many stylists advocate techniques like "silkening," along with other representational strategies to keep professional knowledge beyond the reach of would-be kitchen beauticians.

Remarks by another facilitator, Gwen, shed additional light on this subject. As discussed above, Gwen admonished stylists during a retailing/marketing semi-

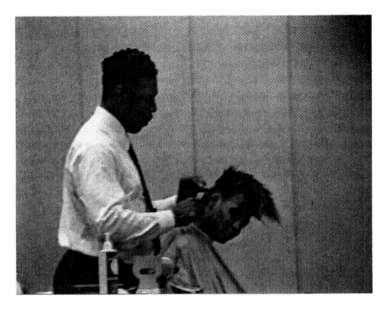

Figure 2.1. Khalif demonstrates hair "silkening."

nar to act as though they "own" their clients' hair. Later in the session, Gwen shared a bittersweet tale about transitioning from a booth rental to her own salon and subsequently losing several clients. Her loss was especially painful since these clients had been loyal patrons for over six years and she had nurtured personal relationships with each of them. Nevertheless, as Gwen lamented, "They left without a word." To add insult to injury, she did not know why. She reported that a client who had remained with her and was a friend of the disloyal patrons eventually answered this question. The client confided that her friends had left because Gwen had raised her prices. Gwen was disturbed by this revelation for several reasons. She felt that establishing her own salon entitled her to raise her prices. Further, she (wrongly) assumed that her patrons would support her entrepreneurial endeavors, given their shared status as Black women. Gwen's sadness eventually turned into anger. In her struggle to make sense of it all, she echoed a sad truth among Black stylists: "Clients will leave at the drop of a dime."

Gwen's admission complicates "hair doctor" stances that presume or actively construct clients as dependent on stylists. Her and Khalif's remarks also socialize cosmetologists' awareness of their professional vulnerability. Cosmetologists learn from such candid remarks that there are limits to the privileged beliefs and stances afforded by the "hair doctor" metaphor. They also learn to appreciate the fact that their clients have a wide range of hair-care options and even expertise insofar as they can consult kitchen beauticians or become one themselves.

Word of mouth can make or break you

Cosmetologists report additional vulnerabilities that are caused by clients' own narratives about their salon experiences. In example 5, students in a South Carolina cosmetology school corroborate their teacher's warning that bad publicity can wreak considerable damage, especially in their tight-knit community. Mrs. Collins brings this point home by discussing a gripe session she overheard during a routine visit to the grocery store (see fig. 2.2). In this reported experience, an unsatisfied customer complained bitterly to a friend about her former stylist within earshot of all who passed by them in the dairy section.

(5) Socializing Novice Stylists' Appreciation for the Power of Clients' Words

```
    1   Mrs. Collins:   The best interest of the client should be your first
    2                   consideration =
    3   Lynn:           Definitely
    4   Mrs. Collins:   = Always your first consideration because you want that
    5                   client to come back. You want them to be satisfied and
    6                   that's your work and your talent that you let walk out the
    7                   door and . . . when somebody asks her who did her hair,
    8                   she's gonna . . . - You know I was in a grocery store
    9                   yesterday in [name of city]. I was at Winn Dixie shopping
   10                   and bo::y it was two ladies standing at the - two Black
   11                   ladies standing at that counter. I don't know WHO this
   12                   cosmetologist was or you know that they go to to get they
```

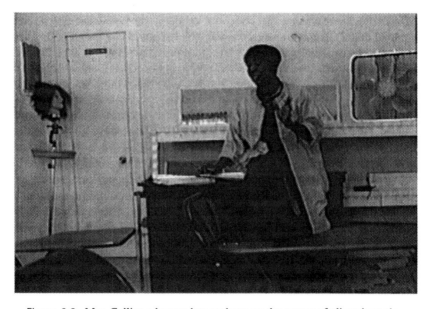

Figure 2.2. Mrs. Collins educates her students on the power of clients' words.

13		hair done but boy they was dogging her name in the
14		grocery store
15	Class:	Heh heh
16	Mrs. Collins:	O::h - I was like WOW ma::n. I mean, ((mimics the angry
17		client)) "And she do this and she gave me a French twist"
18		["up-do"/upswept hairstyle] ... [they were] talking all
19		LOUD up in the grocery store in broad daylight yesterday!
20	Class:	O:::h
21	Mrs. Collins:	((mimics angry client)) "And she gave me a French twist
22		and she didn't do this and girl you know I ain't going back
23		and I got to sit in the salon so long—I told her no!"
24		((someone knocks on classroom door)) Okay, we'll
25		calm it down. ((resumes marking the angry client in a
26		lower voice)) "And I told her, 'No! I'm not gonna I I
27		got to go! I ain't gon' be sitting up in this salon all day
28		long!'" I mean they was going on:::: and on::::: and
29		on::::: about this - I I wanted to ask them so bad, "Who
30		y'all ta(h)lkin' about?"
31	Class:	Heh heh
32	Mrs. Collins:	'Cause I know -
33	Lynn:	I would've asked
34	Mrs. Collins:	I I cain't believe
35	Lynn:	I would've asked
36	Mrs. Collins:	They was just standing up in the in the um::: you
37		know where the milk and the cheese and stuff? I mean
38		they =
39	Lynn:	- They wasn't even at the cash register, man I would've
40		asked her
41	Mrs. Collins:	= Aw ma::n they was loud! They was almost to the cash
42		register though because ... in Winn Dixie in [name of
43		city], it's closer to the front, the door. Aw ma::n everybody
44		heard that one. I don't know WHO this girl was but
45		they was dogging her yesterday, you hear me? And and I
46		was like, "Da:::ng, man. I'm glad I don't do they hair.
47		They don't know who I am." But I sho:::' heard some
48		things out of them ... It had to be somebody in ((names
49		city)) ... either ((names one candidate)) or ((names
50		another candidate))
51	Lynn:	Be quiet, Mrs. Collins. Be quiet, Mrs. Collins heh heh
52	Deirdre:	You on tape
53	Lynn:	Lanita, just edit that
54	Mrs. Collins:	Heh heh it had to be one of them ma::n because they was
55		... dogging that girl bad bo::y but anyway
56	Tina:	Word of mouth can either make you or break you
57	Mrs. Collins:	Make you or break you that's why that's right. So you
58		need to—if you don't have but one client

59	Lynn:	- You need to give a:::LL you *got* to that one client =
60	Mrs. Collins:	To that one client
61	Lynn:	= in that space and time that you have to work on them
62		...they should be your first your main priority
63	Mrs. Collins:	You shouldn't ... and don't try to rush your client 'cause a
64		lot of people do not need you and you know for yourself
65		when you do a rush job, you gonna do a bum up job. So
66		you want to (do your best)

Mrs. Collins weaves in and out of character voices to bring to life one of stylists' worst nightmares: public badmouthing from clients. This nightmare resonates among licensed and student stylists alike—and among clients, for that matter. No stylist wants her or his name defamed in public. In an industry where stylists are already vulnerable given the presence of kitchen beauticians and the omnipresence of professional over-the-counter hair treatments, disparaging remarks by clients can cause irrevocable damage. This is especially true in their local community where gossip travels fast and stylists are easily identifiable by way of deduction (as shown by Mrs. Collins's detective work in lines 47–50 and edited portions of the transcript, as per Lynn's admonition in line 51).

However, many African American women may also be inclined to empathize with the angry client in the grocery store. Her anger about having been in the salon all day reflects a widespread frustration among Black women about the lengthy duration of their salon visits. In fact, as I discuss further in chapter 4, the subject of being "held hostage" in beauty salons for "seven whole days and seven whole nights" has been parodied by Black female comedians such as Adele Givens and Retha Jones, much to the amusement of African American audiences.

The moral to Mrs. Collins's tale is clearly articulated by students Tina and Lynn. In lines 56 and 57–58, they note, respectively, "Word of mouth can either make you or break you" and "You need to give a:::LL you *got* to that one client." Their collaborative coda exemplifies the fact that clients have more power than is often recognized and that stylists' vulnerability is clearly understood, particularly among cosmetology's bona fide apprentices.

Socializing a more inclusive view of hair-care expertise

Appreciating language as a primary site of professional socialization helps us unearth the everyday entailments of the "hair doctor" theme for stylists throughout the English-speaking African diaspora. Specifically, it gets us into the heart of women's being and becoming vis-à-vis discursive engagements with hair-care practice. It also illuminates how Black women and men negotiate and contend with various competencies in the workplace. In the context of training seminars and cosmetology classrooms, these instructive bids to specialized language use socialize licensed and student stylists into professional discourse and representational practices befitting their community of practice.

But this socialization is ever complicated. Many stylists who codify the "hair doctor" trope as a mantra for professional development also feel compelled to qualify this stance. Their cautionary remarks routinely expose their vulnerability as cosmetologists who service a highly knowledgeable clientele and must therefore actively pursue and in some cases cajole their clients' respect. In example 6, Carol hints at these challenges but suggests an alternative to the strategies of client exclusion espoused thus far in "hair doctor" discourse. She proposes that hair doctoring, at its best, involves self-assured stylists who are generous with their "gifts":

You can't take nothing from me ... that God has given me

(6) Constructing Cosmetology as a Gift from God

1	Carol:	. . . In our salon, I don't hide. 'Cause they [clients] look
2		under that dryer. *They be looking under that dryer!*
3	Audience:	They want to see
4	Carol:	*And I just let them LOOK and I hh le(h)t the(h)m look* 'cause
5		I know they can't I mean, ... some of them really can do
6		hair =
7	Audience:	Mm hmm
8	Carol:	= they just don't want to go to school. But I'm thinking I
9		try not to hide from them. Even . . . with Gwen, both of us
10		work in different rooms. I think that we should be able - if
11		she's learning something new, I'm gonna look. What you
12		wanna do? - I mean =
13	Audience:	That's right
14		Mm hmm
15		That's right
16	Carol:	= You gon' hide from me? I'll just come on up to [you] =
17	Audience:	Heh heh
18	Carol:	= You know and it's the same with us. IF we do that to each
19		other and start thinking, "Oh she gon' learn [more than me =
20	Audience:	[more than me
21	Carol:	= or she gon' have more techniques than me, I mean, you
22		can't take nothing from me that God has . . . given me =
23	Audience:	That's right. That's right
24	Carol:	= A talent and a gift to do hair enough to share with you.
25		And if I don't give it away, then I'm not gonna even prosper
26		with God
27	Audience:	That's right
28	Carol:	So I'ma give it back
29	Audience:	That's right
30	Carolyn:	It don't matter. You can't take nothing from me. I'm not
31		intimidated.

Here, Carol champions a very different way of viewing professional hair care. Rather than exclude clients from the exchange of advanced hair-care knowledge and skill, Carol suggests that her success will be ultimately determined by the extent to which she gives freely of her "gifts." The spiritual undertones of Carol's message in lines 24–26 are unmistakable and highlight another way that many African American women make sense of hair in their everyday lives. In the next chapter, I explore stylists' use of metaphor to describe their work as both a "gift" and divine "license to touch" people's bodies and lives. I also consider the implications of such talk for the study of language and gender, particularly how women construct and negotiate between various lay/expert and secular/spiritual competencies at work and in their wider communities of practice.

3

A License to Touch

Cosmetology as a Divine Calling

In the prior chapter, I discussed how African American cosmetologists use linguistic and other strategies to represent themselves as hair doctors. When interacting with clients, for example, stylists substitute lay hair terms like *press* with jargon such as *silken* to reduce clients' familiarity with this popular hair-straightening procedure. Stylists also display their cosmetology licenses and accolades prominently to highlight their specialized training and hence discourage clients from quibbling over prices. By modeling themselves after physicians and urging other stylists to do the same, African American hairstylists seek to differentiate themselves from unlicensed kitchen beauticians.

Carol's comment at the end of chapter 2 exemplifies another frame used by many African American stylists to describe their work. She attributes her skills as a cosmetologist to God and argues that her "gift" must be shared freely with clients and other stylists in order for her to prosper. This is a powerful attribution, not simply because it begs greater tolerance and generosity from stylists in their interactions with clients, but also because it imbues hair care with spiritual significance.

Carol's perspective resonated widely among the stylists I observed. For example, the slogan on my mother's original business cards, as well as the name of her salon, was inspired by the scripture "Therefore if any man be in Christ, he is a new creature: old things are passed away; behold, all things are become new" (2 Corinthians 5:17). Additionally, teachers at the cosmetology school where I conducted my doctoral fieldwork often infused textbook instruction with moral and scriptural addenda (Jacobs-Huey 2003b). Further, many of the

Black hair-care seminars and hair expos I observed in the United States and England incorporated testimony, prayer, and Sunday morning worship services.

Similar to stylists' use of scientific discourse in chapter 2, Christian stylists employed spiritual discourse as a means of professional socialization and representation. Stylists' use of religious discourse also informed a broader array of interpersonal exchanges with other cosmetologists and clients, including fellowship and prayer (Battle-Walters 2004). For many African American female stylists, the use of spirituality to frame their identities as "gifted" or "called" (by God) enabled them to construct and maintain a religious authority that was not always publicly available to them elsewhere (see Gilkes 2001; F.L. Smith 1993; D.K. Williams 2004), and was likewise useful in bolstering their (also tenuous) professional authority.

Throughout my fieldwork, spirituality was most profoundly underscored in monthly Bible study meetings of a nonprofit organization called Cosmetologists for Christ (CFC). I learned of CFC and its charismatic founder, Estelle, while attending a "natural" hair show in Los Angeles. Estelle, who is also a certified cosmetologist, licensed minister, and salon owner, facilitated a workshop entitled "How to Turn Your Talents into Dollars." In the seminar, participants sang gospel songs, testified about their blessings in life and work, prayed, and contributed financial offerings. Estelle also taught a Bible study lesson addressing such themes as "How to Apply Faith to Your Profession"; "How to Increase Your Income by Application of the Word of God"; "How to Remain Committed to Your Profession"; and "And By the Word of Our Testimony." The themes of Estelle's lesson were frequently underscored in CFC's monthly Bible study meetings, which were held after hours in two of Los Angeles's premiere African American-owned salons. I observed these meetings closely over a period of two years and was eventually appointed the organization's historian. I also observed Estelle in the salon she managed after she graciously "blessed" me with discount hair-care service during my initial years in graduate school. As a client, I noticed several occasions wherein she discreetly obliged clients' requests for prayer and anointed the walls of her salon with prayer oil. I came to better appreciate the ideologies behind this spiritual practice as a participant-observer in CFC meetings.

In my primary observations of Bible study meetings, stylists regularly described cosmetology as a "gift," a "calling" and an "awesome responsibility" and socialized other stylists and aestheticians to embrace similar views of their work and professional status. Example 1 exemplifies Estelle's use of such discourse during a typical session. While welcoming a small cohort to Bible study one evening, she elaborated on stylists' "awesome responsibility" by celebrating their divine license to touch people's bodies and lives:

(1) A License to Touch: Hair Care as Ministry

    1   Estelle: Well, we have a lot of things that God has given us to do
    2   and I know that we're gonna accomplish all of our goals
    3   with all of the support that we have and all of the people

4		that love the Lord and that love this industry. There's no
5		reason why we can't accomplish all the goals that God
6		has given us because . . . we have an awesome responsibility.
7		And you know, those of us that have the **talents and the**
8		**gifts, as we minister to people physically, we can also**
9		**minister to their spirits at the same time =**
10	Member:	(That's right huh)/(That's true too)
11	Estelle:	= because we're one of the few professionals that . . . are
12		**licensed to touch people**
13	Member:	Mmm hmmm
14	Estelle:	And when we do, *boy oh boy* [heh hhhh =
15	Member:	[Hmmm hmmm hmmm
16	Estelle:	= a lot can take place right?
17	Member:	[Mm hmmm
18		[Yes
19	Estelle:	You know we can pray over them, we can share with them
20		hhh -I'm telling you there's not a *week* . . . goes by that the
21		Lord doesn't have me to **minister** to somebody about
22		something
23	Member:	Yes Lord
24	Estelle:	NOT EVERYBODY that sits in your chair will need
25		**ministry** but there are some that will and they will ask you
26		questions and it's our job to give them the **word**. But you
27		gotta *know* the **word** to give the **word**
28	Members:	That's [right
29		[Mm hmmm
30	Estelle:	[Right?
31	Members:	[That's right
32		[Right
33		Mm hmmm

Estelle exploits literal and figurative meanings of *touch* throughout this exchange. For example, her reference to stylists' "license to touch" refers both to their state-issued certification and to their divinely appointed "gift" to touch people. Similarly, her use of *touch* invokes the centrality of physical touch as a display of expertise and authority (Synnott 1993), as well as the significance of Jesus' healing touch. In New Testament accounts, Jesus' touch, including the mere touch of his garment, resulted in spiritual and physical restoration (e.g., Matthew 9:20–26; Mark 5:24–34). Moreover, Estelle highlights hairstylists' ability to pray over their clients. In past meetings, she also described instances in which she privately "laid hands" on clients requesting special prayer.

Estelle's use of *touch* may also convey a sense of affecting someone emotionally, as in "I was touched by your testimony." This is because cosmetologists are often more than just service providers. In many cases, hairstylists also act as clients' informal caregivers, lay psychologists, and confidants (Brown 1983;

Eayrs 1993; Getz and Klein 1980; Gimlin 1996; Majors 2004; Weisenfeld and Weis 1979). Stylists' reported "license to touch" may thus represent their ability to touch their clients physically, emotionally, and spiritually. Beyond the heteroglossic meanings of touch exploited in this exchange, Estelle employs other expressions from the King James Version of the Bible to forge symbolic links between cosmetology and ministry. Her use of *talents* and *gifts* in lines 7–8 evokes biblical accounts of God's provision of "talents" and "gifts" to be used for his edification (e.g., Psalms 90:17). Similarly, her use of the verb *minister* in lines 8 and 21 and *the word* to reference the Bible in lines 26–27 (e.g., 2 Timothy 2:15) further exemplifies the multigenred nature of CFC narratives. Members' participation in call and response with Estelle ratifies the tenets of her narrative and collaborates in framing cosmetology as a form of ministry.

Estelle's narrative, much like Carol's testimony in chapter 2, provides a window into stylists' use of narrative to underwrite their membership in a community of divinely "gifted" hairstylists. They indicate that with this membership comes a responsibility to touch people in literal and spiritually transformative ways. In the remainder of this chapter, I explore stylists' testimonies and prayers during CFC meetings as well as a hair care seminar. I show how these narratives socialize cosmetologists' shared conceptions of themselves, their clients, and their work. Much like the "hair doctor" narratives considered earlier that socialize stylists into a self-conception as scientific professionals, these spiritual narratives provide insight into the symbolic meanings associated with Black hair care. They also provide a glimpse of the centrality of language (Smitherman 1977) and hair-care practice (Banks 2000) in African Americans' spiritual and aesthetic "becomings," both as hair-care professionals trying to be godly and successful in a vulnerable service industry and as clients who, as we know from Nana G, actively shape their interpersonal engagements with and aesthetic refashionings by stylists. Finally, stylists' spiritual discourse illuminates the heteroglossia (Bakhtin 1968; Ivanov 2000) noted of religious discourse practices insofar as they entail spontaneous uses of spiritual, secular, and even scientific genres to instantiate symbolic links between cosmetology and spirituality and to further legitimate the field of cosmetology as "expert" practice.

Cosmetologists for Christ

Established as a nonprofit organization in 1988, the Los Angeles chapter of CFC that I observed is a mixed-gender group composed of the city's premiere African American stylists. Several of its more than 25 members own salons in Beverly Hills (see fig. 3.1). Others market professional Black hair-care products. A few CFC members also work as hairstylists in the television and film industry or as cosmetology instructors; some are still students.

Symbolically, the organization represents the convergence of two core African American institutions: the church and the beauty salon. In fact, the CFC's monthly Bible study meetings are actually held in a beauty salon and

Figure 3.1 Cosmetologists for Christ at Bible study.

often begin against the backdrop of contemporary gospel or praise music. The two Bible study leaders at the time of my fieldwork, Estelle and Charles, are certified cosmetologists and teachers at their local church; they sometimes travel to major hair shows to lead Sunday worship services or Bible study meetings.

During meetings, CFC members use a range of African American religious speech styles (Wright 1976), including call and response (Morgan 1994b, 1998; Smitherman 1977), biblical expressions, and terms that are highly symbolic in Christian theology, such as *touch, hands,* and *calling.* Participants also show agreement through expletives such as *Amen!* or *Hallelujah!*, or by waving a hand during testimonials and prayers. CFC Bible study sessions resemble Black church services (see Boyer 1973; Freedman 1993; Kostarelos 1995; Smitherman 1977; Taylor 1994) insofar as they designate time for testimony, song, prayer, financial offering, and a Bible study lesson that applies biblical principles to cosmetological practice. I examine in detail two of these discourse genres— prayer and testimony—in order to demonstrate how African American stylists within and beyond the CFC employ spiritual discourse as a resource in their daily lives. In particular, I aim to show how stylists use these spiritual discourses to reaffirm and socialize their colleagues into collective ways of "being" and "becoming" spiritual in their daily lives.

Prayers

Prayer is a central means through which CFC members frame their professional identities and the nature of their everyday engagements with clients and co-workers. Prayer is a ritualized event that occurs at distinct intervals during the

Bible study meetings. Private intercessory prayer takes place via prayer request cards upon which people privately write a request to God. These cards, along with monetary offerings, are then sealed, placed in a collection basket, and collectively prayed over. Prayer also precedes the Bible study lesson and later concludes the meeting.

While prayer is a conventionalized activity at several distinct intervals during CFC meetings, the discursive form it takes is by no means static or routine. Hairstylists engage in spoken, sung, and collaborative prayers, utilizing call and response, timing and rhythm (Morgan 1998), and, as will be shown, referential and assertive stances that reposition speakers in relationship to God, Satan, clients, and each other. Special intercessory prayer may also be physically enacted on the bodies of CFC members by the "laying on of hands" and "anointing with oil." (I received such intercessory prayer before embarking on my doctoral fieldwork.)

Stylists' prayers also evidence a range of intentions as mediums of praise, petition, confession, and intercession. Stylists report that they use prayer in their daily lives to deter negative engagements with their clients and coworkers. Some members testify that they "lay hands" on the physical structure of their salons and pray silent prayers for their clients in order to maintain a peaceful atmosphere in their workplaces. Other participants write and sell their own business prayers to other beauty industry professionals, exerting poetic license and entrepreneurial agency within these texts by representing themselves as "prayer warriors."

Ochs and Capps (1996) and Baquedano-Lopez (1997) demonstrate that prayers, whether recited or spontaneous, constitute literacy practices that socialize participants into proper roles, beliefs, attitudes, and other ways of being moral in the world. During prayer, speakers enact bold authoritative stances toward the worlds they inhabit and the futures they seek. In example 2, Estelle describes to CFC members how she uses the various prayers she wrote and published in her manual, "How to Turn Your Talents into Dollars," to run her salon as an "outreach" (i.e., intervention):

(2) "I'll . . . Lay Hands on Everything": Charging the Salon with the Power of God

1	Estelle:	. . . and there's one in here [in manual] uh it's to dedicate a
2		business to God uh to operate a business as an outreach. And
3		that's what basically I believe that we're doing here in this
4		business. Because we're reaching out . . . with the **word of**
5		**God** because God is first place in this business. He is the
6		CEO *here*! So therefore the atmosphere is already charged
7		when people come in. Because we've prayed, because we've
8		lifted up the name of Jesus, and because, you know, it's
9		charged **with the Holy Spirit,** then we know that *you* know
10		what takes place here. The **anointing** is already here and
11		when those evil spirits come in or . . . people *bring* them in
12	Member:	Mm hmm

13	Estelle:	Because . . . you know whatever is operating in and through
14		them—because we know that spirits embody people. You
15		know, they just don't walk around . . . but they're . . .
16		walking around *in* people
17	Member:	Mm hmmm
18	Estelle:	And so when those spirits walk through that door because . . .
19		of the prayer, because of the **anointing**. -You know many
20		times what I'll do is just walk around this place and **lay**
21		**hands on everything** and begin to **anoint the place,**
22		you know, **anoint the doorpost** . . . and we play um you
23		know the type of music, *not* all day but at some point during
24		the day, you're going to hear the **word of God** going forth
25		across those . . . airwaves. And that's another way of
26		keeping the atmosphere **charged with the word of God** and
27		the **power of God.** And that's more important than anything
28		else because that way you always know that He's in charge
29		here. So those spirits, *they may come in*, but **they have no**
30		**victory in here**

Estelle's description both markets her business prayers and socializes CFC members to envision prayer as a means of taking authority over problems in their everyday lives, particularly the problem of clients (and presumably coworkers) with negative attitudes (evil spirits, line 11). Estelle's practice of "laying hands" on her clients and anointing the doorposts of her salon recalls biblical accounts (e.g., Exodus 12:7) of the redemptive merit of such actions. Further, her discourse exploits scriptural authority through highly symbolic terms such as *anoint* and *charge*. As she notes, her salon is "charged" with the word and power of God (lines 26–27). This framing situates God as explicitly involved in her business; God is, in effect, its CEO. By extension, profiting financially from hair-care practice is not only a legitimate but also a godly act.

CFC members regularly discuss and practice an intertextual genre of prayer called "confession." When confessing, stylists use spoken, silent, and tactile prayer to inscribe the spiritual and professional selves they seek to become, as well as to effect dispositional changes in their clients and coworkers. Example 3 illustrates that CFC members' uses and understandings of confessional prayer belie traditional understandings of confession as the admission of sin to God or clergy. Rather, as Estelle notes during a subsequent Bible study lesson, confessional prayer does not entail merely repentance, but also "saying what the word of God says about" believers:

(3) "Saying What the Word of God Says about Us": Confession Redefined

1	Estelle:	Confession means that we say what God's word says about us.
2		We're not supposed to speak to circumstances . . . so no matter
3		what the circumstances look like, instead of confessing, you
4		know, "I'm broke," as we will say on occasion

5	Member:	Mm hmm!
6	Estelle:	If we look in our bank account or look in our purse, it's like, "I
7		ain't got no money!" But the word says that that we're blessed
8		abundantly, the blessings of the Lord make us rich and he adds
9		no sorrow [**Proverbs 10:22**]. So we cannot say what the
10		circumstances say and it's very tempting to do that. . . .We have
11		to remember that God's word says everything that we have
12		need of, he's going to supply all of our needs, according to his
13		riches in glory, by Christ Jesus [**Philippians 4:19**]. And he said
14		his mercies are new every morning [**Lamentations 3:21–23**]
15		and we know we have new mercy every morning.

Estelle's commentary provides a powerful reinterpretation of the traditional genre of confession. When confessional prayer is practiced in CFC meetings, members invoke scriptural references as master scripts on which to base their petitions or authoritative claims (see lines 9, 13–14). Confessions are thus intertextual, incorporating stances typically associated with prayers of intercession and praise, along with bold articulations that challenge Satan and provoke God to actualize faith-based claims. Further, CFC members' confessions combine preformulated speech from the prayer genre and unplanned speech in accord with the specific dilemmas stylists face in their everyday lives (see Shoaps 2002). Stylists' highly agentive and performative prayers (Austin 1962; Finnegan 1969; Hall 2000) enable them to assert control over their professional identities, engagements, and destinies; through them, they instantiate news ways of being and becoming successful as stylists, salon managers, Christians, women, spouses, students, and a host of other roles. As Estelle underscores to CFC members in example 4, this is because the prayer genre of confession privileges the symbolic power of biblical text and spoken words:

(4) "Words Are Containers . . . That Carry Faith or Fear": Confession Redefined

1	Estelle:	You know if you're unsure about what to say, begin to pray the
2		word. Pray what the word says. Pray what the word says and
3		that way you can't go wrong. Now words are like containers.
4		Containers, they carry faith or fear so we are to speak faith
5		in words [**e.g., Mark 11:22–24**]. . . . So we have to put him
6		[God] in remembrance of his word, not that he's forgetful but
7		see it's a matter of us continuing to confess it. We're really
8		remembering it ourselves . . . what his promises are to us when
9		we, you know, continue to say it over and over again

Confession is thus a purposeful act among cosmetologists, enabling them to temper fear with faith in their personal and professional lives. In example 5, CFC member and celebrity stylist Debra affirms Estelle's remarks by describing the ways she has used confession to resolve problems at work.

(5) "Framing Your Work with Your Words": Confession Redefined

1	Debra:	It's just like you said earlier, the confession. I see them [clients,
2		coworkers] kind, I see them loving, I see them caring. You
3		know, I even call out their name. I see them fair and . . . what
4		was I gonna say? But um the things that you want them to
5		be, you know, um a good employer or a good coworker, to
6		confess those things. And I started doing that and it really made
7		a difference
8	Estelle:	Praise God
9	Debra:	It made a difference. So, you know, if you start confessing the
10		word over that person. It's like when you say, "I see . . .
11		((client's name)) as a loving, kind child of God and she is um
12		. . . a warm person and . . . I cover her with the word of Jesus
13		and, Lord, I lift her up to you" and so forth and so on and . . .
14		one day she will start you know, because you're putting the
15		word out there in the spirit realm and she will start acting the
16		way that you are confessing
17	Estelle:	So what you're doing is framing your work with your words
18	Debra:	Framing the person with your words

Estelle and Debra co-construct prayer as an alternative spiritual means of socializing clients and coworkers into more socially acceptable behaviors and dispositions. By silently confessing the word of Jesus in the proximity of a difficult person in their workplace, stylists lay the spiritual groundwork for improving client-stylist relations and collegiality among their coworkers. In essence, they take authority, through faith, over some of the adverse aspects of their industry. Examples 6 through 9 attest to some of these adverse qualities, including difficult clients, lack of funds, business slumps, and tumultuous work conditions.

(6) "Clients Sometimes Can Put You in Fear": Applying Confession at Work

1	Estelle:	Clients sometimes can put you in fear=
2	Member:	Mm hmm
3	Estelle:	= because they'll confront you: "Well, my hair this" or you
4		know, like get a attitude and you're like, "OH my Go:d," you
5		know. You have to take authority over it. I had a couple of
6		them last week. You know, they had me almost gettin' in fear.
7		I was like, "Unh unh, I take authority over that spirit in the
8		name of Jesus, you know." And I don't actually have to say it
9		out loud. I say it to myself but I know that it has to come
10		subject to the spirit of God in me. That spirit has to become
11		subject to the spirit that's operating in me. And it will when
12		you speak to it. If you don't speak to it, it will just rise up and,
13		you know, have you thinking that you just totally out of line,

14   that you've done something terribly wrong. But everybody can
15   make a mistake, you know. But you got to communicate about
16   it, you gotta talk about it and uh when you do, when you take
17   authority over it, then it will begin to submit to the spirit of
18   God that's in you. So we have rights, but if we don't exercise
19   them, it doesn't do us any good. Just like we have a right to
20   vote, but if we don't vote, we can't complain if we didn't vote,
21   you know, we have we have rights God has given us. We've
22   been made righteous by the blood of Jesus so we're already in
23   right standing with him

Here, Estelle acknowledges the "fear" cosmetologists experience when encountering dissatisfied clients. She encourages stylists, however, to discuss their "mistakes" in a godly manner, while also remembering their "rights" as believers. This is a powerful formulation that functions much like scientific discourse in re-anchoring stylists' authority with respect to clients. To frame cosmetologists as having spiritual rights, even in the face of their mistakes, provides a model of spiritual ideology and behavior in which silent confession moderates against defensiveness and a loss of face when resolving clients' complaints.

During another lesson, Estelle stressed multiple personal and professional applications of the genre of confession. In example 7, she describes how confession helped her overcome a paralyzing fear that she would be unable to pay her tuition in divinity school:

(7) "I'm Standing on Your Word": Confession at Work

1   Estelle: I remember one time when I was going to school. I was at the
2   school of ministry and I woke up one morning and I was like,
3   "Oh my God." I started thinking about my bills, my tuition was
4   due, my rent was due, my car note was due, my phone bill, I
5   mean, everything! I mean everything was due! . . . So the
6   devil had me afraid to get out of the bed. I was afraid if I got
7   up, I didn't know what was gon' happen. And I had to really
8   minister to myself and just say, "No, devil, I'm not gon' lay
9   here and just let you, you know, put me under condemnation
10   and guilt and fear." I had to make myself get out of the bed, get
11   in the car. I didn't even have, I don't think I had enough gas in
12   my car, I was just on, by faith, believing I was gon' get where I
13   had to go. And just walk and just taking every step, every step,
14   every step, and that's what he wants us to do because if I
15   would've just gave into all that - the the circumstances, I
16   probably would've never finished school. I mean, I would've
17   never done what God had called me to do. Because that's what
18   he [Satan] wants to do. He wants to stop the plan of God. He
19   wants to stop you from operating in faith. He wants to get

20		you over to fear and doubt and unbelief so eventually you just
21		go back into the world. You know, you just go back to
22		wherever you came from. But that's not the plan of God. So we
23		just have to encourage ourselves sometimes in the Lord. It's
24		like, "Father, I know what your word says. I'm standing on
25		your word. I'm gonna be encouraged. I'm gonna look up to
26		Jesus who's the author and finisher of my faith. So you're
27		gonna just have to open up a door. I need a breakthrough right
28		now!"
29	Members:	Amen

In this testimony, Estelle reports that confession afforded her an authoritative stance with which to confront Satan and God. To circumvent the fear of not being able to pay her school expenses, Estelle served notice to Satan (*No devil, I'm not gon' lay here and just let you, you know, put me under condemnation and guilt and fear,* lines 8–10) and God (*I'm gonna look up to Jesus who's the author and finisher of my faith. So you're gonna just have to open up a door. I need a breakthrough right now!* lines 26–28). Her testimony serves to socialize CFC members through and to confession insofar as it instantiates the success of this prayer genre in her own life; in essence, her status as a licensed stylist and minister is proof that confession "works." In Estelle, she provides another example of how confession enabled her to "take authority" over negativity, this time as manager of a hair salon:

(8) "You Have to Take Authority over That Business": Confessing Success at Work

1	Estelle:	You have to get in the mirror and just begin to confess God's
2		Word over your life. "Father, I just thank you that I'm the head
3		not the tail [**Deuteronomy 28:13**], that greater is he that's in
4		me than he that is in the world [**1 John 4:4**], that I'm working
5		in divine and perfect health, that I've been made righteous by
6		the blood of Jesus" [**e.g., Romans 5:9**], you know. You just go
7		for—all over the Bible. I mean, every scripture you can think
8		of, just begin to confess it in your prayer time, you know, over
9		your own life. Over your own home, your kids, your marriage,
10		your business. You know, many times, I have to get in here
11		and just begin to lay hands on the books, lay hands on the door,
12		and plead . . . Jesus, lay hands on all the chairs, you know, just
13		command the enemy to leave and the presence of God to be
14		ushered in. Sometimes when our [receptionist client log] book
15		look like we don't have any clients, you know, I just command
16		the clients to come in from the north, south, east, and west
17		[e.g., **Zechariah 6:1–8**], lay hands on the phone that it's gon'
18		ring, lay hands on the bank account that the money's gon' be
19		there to pay the bills!
20	Members:	*((clapping))* Heh heh heh

21	Estelle:	I mean everythi::ng! And that's what - we have to take
22		authority over it because we have an enemy =
23	Member:	Yeah
24	Estelle:	= and he's always walking about seeking whom he may devour
25		**[1 Peter 5:8]**. And he's gonna come in any way that he - any
26		door. . . If you have a business, you have to take authority over
27		that business
23	Member:	Yeah

Estelle's story provides another illustration of how confession can improve conditions at home and at work. Estelle's confession at work entailed both spoken and silent utterances underwritten by references to the Bible, as well as faith-filled and hence, purposeful "touch" of various items in her salon (e.g., chairs, phone, client log, bank register). This tactile form of confession has helped Estelle manage the salon even during more difficult days. In example 9, Estelle discusses her use of confession and "intercessory" touch when interpersonal strife overwhelmed everyone in her salon, including the receptionist, stylists, assistants, and even an observant client:

(9) "A Spirit of Strife": Using Confession (and Clients) to Resolve Salon Strife

1	Member:	You should anoint your workplace
2	Estelle:	Right, because recently uh we had a spirit of strife that came
3		into our salon not long ago and I mean it was so strong. I mean,
4		everybody was arguing and backbiting and disagreeing with
5		each other - the receptionist, the stylist, the assistants, uh I
6		mean just everybody! And um what happened and how I began
7		to recognize it, someone heh heh came up to me at Bible study
8		one night and they said they had this book they wanted to share
9		with me. And she said, "The Holy Spirit told me to give you
10		this book," and I was like, "Okay, what is it?" And it says *Life*
11		*Without Strife* by Joyce Meyers and I was like, "What?" I was
12		kind of confused because I was like, "I don't really recognize
13		any strife in my life anywhere," but little did I know, the enemy
14		had plotted to bring that spirit into the salon. So when I started
15		reading the book, that's when I recognized that that's what that
16		spirit was that had entered in because the word says, "Where
17		there's envy and strife, there's every evil work" **[James 3:16]**.
18		But not only did strife come in, he brought all his compadres,
19		all the evil works. And, I mean, it was going *strong* up in here
20		so I had to really take authority over it. So, I came in one night
21		and I just began to anoint the place and speak to all those spirits
22		and command them to leave, you know, that they didn't
23		have a place here, because remember, it's not the individual.
24		It's the spirit that's operating in and through him that you have
25		to begin to speak to. And I recognized the strife had brought in

26	so much division and so much there was just unrest and there
27	was no peace in here. I mean, I even had a client that, you
28	know, [is] really strong in the Lord. She walked in one day and
29	she was like, "O::h girl, you need to get some oil and anoint
30	this place!" I was like, "Yeah, I know," so she . . . even helped
31	me with that. But then I even spoke to the individuals that were
32	. . . they didn't realize that this spirit was operating in and
33	through them. So I took each and every one of them out of
34	lunch, sat down, talked to them individually, and now, praise
35	God, that spirit is gone! But it took some work, spiritually and
36	in the natural, to deal with the individual that the spirit of strife
37	was working through and then to deal with that spirit itself.
38	So once I did that and anointed the place, and spoke to them,
39	and we prayed, you know, it's peace now. But it took some
40	time and it took some work to get it out

Lest we assume stylists' confessions merely require faith, Estelle good-naturedly reminds CFC members that confession also necessitates hard work, time, and sometimes the intercession of a spirit-led colleague and an observant and well-meaning client. Stylists, it follows, should be observant and open to intercession from other spiritually inspired sources.

The genre of confession also characterizes other prayers employed by CFC members, including those that precede the Bible study lesson. These prayers are designed to prepare an atmosphere suitable for the reception of biblical instruction. CFC members likewise pray for the instructor and verbally serve an eviction notice on Satan; again, stylists underwrite their faith-based claims with biblical assertions. Example 10 represents a typical prayer of this sort:

(10) Bible Study Prayers: Evicting Satan

1	Estelle:	So why don't we just stand up and uh pray. Let's hold hands
2		and get in agreement. Just invoke the presence of the Holy
3		Spirit. Pray God's anointing on this meeting and . . . Uh oh ((*A*
4		*member drops her purse*))
5	Member:	All my junk went . . .
6	Estelle:	That's okay. We're not in a hurry. . . . . . . Father, we just
7		thank you and praise you for this wonderful opportunity that
8		you have allowed us to come together once again to share
9		around your word. We thank you, Lord God, for the meeting
10		tonight. We just pray for every person that's in this circle and
11		we thank you, Lord God, for what you will do for your people
12		in this meeting this night. Father, we thank you for the presence
13		and the anointing power of the Holy Spirit. Holy Spirit, have
14		your way in this meeting tonight. We give you free course and
15		free rein to move by your spirit, so we just thank you for your
16		presence right now. Father, we just pray right now that the

17		words of my mouth and the meditation of my heart will be
18		acceptable unto you **[Psalms 19:14]** to minister to the needs of
19		your people. And Satan, we take authority over you. We bind
20		and break your power. This meeting is off limits to you. You
21		have no part, no place or lot here in this place tonight, so we
22		evict you from this premises and we say that . . . we render you
23		powerless and we say that you have no authority, you have no
24		right, you have no privileges here. So we take authority over
25		you now and we bind and break your power. The word of God
26		says when we tread on serpents and scorpions and over all
27		power of the enemy, nothing shall by any means hurt or harm
28		us **[Luke 10:19]**, so we have the authority to do that now and
29		we take that authority in the name of Jesus
30	Member:	In the name of Jesus
31	Estelle:	So Father, we just praise you, we thank you, we give you glory,
32		honor, and thanksgiving because truly, you are worthy to be
33		praised. We thank you for that you have brought us through
34		another year. We just pray, Lord God, that we will be led by
35		*your* spirit and no other voice or spirit will we heed to other
36		than the voice of the Holy Spirit because you are our leader,
37		our teacher, and our guide, and we give you glory, honor, and
38		thanksgiving, and we ask it all in Jesus' name our Savior. And
39		we stand in agreement by saying
40	Members:	*((sing-song voice))* Amen
41	Estelle:	[And praise the Lord
42	Member:	[Thank you, Lord
43	Estelle:	Praise the Lord. Glory to God! Hallelujah!
44	Member:	Hallelujah!
45	Estelle:	Hallelujah! *((joyfully))* heh heh

This prayer has several conventional aspects. Estelle's appeal in line 1—
"So why don't we just stand up and uh pray. Let's hold hands and get in agreement"—serves as the official call to pray. CFC members then form a circle,
clasp hands, and bow their heads. Their physical disposition signals their collective alignment and sets the stage for invoking the presence of the Holy Spirit
(Ochs and Capps 1996). This collective prayer becomes an occasion in which
CFC members enact explicit ideologies about prayer and confession as literally saying what the word of God says about believers (example 3) and
"speak[ing] faith in words" (example 4; lines 4–5). The most striking illustration of the performative force of prayer is the members' eviction of Satan in lines
19–26. Evicting Satan is a discursive process that begins with highly authoritative claims like "Satan, we take authority over you. We bind and break your
power" (lines 24–25). This collective claim is further legitimated by invoking scrip-
tures that confer biblical authority on these words and recalls Estelle's use of
confession in example 7 to overcome fears of not being able to pay her tuition.

This prayer is a powerful example of how African American women use situated and emergent talk to persevere, inspire, and assert other ways of being and becoming spiritual in their professional communities of practice. As demonstrated in prior examples, confessional prayers enable stylists to reinterpret their lives and futures. By collectively reciting and enacting (via anointed oil or the laying on of hands) various business prayers on a daily basis, CFC members take power over adverse circumstances in their professional lives. These circumstances include difficult clients or coworkers, self-doubt, low productivity, failures, and relentless kitchen beauticians who lure away clients. One of the more dramatic entailments of stylists' confessional prayers is that they expand traditional understandings of confession as a petition for forgiveness. For CFC members, confession entails bold and authoritative claims about stylists' immediate and future circumstances. Their faith-instantiated predictions are rooted in members' shared belief in the actualizing power of their biblical prayers. In such ways, prayers are texts through which stylists speak words of faith as opposed to fear (see example 4); moreover, CFC members actively socialize a vivid awareness of stylists' spiritual agency to confess words that inscribe the interpersonal relations, professional status, and financial success they desire in their lives.

Testimony

Like prayers, testimonies function similarly among CFC members as mediums of socialization and representation. Testimonials are a routine feature during CFC meetings and resemble the narrative format of spoken testimonies in the Black church. As Freedman (1993) explains, church testimonies are spoken or sung co-constructed narratives in which members of a congregation describe how God has blessed them or delivered them from unpleasant circumstances Taylor (1994) adds that an individual's testimony and the congregation's response to it serve to reinforce all members' collective faith in God. Similarly, Smitherman (1977: 150) argues that "the retelling of occurrences in life-like fashion re-creates the spiritual reality for others who, at that moment, vicariously experience what the testifier has gone through. The content of testifying is, thus, not plain or simple commentary but a dramatic narration and a communal reenactment of one's feelings and experiences." Testimonials are therefore transformative engagements that inspire shared memories and mobilize future actions for both the speaker and the hearer. In example 11, Charles, a CFC instructor and internationally renowned Beverly Hills stylist and salon owner, exploits an opportunity to testify when he is asked by a first-time visitor to introduce himself during a CFC meeting at his salon.

(11) "This Is the House of the Lord": Constructing the Salon as a Spiritual Place

1	Visitor:	I don't know your name
2	Charles:	Oh, my name is Charles

3		I am the owner of this salon
4		This salon is a **testimony** from u:h Estelle's ministry
5		I put in a prayer request and I ga:ve offerings
6		an:d God **manifested** this place [here
7	Members:	[((*chorus*)) A:men
8	Charles:	So this place is here for the [glory of God =
9	Estelle:	[((*softly*)) Ha:::llelujah
10	Charles:	= and [everything I do I give honor and glory to God for this
11		place
12	Members:	[HALLelujah
13	Member:	Ame::n
14	Charles:	This is u:h hh hh the house of the Lord
15	Members:	A:men
16		Mm hmmm
17		Praise God

Charles's introduction begets a testimony in which he describes his salon as a literal testimony (line 4), "manifested" (line 6), in part, as a result of Estelle's ministry on confession, his own prayers and offerings, and, as he explains later in the Bible study lesson, hard work. Charles's testimony serves as a medium of praise as well as socialization; as CFC members ratify his claim that his salon represents the "house of the Lord" (line 14), they also craft a view of doing and being professional that successfully reconciles secular (i.e., business) and spiritual ideals. In essence, by endorsing Charles's framing of his business as purposed by and for God's glory, they also sanction the idea that his financial success is also in line with God's will.

The spiritual discourse of testimony was used not merely in stylists' dialogues with each other, but also in their conversations with clients. Example 12 presents a stylist testimony that was recorded at a free educational seminar for new and prospective clients at an elite Los Angeles salon. Brandi, one of the salon's stylists and seminar presenters, introduces herself in a manner similar to that of Charles—that is, by way of a testimony that recounts her early inspiration and experiences as a cosmetologist.

(12) "The Power Was in My Hands": Cosmetology as Divine Touch

1	Brandi:	I was once a salon owner and I had a huge clientele. My main
2		specialty is growing hair
3	Client:	Mmm hmm
4	Brandi:	Uh and I thank God for one thing. . . He has given me that gift
5		and I have always known that . . . **the power was in my hands.**
6		-But I really didn't know . . . I started taking care of my um
7		stepmom's hair and my dad. And my stepmom, she really
8		never had long hair and I was just - we're talking about like
9		chhhh thirteen years old

10	Client:	Mmm hmmm
11	Brandi:	And um pp-sshhh her hair just started growing and . . . I
12		decided to, you know, finish high school and decided to go to
13		college and . . . I always *knew* what I wanted to become but,
14		in a way, . . . I knew that somewhere deep deep down inside,
15		it was another passion for me. It was something else was
16		*in* me that . . . it just had to come out. So I asked God to,
17		you know, help me, to guide me, to give me directions. And
18		**I decided to go** . - I said, "Oh! I know *exactly what I*
19		*wanna do!"*
20	Client:	Heh hhh
21	Brandi:	And **I decided to go into hair** and I had to put college on the
22		side, just on the side for a few years =
23	Client:	Hmmm
24	Brandi:	= and **I decided to go** ahead and pursue that and . . . and it just
25		started out **being revealed**. And as I was doing hair, I noticed
26		[that] people hair was just growing and and **it was just the**
27		**touch!**

Brandi's testimony follows various conventions noted of African American testimony more broadly. Spoken testimonies in the Black church are characterized by conventional prefaces like "First giving honor to God" (Daniel 1971). Brandi's testimony is similarly cued, as she prefaces her narrative in line 4 by saying, "and I thank God for one thing."

Brandi also employs a range of religious terms and figurative phrases. In line 4, she describes her ability to grow and style hair as a "gift," adding, "I have always known that . . . the power was in my hands" (line 5). Brandi's use of this figurative phrase evokes scriptural accounts of lay people's hands being endowed with the healing power of God (e.g., 2 Corinthians 12:9). Her commentary, along with her mention of her skill with "the touch" in lines 26–27, also resembles Estelle's narrative in example 1 insofar as it invokes biblical and literal connotations of the term *touch*. Her reference here also entails the idiomatic sense of having a knack or skill, which further underwrites her hair-care knowledge and skill as a special endowment.

Brandi's several references to having "decided to go" into a career in cosmetology (see lines 18, 21, 24) are also evocative of scriptural accounts of prophets and disciples accepting a divine mission (e.g., Matthew 4:18–22) in that her decision is presented as the result of her request to God for guidance (lines 16–17). This parallel is reinforced in lines 24–25, when she notes that her purpose in life "just started out being revealed." Brandi's testimony before an audience of clients situates her as a hairstylist who was essentially "called" into the hair profession and granted a special "touch" to grow hair. In this way, Brandi's testimony exemplifies what Myers (1991) terms the "call narrative." As he explains, the call narrative among African American believers has traditionally held and still holds an authoritative canonical status in sanctioning the decision of those who report that God called them into the preaching ministry. In situating her as someone who was essentially called to be a professional stylist, Brandi's testimony draws authority and authenticity from this narrative canon.

The notion of having been called by God is echoed by other female stylists. For example, Estelle once stated during a CFC meeting, "I didn't choose this profession. This profession chose *me*." She added that, contrary to her initial doubts, she learned that she could still be glamorous and financially successful while serving God as a cosmetologist. Her perspective finds resonance in African American Christian theology (see Felder 1991; Freedman 1993; Hoyt 1991; Nelson et al. 1971), as well as in the origins of the Black hair-care industry. Madam C. J. Walker, a preeminent African American hair-care pioneer, attributed her invention of a special scalp ointment to a revelation from God after having prayed for a solution to her own hair loss (Due 2000; Lommel 1993). As A'Lelia Bundles (2001), Walker's biographer and great-great-granddaughter, explains, Walker said she dreamt of a big Black man who told her what to mix for her hair. The remedy reportedly included herbal medicinal ingredients from Africa as well as more locally accessible materials, a description (much like Khalif's "silkening" in chapter 2) that helped to both romanticize Walker's concoction and differentiate it from those of a host of other White-owned and Black-owned hair product manufacturers. Walker described the concoction that reversed her hair loss as "an inspiration from God" and felt spiritually obligated to "place [it] in the reach of those who appreciate beautiful hair and healthy scalps, which is the glory of woman" (Bundles 2001: 60). With this product and its spiritual attribution in hand, Walker established herself as one of the highest paid American women (of any race) to run her own business. Although lesser known, Annie Turnbo Pop Malone, an entrepreneur who patented the hot comb and later established the Poro hair product manufacturing companies and schools, also infused spirituality and philanthropy into her multimillion-dollar business (Smith 1991). Like their predecessors, Estelle, Brandi, and other African American stylists reconcile spiritual and entrepreneurial ideals by framing what they do as a "gift" or "calling" to touch their clients' bodies and lives. Moreover, much like scientific discourse, religious discourse helps stylists legitimate their work to clients who may otherwise be skeptical. Since religious discourse is familiar and respected, this strategy can be very effective in gaining legitimacy. In fact, scientific and religious discourses are often used jointly for this purpose.

In example 13, which is taken from the same seminar for new salon clients as in example 12, Brandi incorporates scientific references to differentiate her and other stylists at her salon from unknowledgeable stylists and kitchen beauticians. She anchors this and related distinctions through her use of the mantra, "The truth [will] set you free." Her use of this colloquial expression is heteroglossic, evoking both spiritual and secular connotations that reify scientific and biblical truths as intellectually and personally liberating and instructive. What is especially interesting about Brandi's comments below is the fact that Black female clients in her audience coauthor and ratify her claims, which presume salon care to be superior to hair care at home.

(13) "The Truth [Will] Set You Free": Heteroglossic Framings of Salon Care

1	Brandi:	We're all artists as far as the styling. We're here to enhance
2		what you guys [clients] need, all right . . . We're here to bring
3		the beauty out and one of the things [that] brings the beauty
4		out is hair . . . I lo:ve to groom hair and I can't stand to see
5		a damaged head of hair on somebody's head. The first thing
6		I wanna do is just cut it off and you guys don't understand.
7		You *really* don't understand. So that's why we're here: to
8		help you understand what's goin' on because you hear this
9		over here, you hear that over there. But if you understand
10		**the theory**, . . . the theory is going to really really make
11		you guys understand and the **truth is gonna set you**
12		**free**
13	Clients:	Right
14		Right right
15	Brandi:	That's the only thing. Once you know the truth, you will be
16		able to understand [that] it's . . . *not nothing* pulling out $200
17		for service
18	Client:	Right
19	Brandi:	But you have to know what you talkin' about first!
20	Clients:	((chorus)) Yeah
21	Brandi:	If you don't know what you're saying as a stylist, you can lose
22		clients
23	Client:	Mm hmmm
24	Brandi:	But as long as you have **proof**, as long as you can execute
25		what you're talking about, they'll [i.e., clients] come back.
26		And that's not a problem here at [X salon] and that's not a
27		problem with my clients' hair. My clients . . . don't mi::nd
28		spending up to two hundred and something dollars. I have
29		a *weekly* clientele and they . . . believe in coming to
30		spend money because uh we're gonna give 'em what they
31		need
32	Client:	Right
33	Brandi:	So that's why we . . . practice . . . everything else, as well as
34		hair grooming and that's the number one thing to me because
35		that's gonna keep you [i.e., stylist] in business =
36	Clients:	Yes
37		Mm hmm
38	Brandi:	= I mean hh hhh th- hair grooming, taking care of hair, will last
39		a lot lo:nger than that little instant stuff
40	Clients:	Mm hmm
41	Brandi:	It's not gonna last for 'bout maybe fi:ve or six months and then
42		you [stylist] gonna lose a client - a who::le . . . clientele out
43		there because people are loo:kin' for healthy hair. And that's
44		what we do specialize in: healthy hair.

Obvious parallels exist between Brandi's comments and those of other stylists considered thus far. Her references to "grooming" hair recalls my own mother's poignant distinction between (merely) "dressing" the hair versus "cultivating" or grooming it. In addition, Brandi's references to the "truth" (lines 12, 15), "theory" (line 10), and "proof" (line 24), as well as her implicit contrasts between "healthy (i.e., well groomed) hair" (line 43) and a "damaged head of hair" (line 5), all work in service of a scientific approach to hair care and recall admonitions by the hair doctors considered in chapter 2. Recall that stylists like Khalif, Carol and Gwen, and Mr. Park stressed to stylists the importance of "knowing what one was talking about," particularly with regard to chemical procedures. They also socialized stylists to employ specialized scientific terminology designed to distinguish lay or home hair products and services from professional or salon products and services in order to socialize clients' greater reliance on stylists. Brandi riffs on this particular theme in lines 31 and 32 when she states, "Hair grooming, taking care of hair, will last a lot longer than that little instant stuff." Her use of the diminutive *little* to qualify *that . . . instant stuff* (line 39) implies a clear distinction between the outcomes clients can expect from over-the-counter hair-care products, and those they stand to gain from professional salon hair-care services (lines 41–44).

The fact that Brandi is speaking with noticeable candor to clients, and not her peers, warrants special consideration—especially when we consider the role played here by clients in endorsing what some might consider controversial claims. These claims include Brandi's statement "The truth is gonna set you free" (line 12), which follows a clear move to differentiate stylists who have a "theoretical" understanding of how to properly groom hair from clients, whom she notes, often "don't understand" this theory of hair (line 6). She localizes this lack by invoking a common complaint iterated by many Black hairstylists concerning some Black women's reluctance to trim their hair regularly in order to improve its health (see lines 4–6). Similarly, Khalif, the stylist discussed in chapter 2, commiserated with other stylists about this challenge in the hair-care seminar he facilitated: "Most Black women don't want to get their hair cut because they spend so much time trying to get it to grow. But this is what makes it healthy. For most Blacks [i.e., Black women], one-fourth of an inch is a cut!" Cosmetology students in Charleston, South Carolina, also regularly faced the challenge of convincing African American women to have their split-ends cut to avoid further hair breakage. Brandi alludes to this issue when she states: "I lo:ve to groom hair and I can't stand to see a damaged head of hair on somebody's head. The first thing I want to do is just cut it off and you guys don't understand. You *really* don't understand" (line 7). Another one of Brandi's claims that might be perceived as patronizing and even manipulative is her implication that it is reasonable for clients to expect to pay upwards of $200 for professional hair care (lines 15–17). However, this, along with Brandi's other claims, are readily endorsed by her audience of clients; who provide agreement expletives in lines 13–14, 18, 20, 23, 32, 36–37, and 40.

The reasons clients may ratify Brandi's claims are worth considering. While Brandi clearly frames her own salon's services as scientifically superior to those provided at other salons and in private homes, she rests this framing on a number of resonant claims. First, she assumes—correctly—that healthy hair is what matters most for many African American clients (especially ones who would choose to attend a two-hour hair educational seminar after work) and, further, that Black women will gladly invest considerable expense for hair care, in spite of the proliferation of over-the-counter hair products and kitchen beauticians. Second, she asserts that cosmetologists should be artists of style (line 1), understand hair grooming theory and then convey that "truth" to clients (lines 7–12), be able to provide "proof" in the form of delivering what they promise to clients (line 24), and, finally, specialize in nurturing "healthy hair" (line 44). Third, she acknowledges clients' agency by noting the fact that dissatisfied clients will leave if they do not receive the kind of care they desire (lines 41–44). Thus, although Brandi's overall claims inscribe hierarchical distinctions between herself and clients, she successfully balances these claims by conveying a genuine understanding of what clients really want, will pay for, and, as she suggests, deserve.

Brandi's invocation of the mantra "The truth [will] set you free" (line 9) also commands clients' empathy insofar as it draws legitimization from spiritual, scientific, and arguably even communal understandings of the complexity and double-edged nature of truth (Collins 1990; Gwaltney 1981, 1993; Hurston 1990). In other words, Brandi's invocation acts as a cultural mandate that requires accountability and responsibility from clients and stylists alike; both must work to facilitate a mutually amicable partnership. We also should not forget that, earlier, Brandi framed herself as "called" by God to do hair. This self-positioning situates her as not merely competent and impassioned but also spiritually vested, thus working in service of constructing her expertise. Understood in the context of her remarks, Brandi's legitimacy becomes grounded not only in spirituality but also in science and communal understandings of truth (see Rooks 1996 for a discussion of how early Black hair ads similarly also appealed to science as well as religion and testimony).

Discussion

The fact that clients are actively socialized by Brandi to appreciate the relative superiority and hence high costs of salon care and, further, to endorse these claims provides another testament to the complexity of ideologies of expertise among Black clients and stylists. For example, we saw in chapter 1 that the construction of expertise is not always limited to stylists but is also (and often) a preoccupation of clients; further, stylists and clients do not always contest each other's expertise, but may shift between novice and expert stances—especially when, as Brandi's exchange shows, such collaborative stances serve to maintain amiable, professional, and personal relations. Chapter 2 provided even more nuanced understandings of the constitution of expertise through a multisited examination of language socialization in women's professional communities of practice. Stylists socialized each other to use their skill and to refine and, in some cases, rename common hair-care procedures and terminology to distinguish themselves from clients and "kitchen beauticians." Language was central to this endeavor as a medium through which stylists learned to represent themselves and in essence be or become "hair doctors."

This chapter demonstrates an even deeper role for language as a model of being and becoming spiritual hair professionals in African American women's communities of practice. Stylists once again employ specialized discourse to socialize and organize shared views of themselves, their clients, and their work. Through testimony and prayer, stylists describe cosmetology as a "gift," a "calling," and a divine "license to touch." These descriptions do more than frame stylists' ideologies of themselves and their work; these texts also nurture stylists' own "becomings" as divinely appointed cosmetologists by affording agentive stances and biblically based assertions that bespeak the ideologies, dispositions, and behaviors that stylists themselves wish to emulate as well as imbue in their clients and coworkers.

Parallels can be seen between Christian cosmetologists and hair doctors. CFC members employ testimony, prayer, and scriptural references in a manner similar to the scientific discourse of cosmetology to actively frame their work with their words. For example, stylists' spiritual attributions function much like medical or scientific assertions to underwrite their professional authority. Additionally, just as hair doctors socialize like-mindedness among their peers via specialized language use and exclusive hairstyling procedures, CFC members similarly inspire other stylists and, by extension, their clientele into moral roles, beliefs, and behavior through their use of scripture, testimony, and authoritative intertextual confessions.

Significantly, compared to cosmetologists who favor the discourse of science, Christian cosmetologists' alignments with God are less concerned with demarcating key differences between themselves and their clients. Rather, to claim hair care as a gift and a calling imbues cosmetologists with an enormous responsibility to alter clients' looks and lives. While this perspective entails a hierarchic distinction between stylists and the patrons they are called to serve and educate, this stance also affords a view of cosmetology as an act of spiritually motivated service that profoundly touches clients and stylists alike.

Interestingly enough, even knowledgeable clients can be complicit in these framings, as exemplified by one client's intercession that helped Estelle to rid her salon of strife (example 9), and clients' ratification of Brandi's use of the idiom "The truth [will] set you free" to socialize their reliance on salon-based "truths," products, and services (example 13). These examples are vivid testaments to the complexity of spiritual and scientific framings and the degree to which stylists and clients participate in such framings in pursuit of their respective agendas. To the extent that Brandi's exposition invokes spiritual and scientific understandings of hair-care knowledge and skill to disambiguate expert hair-care service from hair done at home or with the aid of over-the-counter products, she shows that scientific and spiritual discourses are not always independent of one another. Nor, I should add, are these discourses merely used by stylists as strategic bids for professional legitimization and financial success. Stylists certainly employ medical/scientific and religious/spiritual discourses to cope with difficult clients, but they also use these discourses to socialize members of their communities of practice to view themselves and their work as legitimately scientific, spiritual, artistic, and even, as we will see in later chapters, political.

Hair expertise is thus predicated not merely on scientific tropes but also on spiritual speech acts and complex articulations between secular and spiritual stances and discourses. Such complexities imply that there is no one single "truth" about hair, but rather multiple truths that are actualized through an array of genres (e.g., spiritual, scientific, communal), performative speech acts (e.g., spoken, silent, or tactile prayer, testimony), and discursive collaborations between clients, stylists, and other vested parties.

Conclusion

Brandi's claim "The truth is gonna set you free" offers a fitting segue for the next phase of this multisited journey. This idiom acts as a mandate to enact new ways of being and becoming knowledgeable clients and stylists insofar as it draws intertextual legitimacy from spiritual, scientific, and communal ideological canons. Chapter 4 explores another discursive site that regularly plays on an array of intertextual meanings, symbolic terms, and communal "truths" about black hair and hair-care experience: African American stand-up comedy. African American comedic performances exploit in-group and gendered understandings about hair in ways that speak back to the experiences of Nana G, hair doctors, and stylists who are "licensed to touch," and also inform the analysis of Internet and cross-cultural hair-care conversations to be provided in chapters 5 and 6.

4

Gender, Authenticity, and Hair in African American Stand-up Comedy

P rior chapters demonstrate how hair and language together act as resources in speakers' varied beings and becomings as hair doctors, stylists with a divine "license to touch," and clients, like Nana G, on an impassioned quest for a new look. They also offer insights into language as a resource in constructing identity and mediating expertise in women's communities of practice. In this chapter, I extend my examination of discourses about hair—and hair itself as discourse—through an analysis of pre-recorded and live comedy sketches concerning African American hair and hair care. These comedic commentaries represent another performative stage through which gendered, political, and other symbolic meanings of Black hair and hair care are negotiated. They also contribute to a small but growing body of linguistic work on women's humor (Barreca 1991; Crawford 1989; Ervin-Tripp and Lampert 1992; Hay 2000; Kotthoff 2000) by illuminating the discursive dynamics of Black women's public humor within the male-dominated realm of Black stand-up comedy (see also Avins 2002; Dance 1998; Dresner 1991; Williams 1995). Black comediennes challenge early findings that suggest that (Black) women do not engage in aggressive verbal humor (see Abrahams 1970, 1976; Apte 1985; Folb 1980); they routinely bring gender center stage and challenge hegemonic masculine ideologies in their hair-related routines (see also Kochman 1972, 1981; Mitchell-Kernan 1971, 1972).

African American stand-up comedy as communal forum

Black stand-up comedy, which is also the site of my current ethnographic research (Jacobs-Huey 2003a), is an especially fitting stage for examining the
cultural significance of hair. Black humor and laughter have long provided
African Americans with a means to critically reflect on in-group practices and
ideologies (Dundes 1973; Hurston 1990; Levine 1977; Watkins 1994, 2002).
As dialogical performers, comics actively engage African American audiences
as co-participants (Duranti and Brenneis 1986) through their use of in-group
cultural knowledge and cultural discourse styles (e.g., call and response, playing the dozens or capping, signifying, indirectness; see Coleman 1984; Morgan 2002; Williams 1995; Williams and Williams 1993). Black audiences'
ability to interpret culturally laden jokes likewise relies on their local knowledge and communicative competence (Hymes 1972).

      Black audiences mark their co-participation in joke telling through such
responses as laughter, silence, heckling, and applause. Insofar as comics frame
themselves and their audiences in terms of a collective "we," and audiences
corroborate this framing through applause and other forms of agreement, Black
(also called "urban") comedy clubs readily act as communal forums. Further,
comics' and audiences' shared musings on intimate subjects like hair reflect
critical engagements in knowing and being through gendered engagements with
the body.

Hair jokes in Black stand-up comedy

The subject of hair routinely emerges in Black humor. Jokes about hair often
rely on the audience's shared cultural knowledge and experiences with Black
hair textures, styles, procedures, and terminology. African American comics
exploit this in-group knowledge in humor that plays on cultural discourse styles,
innuendo, and comedic strategy. In doing so, they expand our understandings
of how and why hair matters in African Americans' everyday lives.

      Thematically, hair jokes often focus on artifice (e.g., weaves, extensions),
communal debates about "good" versus "bad" hair, Black women's hair rituals in beauty salons and kitchens, and common Black hairstyling dilemmas.
Hair and head coverings (e.g., wigs, bandanas) also emerge in some jokes as
signifiers of "authentic" racial and gendered consciousness. Questions of authenticity permeate these and other thematic threads in ways that both idealize
and interrogate "realness" as a cultural value and aesthetic ideal, with gender-
specific implications for Black women and men alike.

Is that your hair?

The query "Is that your hair?" epitomizes this trope of authenticity, relying on
indirectness as a comedic filter. The issue of how one wears one's hair, and
specifically whether or not one's hair is "real," enters the public domain in the

comedy club. Comics who are well known for their skills at the dozens—that is, the art of ritual insult—routinely play (or prey) on hairstyle fashion victims in the audience by making their hair the focus of humor. Sometimes audience members even assist comics by calling attention to those around them who they feel would make ideal candidates for comics' acerbic wit. Women are particularly vulnerable to such exposure and jokes since they are more likely than men to wear artificial hair or hair attachments (e.g., wigs, extensions, weaves).

Significantly, comics' queries about the authenticity of an audience member's hair are not restricted to the indexicalities of hair as a marker of racial authenticity; rather, hair is also viewed as a reflection of aesthetic and personal aspects of an individual's identity. Great stakes are placed on people's presentation of self. The humor derived from this question is thus rooted, in part, in its transgressive nature. To ask a stranger about the authenticity of their hair is a delicate maneuver. Within the comedy club, this query can coax laughter in the very violation of implicit norms of etiquette—especially since many African Americans consider hairstyles a matter of personal choice and view fake hair, in particular, as a private matter.

As the inaugural host of *Russell Simmons' Def Comedy Jam*, a popular urban stand-up comedy show that aired on HBO from 1992 to 1997, actor/comedian Martin Lawrence often ribbed members of his audience by making fun of their hair or clothing. One such "friendly" interrogation of an unnamed female audience member who sported an elaborate Afro style embellished with a flower illustrates how personal hairstyle choices become comedic texts. Lawrence asked her, "What the fuck is this hairstyle? The bush with the rose in it? You look like a late great fucked-up Billie Holiday. God bless the child that's got her own!" (see *Def Comedy Jam: Best of Martin Lawrence 2002*). After a brief spell of laughter, Lawrence asked, more seriously, "Baby, is that all yours?" while motioning near the top of his own head. Her reply, a sheepish "No" and a pleading expression, compelled the woman sitting next to her to bow and shake her head sympathetically. Lawrence continued his interrogation: "So you brought somebody else's hair and put it into a BUSH?!" This comment induced widespread laughter from the audience. When it subsided, Lawrence qualified his query and offered one final quip, "All right, I just had to know… I just noticed it from on camera and wanted to know where we were at…. Angela Davis in the hou:::::se!!" His guest responded good-naturedly with a smile and a raised fist, the Black Power salute.

Part of what is funny about this exchange is the guest's reliance on artifice to achieve a hairstyle heralded in the 1960s as emblematic of a "natural" aesthetic and Black pride (see Mercer 1994). Afros are among several of the hairstyles most amenable to naturally kinky hair textures. For people with thick curly hair, Afros can often be achieved with little or no reliance on chemical or thermal hair straighteners and weaves. Lawrence's query therefore interrogates the use of artifice to effect an Afrocentric hairstyle—an Afro—by exposing his guest's aesthetic versus (merely) political intentions.

The guest's use of additional hair to embellish her Afro is also atypical since weaves and other hair attachments are typically used with great subtlety in order to make women's hair appear longer, straighter, and/or slightly wavy versus "blown out" in a manner consistent with an Afro. (However, in my observations of Black hair shows, I witnessed numerous dreadlock and braided extensions and other forms of "natural"/Afrocentric artifice.) Needless to say, these ironies are not lost on the audience, who express shared amusement following Lawrence's incredulous query, "So you brought somebody's else's hair and put it into a BUSH?!"

Lawrence's question "Is that all yours?" is an example of strategic indirectness insofar as it entails meanings beyond those suggested by the surface content. Thus, in asking his question, Lawrence is not merely gauging whether the guest's hair is authentic so much as he is setting the stage for further comedic quips about her aesthetic sensibilities and presumed racial consciousness. Moreover, as his guest and his broader audience well know, Lawrence's question allows him to stage an insult before an audience without appearing culpable for implied and/or subsequent critiques (see also Morgan 2002). His audience acknowledges the indirectness at play through preemptive laughter, which functions pragmatically as an anticipatory completion (Lerner 1996). In short, they (and his hapless guest) foresee his comedic intentions as soon as he asks the question.

Yeah, I bought it!

Interestingly, while African American comics—most of them male—frequently lampoon women who wear fake hair, comedienne Dana Point offers a gender-nuanced retort that celebrates weaves as one of many hairstyle options for Black women. While performing on *Russell Simmons' Def Comedy Jam* in 1995, she quipped:

> Black women. Wear yo' weaves. Fuck what everybody else say. If it makes you happy, wear [it]! My man wanted me to have some long hair, so I went and got a weave. Now he don't like it. [He] say, "It's not yours." I say, "Why? I bought it, didn't I!" (see *Def Comedy Jam: Best of Martin Lawrence 2002*)

Point's joke frames male desire as a compelling force in her own decision to wear a weave. But she doesn't stop here. Her sardonic rejoinder "Why? I bought it, didn't I!" strategically resists her partner's attempts to police how she achieves the look he desires. Her snap also has a broader appeal, as evident in her comment "Fuck what everybody else say." Essentially, she tells Black women to be happy with their hair, whether purchased or not, adding that if they feel compelled to oblige a personal desire for longer hair, then they should do so by any means necessary—without apology. Point's joke was well received, especially by Black women, who shouted their approval and clapped enthusiastically.

In his one-hour HBO comedy special, *Brain Damaged*, comic/actor Sinbad also joked about weaves (Sinbad 1990). His joke garnered enthusiastic applause from women and men alike, despite the fact that it represents another pointed admonition by a man to women who wear weaves. His reception may very well be due to his stance, which is neither hostile to nor celebratory of weaves per se. He states:

> Ain't nothing wrong with a weave. If you wanna get yourself some hair, go 'head. But at least try to fool somebody! Why say, "I got a weave on my head?" If you baldheaded on Monday ... *((Audience roars))*—LISTEN to me now! If you baldheaded on Monday, you cain't have hair down to yo' butt on Wednesday. Don't get excited when you sit in the weave chair! At least try to fool the people. Get like an inch a month. People'll think your hair growing. They compliment you. *((impersonates female speaker))* "Girl, your hair lookin' good. What you been doing?!" *((impersonates female addressee))* "Yeah, I just been washin' it and conditioning it."

Sinbad's joke extends Dana Point's central thesis. He, too, frames weaves as a personal choice, but also asserts that hair weaves should be worn with great subtlety in order to effect a more "natural" look. His gender-diverse audience corroborates this stance through enthusiastic applause, underscoring shared cultural ideologies around aesthetics and authenticity (see Favor 1999; Jackson 2001; Morgan 2002).

Good hair

Notions of "good hair" also become subtexts in cultural humor about Black hair. As will be discussed in subsequent chapters, Black women critique communal notions of "good hair" (i.e., wavy or straight hair) that are strictly based on Eurocentric standards of beauty. Chapters 5 and 6 show how women redefine the concept of "good hair" and terms like *nappy* to subvert early derogatory associations (see also Bonner 1991; Jones 2003).

Among African American comics, however, some jokes privilege conventional, narrow understandings of "good hair" to make larger claims about racial authenticity. In particular, comics may target individuals who uncritically ascribe their own "good hair" to Native American ancestry as cliché, "ghetto" (i.e., lower-class), or alternatively as elitist or racially "inauthentic." In these critiques, comics actively welcome Black audiences' corroboration but also open themselves to critique in their own turn since they ultimately leave the category of "good hair" unproblematized. Martin Lawrence's (1994) performance in his stand-up comedy film "You So Crazy" presents a vivid case in point. In the mock dialogue below, Lawrence expresses the cynicism that many African Americans feel about women who attribute their "good" hair to Native American ancestry, although he fails to unpack the entailments of the category itself:

> We see Black people we don't like with good hair, we always make some goddamn excuse, don't we? You know, say, "Excuse me, damn, baby, you got some, that's your hair?" She say, "Yeah that's all me." Say, well, "Damn, that's real pretty,

got nice hair." [She says,] "Uh-huh, well, you know, we got Indian in our family." *((cynically))* "Get the fuck out of here!" *((Audience laughs))*

Lawrence imports the familiar "Is that your hair?" question into his routine to
mock, in this case, a pretty woman who appears to brag about her Native American racial heritage. His critique may have less to do with Black folks' claims of
Indian ancestry, given that many African Americans do indeed possess a partial
Native American heritage, than with the imagined female character's unsolic-
ited elaboration about her mixed ancestry. Still, Lawrence's critique is directed
more toward the woman who banks on the aesthetic privileges of so-called "good
hair," and less on the man who privileges such standards of beauty.

Scruncho, an up-and-coming, Los Angeles-based African American comic
I have observed over several years, echoes Lawrence's cynicism toward Black
people who profess Indian ancestry. In particular, he exposes the broader communal basis for Lawrence's critique in a joke that contrasts "real niggahs" with
"fake niggahs." Scruncho's use of the term *niggah* is complicated; while telling this joke, he shifts between positive (i.e., communal) and derogatory (i.e.,
class-marked) connotations of the N-word (Kennedy 2002). He also implies, à
la Chris Rock in his infamous comedic film "Bring the Pain" (1996), a clear
preference for "Black folks" over "niggahs." Scruncho's distinction is further
nuanced since he reveals *niggah* to be a race-neutral term (i.e., someone from
any racialized category can be a "niggah"), as well as a generic signifier for an
individual or person. He employs the former race- and class-specific connotation
of *niggah* in a 2004 performance at the Comedy Union, an African American-
owned comedy club in Los Angeles:

> You got "real" niggahs and "fake" niggahs. If you ask a *Black* person what they
> mixed with, they're gonna say, "I'm Black. I'm not mixed with nothing." But if
> you ask a *niggah*—a straight-up niggah—what they mixed with, what they gon'
> say? *((extends microphone to audience))* [Audience responds in unison: "I'm In-
> dian!"]—Yeah right, "I'm INDI::AN! Cherokee:::!" Can I share my philosophy
> on that? *((Audience: "Yeah!"))* In-de-end, you still a niggah! (September 13, 2004)

Some of the assumptions apparent in Lawrence's joke are reinscribed here. Both
Lawrence and Scruncho reify the "one-drop rule" in the history of American
law, which purported that one drop of Black blood racialized an individual as
Black (Davis 1991). Additionally, they both express cynicism toward Black
people who self-identify in any way but as "Black." While Lawrence indicts
people who attribute their "good hair" to Indian ancestors, Scruncho criticizes
"straight-up niggahs" who, unlike "real" Black folks, emphasize or confidently
assert their multiracial heritage. Claims of Indian ancestry become opposed,
in both jokes, to racial consciousness and Black pride.

Significantly, Black audiences corroborate the subtext of Scruncho's joke
not merely through laughter and applause, but also through a telling anticipatory completion. When he asks them to specify how so-called "fake niggahs"
respond to questions about their ethnic background, the audience shouts in

unison "I'm Indian!" Scruncho uses the African American discourse genre of call and response to elicit this response, thus situating his audience as literal "coauthors" (Duranti and Brenneis 1986) in the construction of his critique.

Scruncho draws heavily on shared cultural knowledge in constructing this joke. Indeed, his very punch line relies on the audience's provision of the word *Indian*. Their response allows him to cement his poignant observations about the sociopolitical legacy of the "one-drop rule." In a coda rich in phonetic parallelism and dialectal play, Scruncho insists that while African Americans may claim to be part-*Indian*, *in-de-end* (i.e., in the end), they are still "niggahs." Scruncho's joke, like Lawrence's, rests on the cultural recognition that some African Americans highlight an Indian heritage; as Lawrence's joke indicates, hair in particular is a focal point for such claims.

Bandanas, wigs, and questions of authenticity

In additional performances by Scruncho, as well as comedienne/actress Laura Hayes, hair and head adornments similarly become a literal stage for constructing authenticity. For example, in the same Comedy Union performance, Scruncho used a bandana as a prop to distinguish "real" men from "fake" men. His joke was multifaceted. First, he performed caricatured renditions of Black and Latino gangsters, imitating their gait, posture, and bandana styles. (The symbolic use of bandanas or headscarves is a longstanding gang practice; see also Mendoza-Denton 1999 for language and gender issues in gangs' use of bandanas.) Having established these groups as prototypes of "real" men, Scruncho then presented an image of an "inauthentic" wannabe thief who tied his headscarf in a manner completely unlike the other groups he had discussed. Here is an abbreviated version of his joke:

> All my real men say "Man up!" *((Male audience members reply in unison; "Man up!"))* Something's going on with men. They're getting watered down and losing their edge. Let me tell you something. The bandana was designed to give men an instant edge. It was NOT meant ... for rhinestones! Let me show you how to wear this thing. Now brothers (i.e., Black men) and Mexicans wear theirs like no one else in the world. We [Black men] wear ours just above the eyebrow. *((Ties scarf on head to demonstrate))* Instant edge! Now Mexicans have the same mentality. They wear theirs right below the eyebrow. *((Adjusts scarf so it rests just below his eyebrows))* ... Now if you gon' make a conscious decision to rob me, you better have it on right! I SWEAR FO' GOD I'd rather DIE than—*((Unties knot and reties it under chin; wields imaginary gun with one hand on his hip))*—[If] you come at me this way, you better kill me! I'd rather die!! *((Audience laughs uproariously))*

As in his prior joke, Scruncho sets the stage for his punch line by enlisting (male) audience members' corroboration for its central thesis (i.e., "Man up!"). His purpose is the exact opposite of Dana Point's in her joke above. While she celebrates women's right to wear weaves without apology or regret, Scruncho actively polices men's aesthetic practices, outlawing rhinestones on bandanas and prescribing other standards by which "real" men should don headscarves. The crescendo of his joke occurs when he assumes the stance of an awkward thief who knots his scarf below his chin before engaging in an attempted robbery. Scruncho jokes that to be robbed by such a nonmasculine figure would be worse than death, telling his audience that he'd "rather die" than be subject to this kind of ambush.

Prescriptions for gendered authenticity are being authored here. Scruncho's performance situates bandana styles associated with Black and Latino men, particularly gangsters, as characteristic of hypermasculinity (Bucholtz 1999b; Connell 1995; Harper 1996; McElhinny 1995). His performance juxtaposes representations of Black and Latino men who contrast comically with the final character he presents, a most awkward thief whose bandana is affixed below his chin and who keeps one hand on his hip while staging a robbery. Scruncho's joke inscribes models of culturally authentic masculine aesthetics and succeeds on the basis of these incongruous juxtapositions. Here, head adornment comes to represent gender appropriateness for men in much the same way that hairstyle in the jokes above comes to represent racial appropriateness for women.

Whereas Scruncho's parody implies an aesthetic blueprint for authentic hypermasculine posturing, Laura Hayes's comedy constructs a much less prescriptive model of authenticity for Black women. Her joke suggests that "real" sisters, in both a familial and figurative sense, stick together in times of trouble. Hair figures prominently in this joke by way of a calculated "unveiling" that dramatizes these core values. In essence, Hayes turns quips about fake hair on their head (so to speak) by revealing her own hair to be artificial: she removes her wig onstage (see figs. 4.1 and 4.2). Like Scruncho, Hayes plays up the drama of this highly incongruous gesture by making it the unexpected capstone of a story-in-progress. As host of *The Queens of Comedy* (2001), she begins her joke by reflecting, not uncynically, on her and her sisters' upbringing as the basis for their camaraderie today:

> I come from a big family of girls. My daddy raised us tough. He was like, "I ain't raising no punk bitches." And you couldn't go to my daddy with . . . what he called "sissy shit." You couldn't go up to him and say, *((little girl voice))* "Daddy, can I go outside and play with Barbie?" *((mimics Dad's retort))* "Fuck Barbie! [You] better get out there and build me a sofa!" And he taught us to stick together, too. You marry one of us, you marry a::::ll of us . . . And when there [are] some problems, we'll get together, baby, 'cause Moms is the dispatcher.
>
> My little sister got in trouble and had to call Mama. *((impersonates tearful sister))* "Mama . . . this . . . niggah . . . HIT me." . . . Mama was cool, though. She said, *((deep voice))* "Don't worry about it, baby." Moms hung up the phone, dialed one number, and ALL our phones rang. *((mimics mother))* "Bertha, Laura, Eula, Ruthie, get on over to Alice's house. That niggah done gone crazy." That was all we needed. We jumped in the car, we rollin'. We slapping 5's [i.e., slapping hands] over the seat . . . . . . Get to the house. Screech up real fast. Walk in the door. The niggah was just about to hit my sister. We go: *((Takes off wig))* "Aww na::w, not tonight, niggah! *((rhetorically))* What?!" *((Audience laughs wildly; Hayes saun-*

Figure 4.1. Laura Hayes with wig intact in *The Queens of Comedy* (2001).

Figure 4.2. Laura Hayes's de-wigging in *The Queens of Comedy* (2001).

ters around onstage wigless)) . . . "Niggah what? Niggah who?" *((to audience))*
Unh-unh. We didn't play that!!

Hayes's onstage removal of her wig is a radical gesture, especially considering the primacy of authenticity endorsed by Black audiences in the jokes discussed earlier. Her gesture is also highly symbolic within her narrative insofar as it effectively announces her intention to fight. Her wig removal is a vivid exemplar of comical depictions of tenacious "ghetto" (i.e., street savvy) Black women and men who remove extraneous accessories prior to fights and are defiant even in the face of threats of domestic violence. Specifically, her gesture enacts core communal and, to some extent, distinctly class-marked values concerning the importance of protecting family honor at all costs.

Hayes's "unveiling" also acts as a climactic coda. It provokes laughter as an explicit breach of societal as well as communal standards governing the presentation of hair and hence of self. Hayes is poignantly aware of the implicit aesthetic rules she has violated. After a brief pause, and with wig still in hand, she goes on to quip:

> *((to audience))* No, baby. I have no shame in my game. I have forty or fifty of these [wigs] at the house. *((Reaffixes her wig))* . . . I'll fix it better when I get in the back but uh I was young and wi::ld. Now I could do this shit in the dark. My drawls [i.e., drawers, underwear] might be on backwards, but this hair gon' be straight!

By reaffixing her wig onstage, Hayes violates additional prescriptions about the manner and context in which to fix one's hair—particularly if it is "fake." If Sinbad's communally ratified instruction to women with fake hair (i.e., "at least try to fool the people") is to be followed, Hayes's wig should be donned in private. Hayes flouts this advice for comic effect, although her rejoinder to the audience's laughter reveals that she is fully aware of her violation.

In one of several interviews I conducted with her, Hayes told me that this joke was inspired by a real-life experience. During her early and more tumultuous years as a comic, Hayes encountered an obstinate heckler. She employed several tricks of the comedy trade to silence him, including quips about his appearance and gracious appeals that he let her do her job. When none of these strategies worked, Hayes took off her wig and proceeded down the steps of the stage toward the heckler, adopting for the first time in her routine a fighting stance through the use of her wig as prop. Almost immediately, the audience began laughing hysterically, including the very heckler she intended to throttle. Their unexpected laughter was thus quite fortuitous. Not only was a fight with a male heckler averted but, for Hayes, a hilarious comedy sketch was born.

Out of the mouths of babes: Black women, hair, and self-esteem

In her 1991 "Live on Broadway" show, Whoopi Goldberg, one of the most successful Black comediennes currently working, brings an array of characters to life in monologues that tackle such issues as drugs, race, politics, and the "whitewashing" (i.e., overrepresentation of White actors) of mainstream television. Each of her characters expresses idiosyncratic perspectives and desires, displaying Goldberg's improvisational skills as a comedienne.

One of the characters Goldberg embodies is that of a little Black girl who wears a white shirt on her head as a stand-in for the "long flowing" blonde hair she desires. Goldberg's character offers an interesting point of contrast to some of the positions toward hair considered in this and earlier chapters. She lacks the sassy ingenuity and *esprit de resistance* embodied both in Laura Hayes's defiant de-wigging and in Dana Point's retort, "Yeah, I bought it!" Goldberg's character is also the antithesis of the character Brenda in Carolivia Herron's (1997) controversial children's book *Nappy Hair*, which I discuss in chapter 5. Whereas Brenda celebrates her gloriously curly hair and the controversial term *nappy,* Goldberg's character resembles the tragic Black character Pecola in Toni Morrison's (1970) powerful novel *The Bluest Eye.* Growing up in the Midwest in the 1940s, Pecola loves Shirley Temple and thinks having blue eyes will make her pretty. Similarly, Goldberg's character buys into Eurocentric representations of beauty on television and wants to have blonde hair and blue eyes and to be White "like Barbie."

((Swinging white shirt on her head)) This is my long and luxurious blonde hair. Ain't it pretty? *((Audience: Yeah!))* I can put it in a ponytail. Wanna see? *((Goldberg turns around, grabs the shirt and swings shirt sleeves))* . . . My momma made me go to my room 'cause she said this wasn't nothing but a shirt on my head and I said, "Nuh unh, this is my long luxurious blonde hair." She said, "Nuh unh, fool, that's a shirt!" And I said, "You a fool. It's my hair." She made me go to my room. But I don't care because when I get big, I'ma get fifty million trillion million million elephants and I'ma let 'em go in the house so they can trample on everybody. And then she gonna want me to make 'em stop but she ain't even gonna know I'm there because I'ma have blonde hair, blue eyes, and I'ma be White. . . . I AM! Uh huh! And then I'ma have a dream house, and a dream car, and dream candy and a dream house and me and Barbie are gonna live with Ken and Skipper and Malibu Barbie. . . . We ARE!

Goldberg's character's fantasies of looking like and hence living as Barbie are, in many ways, similar to complaints made by the Black cosmetology students in South Carolina whom I followed. As I will discuss in chapter 6, several students shared sad memories of the dearth of both Black dolls available to them as children and of Black mannequins available to them years later as cosmetology students. Goldberg's character's monologue is especially tragic for the reasons candidly expressed by the child's mother. Her dreams of becoming White will never be realized, nor perhaps should they be. Although Goldberg's little girl character is naïve, she is astute enough to anticipate her audience's cynicism. She couches her expressed desires with defensive ripostes such as "I AM!"; "Uh huh!"; and "We ARE!"

Later in the sketch, Goldberg stages a dramatic unveiling that recalls the calculated and symbolic nature of Laura Hayes's defiant de-wigging: she

removes the white shirt draping her head. But whereas Hayes' gesture acts as
a dramatic climax, Goldberg's unveiling constitutes a performative segue. Having removed the shirt, she then provides a candid critique of her own hair in
relation to depictions of beautiful straight hair in television commercials:

> And [my mother] say I just gotta be happy with what I got, but look: *((Removes
> shirt from head))* . . . It don't do nothin'. It don't blow in the wind. And it don't
> casca- casca-ca-dade down my back. It don't and I put that bouncin' and behavin'
> stuff in it and it didn't even listen! And I want some other kind of hair that do
> something else. I do.

Goldberg's character's childlike innocence is reflected in her frank assessment of her kinky hair, in the trouble she has pronouncing *cascade*, and in her
literal interpretation of hair product advertisements. Like Nana G in chapter 1,
she animates her hair in order to problematize its stubborn resistance to products that promise to make her hair "bounce and behave." These confessions
reveal a near-comical naïveté. When carefully considered, however, Goldberg's
character's lament hints at the harmful effects of televised depictions of
Eurocentric beauty on young African American viewers.

The relationship between Eurocentrism and the character's own hairstyle
dilemmas are further accentuated when Goldberg, in character, addresses an
African American man seated in the front row. His selection is by no means
arbitrary; Goldberg identifies him on the basis of their visibly similar hair textures. She states:

> *((Addressing African American man in front row))* Hi. You got hair like mine,
> huh? *((He nods))* How come you don't got your shirt on [your head]? You came
> out without it? Nobody said nothin? *((He shakes his head))* No?

Goldberg then engages other audience members with curly hair, not all of
them Black. Playing an impulsively observant child, she is ever the comic:

> *((Points to another audience member with curly hair))* Ooh, she got our kind of
> hair, too. Is that your hair? On the top? Somebody in your family look like me?
> *((Audience laughs))* . . . It's just naturally like that? I guess nobody on TV look
> like you neither. *((Points out other audience members with curly hair))* And she
> got it. And he got it. And nobody got no shirt on [their head]. And don't nobody
> on TV look like none of y'all. *((Audience laughs))* . . .

Goldberg's broader appeals to non-Black audience members with curly hair
allow her to successfully navigate an array of racial, political, and comedic
stances. Specifically, by making other guests the brunt of her humor and slyly
referencing America's insidious history of race mixing (i.e., "Somebody in your
family look like me?"), Goldberg moderates the more serious aspects of her
monologue with humor. Further, by speaking as a child, Goldberg can assume
an unapologetically naïve positionality and frankness (e.g., "And don't nobody

on TV look like none of y'all.") Her innocence summons greater empathy from
the audience concerning her plight and its relation to the lack of racial diversity on television and in children's toys.

Like several of the comedy sketches previously discussed, Goldberg's
humor plays on visual and highly symbolic incongruities. The white shirt, for
example, is a comical substitution for both the long blonde hair she covets and
her own curly hair. Goldberg plays these vivid signifiers against each other
with great comic effect. Moreover, her monologue works as a critical engagement between her character (a child) and her audience (authoritative adults),
particularly as she personally engages members of her audience. Goldberg's
final comments exemplify this best. Although (as the sketch continues) her
audience ultimately manages to convince her that she doesn't need the white
shirt, she dangles it close by just in case they have "lied to [her]." But even this
coda is playful and coy; it reinforces her audience's role as responsible adults
in this dialogical and political performance. In Goldberg's hands, questions of
artifice and authenticity, gender and beauty, center on African American
women's complex relationship to their hair.

Hair-straightening dilemmas; or, riffs on a "burning" question

Hair dilemmas are not restricted to women, however; men too suffer social
discomfort and even pain during hair treatments. This is especially true of
common Black hair-straightening procedures (e.g., relaxers/perms, pressing/
silkening), all of which entail the risk of burns. Sinbad exploits cultural knowledge about these risks in a joke about his first experience with receiving a relaxer. This routine also comes from his performance in Brain Damaged (1990):

> Have you ever had some relaxer put on your hair after you scratched it? That's a
> pain worse than labor! *((Female audience member: "WHAT ABOUT YOUR
> HEAD?!"))* I *had* some in my head. We've had some relaxer. Don't you lie! We've
> all had a *full-of-waves* cap [i.e., silk cap for men often worn at night to preserve
> "natural" or chemically effected waves] on one time in our lives. Man, that girl
> put that relaxer on my head. And I didn't know it burns. I was like, *((calmly))*
> "Yeah, I'll do it. Let's try that." I had scratched my head all day long. *((Audience
> laughs))* My foot went through the floor. [My] butt tightened up, [I] grabbed the
> chair. I was [like] . . . "YOU GOT TO TAKE IT OUT NOW! It's—you" *((imper-
> sonates effeminate male hairdresser))*—"It ain't cook yet. Wait. It ain't ready!" I
> ran to the sink. [Some of my] hair was nappy. [Some of my] hair was relaxed and
> [I'm] like, "It's okay!" Scabs was fallin out my head. Ha. Burn you up, Jack!
> Whew!

Sinbad's joke exemplifies stand-up comedy as personal narrative. He
embellishes his own personal experiences with hair treatment for great comic
effect. He also draws on his audience's shared experience and knowledge that
scratching increases one's vulnerability to scalp burns during relaxer application (note their laughter immediately after he admits he had scratched his hair

"all day long" before his chemical service). His joke is therefore an engagement in cultural memory insofar as it compels audiences to consider such do's and don'ts of hair-straightening and personally identify with the horror of his hair-straightening encounter.

Sinbad's joke has a personal appeal for me. During my early years in graduate school, my mother would occasionally relax my hair for free. Once I showed up for my bimonthly treatment, having scratched my scalp intensely the night before. I kept this information a secret because I wanted to proceed with my treatment. Needless to say, my scalp began to burn almost as soon as my mother applied the product, and I began to complain. Soon, my complaints escalated to a dramatic, almost religious, appeal to "go to the water" (i.e., to rinse out the chemical). My mother was not happy. As she rushed me to the shampoo bowl, she snapped that I had wasted both her products and her time since my hair—indeed her work—would likely look a mess.

My appreciation for both my mother's complaint and Sinbad's joke deepened during my observations at the African American cosmetology school I studied in South Carolina. Since scalp burns are funnier in memory than when they actually occur, and hair-straightening products are costly, students are trained to ask an array of preemptive questions before chemically treating clients' hair. One of these questions—"Have you scratched your hair lately?"—enlists clients as coexperts in the diagnosis and care of their hair. Clients' answers affirm their state of readiness for chemical services. They also permit stylists to compel offending clients (i.e., those who have scratched) to share culpability for the risk of burns.

Hecklers and hair

Cases of heckling during stand-up comedy performances provide additional opportunities to understand hair as a meaningful signifier and site of cultural practice. When comics encounter hecklers, they often attack visible cues, such as the heckler's hairstyle or clothing. These quips are insightful on multiple grounds. First, they illuminate how comics invoke hair to restore their balance of power on stage. Further, heckling also illuminates audience members' attempts to police who can speak on the subject of hair, even in the transgressive space of stand-up comedy.

The late comedian/actor Robin Harris's performance in his comedy album "Be-Be's Kids" (1990) offers a hilarious case in point. When confronted by a loud heckler, Harris diffused the attack by lampooning the heckler's hairstyle. The style, a "jherri curl," presented an easy target for several reasons. The jherri curl is a curly perm that enjoyed prominence in the late 1970s and 1980s and is considered outdated today. The hairstyle is also often ridiculed on other grounds, including the fact that it requires a daily moisturizing regimen. For example, in 2000, comic/actor J. Anthony Brown performed a joke on *Russell Simmons' Def Comedy Jam* that parodied the way people moisturize their jherri curls in the morning (*Best of Def Comedy Jam* 2002). Brown reduced his audience to hysterics by transforming a morning ritual involving a spray battle into a hyperextended affair. His performance was decidedly cultural; he incorporated nuanced gestures and techniques that only a true jherri curl wearer would know. For example, after he sprays his hair for what seems to be an inordinate amount of time, Brown's bottle seems to run dry. Brown then shakes the spray bottle purposefully, drawing widespread laughter from his audience, only to resume spraying his hair yet again. His joke resonated widely and emphasized just how difficult it was for people who wore a jherri curl to achieve sufficient moisture. Riffs along these lines permeate Black popular culture. Actor Eriq La Salle's character in the comedic film "Coming to America" (1988) wears a jherri curl and routinely leaves evidence of his daily moisturizing regimen on couch and car upholstery. The camera rests on the grease stains left in his wake to satirize both the character's hairstyle and his outdated fashion sense.

Returning to Harris's handling of the heckler, whom he likened to "E.T. with a jherri curl," we find yet additional riffs:

> [You] better go home and fuck up somebody pillow case. *((To audience))* You know people with jherri curl cain't do no crime . . . Police find they ass. They . . . follow the drip, follow the drip! *((Audience laughs))* Just messin' up people's pillow cases and carrying on . . . I wish they had . . . a jherri curl when I was going to my prom. I would've made it. I couldn't even go. I went to pick up the girl, man. Her mother had burned all her hair up. . . . HOT COMB! *((Audience laughs))* . . . Fo'head all fucked up. All the earlobes all burnt up. She in there crying. "WAAAAAA—I CAIN'T GO!" Mother standin' there with the hot comb talking 'bout, *((indignantly))* "SHE SHO' CAIN'T!" I started to burn *her* ass up . . .

After his quick and efficient assault on the heckler, Harris moves to a more general discussion of jherri curls and other hairstyles. His joke invokes cultural subtexts underlying other comments on hair discussed in this chapter. For example, Harris's story about missing his prom recalls Sinbad's joke about his first experience getting a relaxer. Harris condemns both the hot comb and his prom date's mother for making him miss his prom. His very mention of the term *hot comb* invokes collective memories and shared laughter from his predominantly Black audience.

Black women, Black men, and hair care

Harris and Sinbad, both male comics, satirize the risks associated with Black hair-straightening procedures and styles, while comediennes Point and Goldberg politicize such parodies by considering these subjects in relation to mainstream and communal standards of beauty and women's freedom of choice. However, this does not mean that Black men do not display a nuanced appreciation for the significance of hair in Black women's lives.

Harris's joke, for example, hints at the importance of hair to both his prom date and her mother, who shouts, despite her own obvious culpability, "SHE SHO' CAIN'T," after her daughter tearfully admits she will be unable to accompany him to the prom. Additionally, in "Brain Damaged" (1990), Sinbad earned widespread laughter and applause when he joked that "bad hair days" are worse for women than men:

> But hair is important, though. . . . Women take hair serious. Men put a hat on! Men look in the mirror [and say], "Forget that, Jack!" A woman's whole day is messed up when her hair is messed up. Whole day is messed UP! You come home. Don't know what's wrong with her. [You ask], "Honey, what's wrong?" *((impersonates angry woman))* "LOOK, LOOK at my head!' And we don't know so we're going—the dumbest thing you can say, "It looks okay to me." Then they go off. "YOU THINK THIS LOOK GOOD!" They call her hairdresser like he's a doctor. *((impersonates desperate woman))* "Willie, you *got* to take me! I got to quit my job! I cain't come in like this!" They get to the hairdresser; it's like a fix. *((impersonates drug addict))* "OOOOH GIRRRRL, do something with it!" And hairdressers is brutally honest . . . especially a gay hairdresser. Gay hairdressers be like, *((feels imaginary hair with grimace and effeminate mannerisms))* "Who cut this last? Wash her please! . . . I'll see what I can do. I can't promise nothin'.'"

Whereas Sinbad highlights the importance of hair to Black women, actress and comedienne Adele Givens takes this knowledge for granted and instead satirizes the dilemmas many women face in Black beauty salons. While flaunting her then blonde-colored hair during her *HBO ½ Hour Comedy Special* (Givens 1996), Givens dramatized the extensive length of time that many Black women spend in salons:

> I am so glad to be here! Y'all looking good. *((Audience applauds wildly))* Thank y'all . . . Y'all like my little new hair color there? . . . I did this myself, you know . . . Hairstylists in the house, tell me what you think . . . I did a good job? *((Woman in audience replies "Yes"))* . . . . . . Hairstylists, you know y'all ain't shit, don't you? *((Audience laughs))* Hairstylists is wro:ng! They wrong, ain't they, ladies?! *((Audience: "Yeahhhhhh"))* Every woman here knows when you go in the beauty shop, you better bring a lunch and some books, bitch, cause you—*((Audience: "Right! Yeah! Ha!"))*—you gon' be in there all da:y!

Black women in the audience provide ready support for Givens's claims. Their laughter and affirmative cries mark her commentary on lengthy salon visits as decidedly in-group humor and shared experience. The rest of her joke offers a hilarious and detailed critique of how stylists perpetuate this trend:

> *((to stylists))* Baby, why do we have to sit there all day with y'all? ... Tell me this—how in the hell can you book two hundred and twelve heads—in one day?! *((to audience))* You hear 'em [stylists] on the phone, don't you! You get your dumb ass there early—you hear 'em on the phone going, "Naw, girl. I got a four o'clock [appointment]. You gotta come at 4:02" *((looks at watch))*. They [stylists] make me so damn mad! That's why I do my own hair now!

Like Goldberg, Givens deftly toes the line between serious critique and playful jesting. Her comment about doing her own hair, however, is a poignant reminder of African American hairstylists' laments in chapter 2. Many cosmetologists complained about their need to compete with kitchen beauticians who did their own or others' hair at home. Givens boldly claims to be one of these practitioners and muses at length on the reasons why, her audience laughing all the while.

Discussion

In the jokes considered above, African American comics address how and why hair matters in African Americans' everyday lives. Hair acts as a figurative and corporeal stage for analyzing how Blackness, gender, class, and beauty are performed, in essence "done" (Fenstermaker and West 2002; West and Zimmerman 1987), within the comedic conventions and tropes of Black humor and language.

Comediennes Whoopi Goldberg, Adele Givens, and Dana Point explicitly inject racial and gendered concerns in their comedy by discussing painful experiences as well as pragmatic considerations associated with Black women's hairstyling decisions. Point offers a witty retort (i.e., "Yeah, ... I bought it!") to Black men's queries about the authenticity of her hair, thus celebrating her own and other women's freedom to choose hairstyles that make them and their partners happy. Givens explores pragmatic concerns surrounding Black women's experiences in salons, focusing on a common complaint among Black women regarding the length of time they spend in salons. Goldberg explores the self-esteem issues young Black girls may face after being inundated by Eurocentric images of beauty on television.

None of these comics present singular stances about Black hair politics or aesthetics. Point, for example, avoids a strict polarized assessment of hair as a marker of racial authenticity on the one hand and evidence of Black women's Eurocentric assumptions on the other by framing her decision to wear a weave as a matter of personal choice. Hayes similarly exposes her wig as a fashion accessory, to be abandoned and reaffixed as situations demand. Givens's joke also pays little regard to gendered prescriptions for aesthetic "realness," and instead privileges the humor implicit in Black women's everyday dilemmas in the salon. Moreover, the political significance of Goldberg's monologue extends well beyond one Black girl's negative self-image to indict the lack of racial diversity in mainstream media representations of beauty.

Male comics also incorporate hair as a subject in their stand-up comedy. Sinbad, Martin Lawrence, and Robin Harris offer comical critiques of weaves, hot combs, and relaxers. Lawrence's stand-up routine, in particular, hints at the ideologies underlying the very notion of "good hair" in African American culture. In doing so, he suggests that one's racial affinity can be assessed through the question "Is that your hair?" Scruncho's joke enacts strategies of racial and gendered representation that strictly adhere to the tenets of the "one-drop rule" and hypermasculine aesthetics and postures. Sinbad and Harris mine the terrain of in-group humor around hair through jokes with gender-specific as well as more universal appeal. Collectively, male comics lampoon artifice and elaborate on hair-care rituals, at times privileging questions of choice, to illuminate the comedy of Black hairstyles and hair care in everyday life. They also frame hair as more of a preeminent concern for women, at times policing women's aesthetic choice with regard to artifice, hair length, and ritual.

Conclusion

African American comics and their audiences remind us that there exist many complex truths and realities surrounding Black hair and that these multiple truths are further shaped by gender. Comics privilege such shared in-group knowledge, cultural discourse styles (e.g., call and response), and hair terminology (e.g., "good hair"), all of which rely on Black audiences' interpretive investments. Comics' hair jokes also summon audiences' appreciation for imposed and comical incongruities, veiled meanings, and hair itself as a resource in the construction of racial, cultural, gendered, and class-marked "authenticity." Black audiences frequently corroborate comics' jokes through laughter, applause, and agreement expletives (e.g., "That's right!"), as well as through silence and heckling. In this sense, jokes about hair are highly dialogical. Moreover, as critical engagements in ways of being and doing gender and Blackness vis-à-vis hair, they tell us even more about how and why hair matters in Black folks' everyday lives.

The next chapter extends these insights by examining a series of online debates about hair on a listserve dedicated to African American life and culture. Much like the jokes by Black comediennes discussed above, African American women's posts in this forum overwhelmingly home in on the ways hairstyles and hair-care politics are nuanced by race and gender (Rooks 1996). They also strategically invoke an array of in-group hair terms, gendered experiences, and cultural discourse styles to establish their individual and collective rights to speak. Significantly, many women actively preclude the discursive rights of others (specifically Black men and White women) based upon their race, gender, and professed views on hair straightening. Their dialogues once again illuminate how hair and language act as resources through which speakers construct a sense of themselves and inscribe visions of their past and immediate "becomings" vis-à-vis hair-care experiences.

5

"BTW: How Do You Wear Your Hair?"

Gender and Race in Computer-mediated Hair Debates

I
n prior chapters, we have seen how African American cosmetologists use religious and scientific discourse to underwrite their professional authority. Specialized language use and hair-care practices ground both of these representational paradigms; they form the foundation upon which stylists foster new ways of being and becoming professionals. Comics broaden our understandings of hair and language as resources in African Americans' "being" and "becomings" even further. Their jokes get at the heart of how gender shapes the meanings of hair in Black women and men's everyday lives. As communal conversations, jokes about hair explicitly play with cultural attitudes about hair, highlighting the performative nature of hair and language in constructing notions of racial and gendered identity and experience.

In this chapter, I consider many of the aforementioned themes in relation to a hair debate among scholars, cosmetologists, and the general public on an electronic discussion list dedicated to African American life and culture, AFROAM-L. This discussion was provoked by a letter, originally submitted to *Essence* magazine and later forwarded to AFROAM-L, questioning whether or not Oprah Winfrey's hair as depicted on the magazine's (May 1995) 25th anniversary cover was real. To the surprise of several disgruntled list subscribers, as well as many hair enthusiasts like me, the letter incited almost a month of impassioned exchange about hair. Much of the discussion centered on hair straightening among Black women, recalling historical debates about the politics of hair (see Lommel 1993; Mercer 1994; Rooks 1996). Although this issue was of intense personal and political interest to all those who contributed to the debate, it was also of professional concern for cosmetologists, since the arguments against hair straightening served to undermine their professional legitimacy and cultural authenticity. However, my focus in this chapter is not merely on cosmetologists, since all African American women face profound issues concerning gender and racial identity when making decisions about hair.

A closer examination of the discussion, including who contributes and to what end, provides revealing insights into hair as a perceived marker of racial identity and cultural consciousness. At a discursive level, these computer-mediated exchanges illustrate how hair is invoked as a symbol of racial authenticity on the Internet, an environment that is often claimed to mask identity (e.g., Rheingold 1993). Many participants who overwhelmingly present themselves as Black reference their own hairstyle and texture to make larger claims about their racial consciousness. Personal references to one's own hair thus also serve as bids for cultural authority. By exploiting language and the cultural discourse of Black hair (Mercer 1994) in such ways, AFROAM-L subscribers circumvent the nonvisual and nonaural properties of the medium.

The discursive and linguistic strategies adopted by speakers to accomplish this end are varied and include the use of cultural hair terms (Smitherman 1994) to describe a wide range of African American hair textures, styles, and treatments. Because this lexicon includes in-group hair terms, participants' fluency with such terms displays their knowledge of and experience with Black hair and hence augments their claims of legitimacy. Participants also rely on discourse styles characteristic of African American speech communities. For example, several participants employ indirectness (Morgan 1991, 1996a) by asking others (including me) a simple yet loaded question: "How do you wear your hair?" Given the semiotics associated with Black hair (Bonner 1991; hooks 1992, 1994; Jones 1994; Mercer 1994; Weekes 1997), this question interrogates the addressee's racial authenticity via their hairstyle choices.

Language is an important mediator of speakers' social identities in this debate. As Ochs (1992) explains, while speaker's identities are never static and can shift at any given moment, they can be constituted and mediated by the indexical relation of language to stances, social acts, social activities, and other social constructs. Given the visual constraints imposed by the "cyberspace curtain" (Hunkele and Cornwell 1997), language and discourse style are crucial resources through which AFROAM-L members construct their race as African American women and levy cultural knowledge in the hair debate. Using text-based representational conventions available in computer-mediated communication (CMC), along with African American discourse styles and hair terminology, participants "do" racial and gendered identities (Fenstermaker and West 2002; Herring 1994; Kolko et al. 2000; West and Zimmerman 1987) in ways that belie reports of the invisibility or flexibility of race and gender on the Internet (Haraway 1985).

Werry (1996) describes the textual and graphic modes of representation that enable cyberspace conversationalists to embed paralinguistic (e.g., action, gesture, gaze) and prosodic (e.g., voice, gesture, intonation) features within their posts. For example, capitalized letters can simulate the African American discourse style of loud talking (Fordham 1993; Mitchell-Kernan 1972; Morgan 1998, 2002), and words in asterisks or quotation marks can convey irony or emphasis. As in face-to-face communication, these features are widespread in CMC and were heavily employed during the hair debate on AFROAM-L to enrich the persuasive, humorous, or mitigated rhetorical force of posts.

In this chapter, I examine several exchanges that highlight participants' use of language and invocation of personal experience with Black hair care to display their racial identity and cultural knowledge. Participants' shared use and interpretation of African American discourse styles and hair terminology reflect norms governing talk in African American speech communities more broadly. As such, the listserv can be characterized as an electronic speech community (Kirshenblatt-Gimblett 1996) that is constituted, in part, through narrative tropes of and stances about hair.

Significantly, Black women's posts during the AFROAM-L hair debates played a central role in shaping the interactional contours of this electronic speech community, determining who could or could not speak on this issue. Additionally, while Black women did not necessarily align with one another in their hair debates, they also problematized Black men's expertise and right to speak about women's hairstyle options. In the AFROAM-L hair debate, Black women's discourse and interactional styles exemplify both more direct and strategically indirect discourse styles apparent in prior studies of Black girls' and women's speech (Goodwin 1990; Jacobs-Huey 2001; Mitchell-Kernan 1972; Morgan 1996a, 1996b) and further suggest that "doing gender" online is mediated by race. These findings qualify descriptions of (mostly White) women's online discourse as polite and nonadversarial (e.g., Herring 1993, 1994).

Data

The messages analyzed in this chapter were selected from a corpus of 258 pages of hair-related exchanges that occurred during April and May 1995 on AFROAM-L. Participants' exchanges occur asynchronously rather than in real (synchronous) time and are mediated by a LISTSERV discussion list. At the time of the hair discussion, there were more than 200 AFROAM-L subscribers. Dr. Lee D. Baker, who established AFROAM-L in 1990, notes (personal communication, October 2, 2002) that the list's constituency shifted notably around 1997 from university-based email accounts (i.e., those with .edu extensions) to corporate accounts (i.e., those with .com extensions); he adds, more generally, that although women historically outnumber men with respect to membership, men often participate more often in online discussions on this list (see also Herring 1994, 1995). It is telling, then, that Black women monopolized the hair discussion, at times restricting the rights of Black men and White women to weigh in on subjects most directly relevant to Black women's bodies. It is equally telling that these other groups acquiesced to their own marginalization within the debate.

Most of the posts in the hair debate are between one and two screens in length and describe subscribers' personal experiences with and beliefs about Black hair. They also attest to racial and gender diversity among subscribers. In example 1, taken from the middle of the debate, Njeri, a major player in the hair discussion, belatedly acknowledges the apparent ethnic diversity of AFROAM-L (line 14). Her post, along with previous posts embedded in her reply, explicitly situates hair texture and color (e.g., "kinky hair at the roots," "straight & blond") as indexes of racial identity. (Njeri's own words appear at the bottom of the message, in line 14.) In keeping with a widespread online practice, Njeri first quotes part of Sam's prior message, which in turn quotes and responds to Lena's and Njeri's own earlier posts. Each level of embedded quotation is marked by one or more > symbols.

(1) Ethnic Diversity on AFROAM-L

1	At 09:04 AM 5/8/95 -0500, Sam wrote:
2	>*Lena said:*
3	> *. . . what is interesting is the makeup of individuals on this*
4	>*list it appears we are educators, students, college professors,*
5	>*parents, entrepreneurs, workers and we all are articulate*
6	*And Njeri added:*
7	>>*AND WE ALL HAVE KINKY HAIR AT THE ROOTS/ . . .*
8	>>>>>>>>>>>>>>>>>>>>>>>>>>
9	This forum is also home to people of many different religious
10	affiliations, ethnicities **and** races. Actually, not **all** of us have
11	kinky hair – mine's straight & blond :-).
12	Peace,
13	Sam
14	**Sorry to leave y'all out Sam. I stand corrected. ;-)**

This intertextual exchange illustrates the racial diversity of the list, as well as subscribers' cordial tone, despite their use of emphatic markers. Note both Sam's and Njeri's use of emoticons, or iconic representations of facial expressions (lines 11 and 14), to soften the illocutionary force of their comments. It is also telling that until Sam's comment (quoted in lines 9–11), Njeri (and perhaps Lena) was able to assume that AFROAM-L subscribers were all Black. (Although the actual gender and racial identities of many participants cannot be objectively confirmed, contributors leave no doubt as to how they want to be viewed within the discussion. For the purposes of my analysis, I accept subscribers' self-presentations of their racial and gender identity.)

Hair was also pivotal in my own attempt to gain access to the post that initially provoked the hair discussion. Because I entered the forum as a participant-observer shortly after its inception, I did not know what had originally incited the discussion. Seeking clarification, I privately contacted Njeri, a major figure in the month-long exchange, with whom I had already briefly interacted during the hair debate. (While I did not know it at the time, I could have also consulted the listowner for access to the archives; my ignorance had fortuitous outcomes, since it afforded an illuminating conversation with Njeri). Njeri responded to my inquiry with several questions, including "What do you hope to prove by your research?" (see also Banks 2000) and "What exactly are you looking for in [the] archives?" Her most poignant query was "How do YOU wear your hair?" Given the physical constraints of our computer-mediated dialogue, I interpreted Njeri's question as an attempt to assess my racial identity and political allegiance in the hair-straightening debate. I likewise answered her question strategically by stressing my own diverse hair-care history and passion for understanding the complexities of notions of "good" and "bad" hair among African Americans. I hinted at such complexities by noting that many African American women define "good" hair as thick, strong hair that can hold a curl, and I invoked Oprah's hair as an example. (This proved to be a provocative admission since, as I later learned, Oprah's straightened hairstyle is actually what had incited the month-long debate on AFROAM-L.)

In our subsequent private email exchange, Njeri asked point-blank, "Lanita. I believe you are a Black woman. Am I correct?" I won Njeri's confidence after confirming her hunch and answering an additional set of questions about such topics as the potential influences that Winfrey and African American singer Whitney Houston have upon African American women, and the long-term physical and emotional costs of chemical and thermal hair-straightening procedures for African American girls. Njeri then provided me with a huge computer file that included the antecedents of the hair debate. Still, I wondered about our own exchange, particularly the extent to which the interactional dynamics and uses of indirectness that I observed among women in the AFROAM-L debate had also played out in our one-on-one dialogue. Once I got to know Njeri better, I asked her what she had intended by the question "How do YOU wear your hair?" Njeri conceded that it was indeed an indirect way of asking, "Who goes there?" The question thus functioned pragmatically as a screening by monitoring my access to the original posts in the online debate.

Black hair and discourse styles were invoked in many other posts as a means of legitimating subscribers' ethnic identity and racial consciousness. The posts I discuss below reflect key themes in the hair debate and exemplify the ways in which language and hair together serve as mediators of identity and ideology regarding African American women's hair.

The Black hair discussion on AFROAM-L

As noted earlier, the hair debate on AFROAM-L was stimulated by an unpublished letter submitted to *Essence* magazine and later reproduced on the list that questioned whether or not African American talk-show host Oprah Winfrey's then straightened hair was in fact real. The letter resembled the comedic query, "Is that your hair?" but with decidedly more serious

implications. Njeri, the letter's author, expressed adamant disapproval of the
use of chemical and thermal-based hair-care procedures by Winfrey and other
African American women. Unable to solicit a response from either *Essence*
magazine or Winfrey's representatives, Njeri posted her letter on AFROAM-
L, where it first garnered commentary from African American men on the list,
and later from women. The fact that the hair discussion persevered for almost
a month can largely be attributed to Njeri, who vehemently defended her right
to question Winfrey's aesthetic presentation:

> The world is what we CREATE it to be . . . . that's why I looovvee me some
> Oprah Winfrey! She knows this, I think . . . If Oprah changed her hair, she would
> change some MINDS all around the world. Oprah's hairstyle (along with other
> Black people in the "limelight") . . . is as significant as the closure of apartheid in
> South Africa. (May 1, 1995)

Further, when discussion on the topic seemed to wane, Njeri would forward to
the list hair-related exchanges she had participated in offlist (privately). This
often served to jump-start the discussion, sometimes engendering the discon-
tent of male (and female) members who had grown weary of the topic. Men's
fatigue may have been due to the fact that during the middle and latter stages
of the thread's life on the list, women, mostly African American, dominated
the interactional floor.

   Many of these women invoked personal narratives about their own hair-
care histories to instantiate their credibility in the hair debate. In fact, women's
knowledge of and experience with kitchen and salon hair rituals were critical
in establishing their right to speak on the politics associated with hair straightening. Significantly, many Black female participants unveiled similar hair-care
histories, but differed strongly about the degree to which hair symbolizes racial consciousness and loyalty to Black issues. Some women viewed hair
straightening as a mimicry of Whiteness and evidence of self-hatred (see Grier
and Cobbs 1968). Others appreciated hair straightening as an act of practical-
ity, providing Black women with an alternative means of managing their curly
hair textures and negotiating their professional and sexual identities (Banks
2000; Boyd 1993; Feagin and Sikes 1994; Powlis 1988; Wynter 1993). These
diverse perspectives played out with fervor in the hair debate, sometimes spark-
ing offlist debates between subscribers.

Discourse strategies in the "Black hair" discussion

AFROAM-L subscribers employed a number of different discourse strategies to construct their gender and ethnic identity and cultural authority in the
hair discussion, including the use of African American discourse styles and
verbal genres, cultural hair terms, in-group referents, acronyms, and email
addresses that incorporated references to hair and race. In addition, many sub-

scribers used culturally laden signatures such as quotations by famous African American poets (e.g., "One ounce of truth benefits / Like a ripple on a pond"—Nikki Giovanni). Each of these strategies, which I discuss and illustrate below, helped to create a discourse context in which African American women's issues, experiences, and identities took precedence over those of other list members.

Indirectness

It is well established in the field of linguistic pragmatics that indirectness can be used strategically as a request for action or information as well as to make an assertion (Searle 1975). Targets of indirectness may involve co-present participants or an absent third party and can include individuals or larger groups. Indirectness is cultural insofar as it relies on conversationalists' shared knowledge of how to properly interpret indirect speech acts such as "Can you reach the salt?" to mean "Pass the salt" (Duranti 1997).

Scholars of African American English and African American discourse styles note that Black women's use of indirectness may serve to indict individuals or larger groups for a perceived slight, such as acting out class- or race-based privileges or failing to acknowledge elders (Morgan 1994b, 1998). Unlike African American girls (see Goodwin 1990), African American women tend to avoid using indirectness to target absent parties because doing so is often viewed as disrespectful and provocative to such targets, who are unable to defend themselves (see Morgan 1996a). Morgan (1996a, 1998) identifies two forms of indirectness used by African American speakers: pointed indirectness and baited indirectness. While targeting is a distinguishing feature of both varieties, pointed indirectness occurs when a speaker says something ostensibly to a mock receiver that is actually intended for a co-present third party and is so recognized, whereas baited indirectness occurs when a speaker directly and accurately attributes a feature to the target, who is also the addressee. Both forms rely on the speaker's and hearer's joint investment in determining the meaning and intentionality of the message (Duranti 1993, 1999; Grice 1957; Searle 1983). Moreover, although indirectness has been widely associated with White women's speech as a marker of powerlessness and/or politeness (e.g., Lakoff 1975; Holmes 1995), African American women's strategic indirectness allows for a very powerful moral stance toward the target.

Within the AFROAM-L hair discussion, African American women rely on these and other forms of indirectness to establish their own or interrogate others' ideological positions on hair straightening among Black women. This practice is illustrated by the direct question "How do you wear your hair?" which serves to interrogate the addressee's perceived racial authenticity via her hairstyle. The query exemplifies strategic indirectness because the speaker references shared cultural knowledge about the indexicality of hair as a racial and political signifier without making these associations overt, and because the speaker's query is not mediated by a mock receiver but is rather directed toward a specific and present target. Indirectness figured prominently in the hair debate as a strategy for promoting or contesting particular ideologies about hair straightening. In the following exchange, Mary, a cosmetologist and acquaintance of Njeri in "real life" employs baited indirectness to criticize Njeri's ardent stance against hair straightening. Since Mary's critique invokes personal knowledge of Njeri's past chemical hair service, which Mary provided for her in Hawaii, where both women live, she diplomatically sent her comments to Njeri's personal email account rather than the entire list. I and other subscribers became aware of Mary's critique after Njeri posted Mary's message, along with her own reply, to AFROAM-L. Njeri's reasons for doing so become apparent in example 2. (Njeri quotes parts of Mary's prior message in her reply, as indicated by the > symbol preceding Mary's comments.)

(2) Assessing the Relevance of Njeri's Chemical Hair Service in AFROAM-L

    1   Thank-you for coming forth to reply, Mary. I have commented below:
    2   *At 10:24 PM 5/8/95 -1000, Mary wrote:*
    3   *>Aloha Njeri,*
    4   *>I have been reading this discussion on hair for the past few weeks. Not*
    5   *>really sure how it got started nor am I sure why it was continued.*
    6   It only continued as long as replies continued to be generated by
    7   members of this listserv. I have not been talking to myself all this time;
    8   rather, I have been discoursing with many brothers and sisters of varying
    9   persuasions. :-) If you would like me to send you the file so that you can
   10   follow the progression of the discussion, I would be glad to forward them
   11   to you.
   12   *>Njeri, perhaps you will remember how we met. It was not as TV*
   13   *>producers at Olelo nor any of the other projects that we have dreamed*
   14   *>of. It was at HAIR FAIR in Waikiki.*
   15   Yes, I got a jheri curl in your shop. No offense, Mary, but that night I
   16   washed the perm out and cut my hair down to the skull. I was so
   17   embarrassed by how the "curl" looked and FELT that I swore that I
   18   would never do that again to my head. . . . and I haven't to this
   19   day. As you recall, I never returned to your shop after this incident. I
   20   never mentioned why I never returned because I did not believe that you
   21   would understand . . . I had no desire to insult you or your business . . .

In lines 12–14, Mary uses baited indirectness to expose a potential contradiction between Njeri's previously expressed hair ideologies on AFROAM-L and her actual hair practices by reminding Njeri of their first meeting at a hair expo in Hawai'i. To AFROAM-L subscribers, Mary's reminder may appear to be merely a contextual prompt to trigger Njeri's memory of her. However, when Njeri admits in line 15 that she received a "jheri curl" (i.e., a hairstyle that requires chemicals to first straighten and then curl the hair) in Mary's salon, Mary's reminder is exposed as a subtle form of baited indirectness. In essence, she is questioning the integrity of Njeri's opposition to hair straightening in light of her recent chemical service.

Njeri thwarts the punitive entailments of this veiled revelation by first acknowledging receipt of a chemical hair treatment and then expressing profound dissatisfaction with it. Specifically, she states that her curl looked and felt so bad that she cut off all her hair and vowed to never straighten or chemically treat her hair again. Thus, rather than undermine her right to speak against hair straightening as Mary's baited indirectness is designed to do, Njeri's admission dramatically strengthens her vociferous advocacy of "natural" (i.e., chemical-free) hairstyles for all women. Further, her willingness to broadcast this self-incriminating post to the list is a bold step that fortifies her legitimacy in the overall hair debate.

Signifying

Participants in the debate also employ another indirect African American speech style known as *signifying*. Morgan (1994b) describes signifying as a verbal game of indirection also known by the regional names of *sounding, the dozens, joning, snapping, busting, capping, bagging,* and *ranking*. In an early and influential study, Mitchell-Kernan (1972: 317–318) defines signifying as "the recognition or attribution of some implicit content or function which is obscured by the surface content or function." Language play is essential to signifying, and a high premium is placed on verbal cleverness.

Following Mitchell-Kernan, Morgan (1996a, 1999) distinguishes signifying as a form of boys' verbal play involving ritual insults from conversational signifying, which is more often used by adult women. During conversational signifying, one or more participants is indirectly targeted by a speaker who associates personal attributes of the target with culturally marked signs—such as African American hair texture and styles. Conversational signifying entails inherent interpersonal risks because it is governed by broader cultural norms and expectations that place constraints on who has a right to speak or pass judgment on a topic, and what can be said when all relevant interlocutors are not present (see also Goodwin 1985, 1992). Conversational signifying can often invoke another's prior statements or claims in order to negotiate their truth. As illustrated in example 3 below, conversational signifying can also be keyed through dialect opposition, wherein interlocutors exploit multiple readings of words in American Mainstream English and African American English, often toward strategic ends. In these re-readings, both dominant and subordinate cultural lexical interpretations are highlighted and politicized, exemplifying what Morgan calls "reading dialect" (1998: 265).

These strategic and pragmatic features of signifying were exploited throughout the hair debate. Many Black female subscribers signified on what other participants had said about hair in previous posts in order to make claims about their own or others' racial consciousness. Likewise, in the following exchange, Katrina maintains that her permed hairstyle does not indicate her lack of racial consciousness. Njeri nevertheless takes Katrina to task for her chemically straightened hairstyle by signifying on risks associated with two common Black hair-straightening procedures (i.e., the "press" and the "relaxer" or perm). As most Black women learn from personal experience, even the most careful application of the pressing comb or of chemicals in relaxers or perms can cause burns and scalp abrasions. (As above, Njeri quotes excerpts of Katrina's prior post, as evidenced by the > symbol preceding Katrina's comments.)

(3) Assessing Politics of Personal Hair-straightening

    1   Dear Katrina,
    2   Thanks for replying. And thank-you VERY much for identifying your
    3   hair choice and your position. I've commented below:
    4   *At 04:11 PM 5/8/95 -0400, Katrina wrote:*
    5   *>Hi All,*
    6   *>I just want to add my cents worth to the hair discussion. I know this is a*
    7   *>topic that has been beaten to death but after listening in on this*
    8   *>discussion several times over I want to comment. My thoughts are just*
    9   *>that, my thoughts they are not meant to condemn or to judge any*
   10   *>others on the list, I believe we are all entitled to our opinions and can*
   11   *>respectfully agree to disagree. As a person who has a perm or fried hair*
   12   *>as it has been referred to I'd like to state that I do not hate myself, I do*
   13   *>not hate my race. I don't believe that the way I wear my hair is any*
   14   *>indication of my love or hate for my people. I believe it is my action that*
   15   *>should be the indicator that measures my care for myself and the people*
   16   *>of my race.*
   17
   18   Sister, every time that you lift a pressing comb to your head or apply
   19   chemical straightening agents to your hair you are taking ACTION and
   20   thereby indicating where your consciousness is with respect to how you
   21   take care of your body, the temple of the divine.
   22
   23   *>As a person with a perm I am committed to equity as well as the*
   24   *>liberation of my people. When I was a child I thought as I child. I*
   25   *>thought that the "wash and wear" long flowing/glowing hair was*
   26   *>what I wanted. I must confess that I thought that being able to shake*
   27   *>and flash my hair a la [singer] Diana Ross, was the thing to do. Now*
   28   *>that I am an adult and I have knowledge I know that I would not want*
   29   *>to have anything else. I love being able to wear my hair short, long, up,*
   30   *>down etc., etc., I have even worn an Afro at one point. I frequently hear*
   31   *>WF [White folk/females] tell me as well as AA [African American]*
   32   *>students that we are so lucky to be able to do so many things with our*

33   >*hair.*

34

35   The systematic destruction of our race is not a simple issue. When I think
36   back to my childhood I think about the "burning" question on my mind
37   every time my mother or grandmother straightened my hair: "If they love
38   me, why are they hurting me?" "Am I so ugly that I am not acceptable as
39   I am?" I have "European American" (that's for you Sam :-)) blood and
40   Native American blood, so I grew up with what was called "good hair." It
41   still wasn't "good enough" until it got straightened. Keep perming your
42   hair if you so choose. I don't love you any less for it. I hope you
43   understand where I am coming from, Sis. . . . .

In lines 11–16, Katrina disagrees that hair straightening is a sign of self-
hatred. Her preface is an intertextual and preemptive callback to Njeri and
others in the debate who sardonically refer to chemically straightened hair
as "fried hair." She subtly marks them (i.e., parodies their quoted speech)
when she states, "As a person who has a perm or fried hair as it has been
referred to I'd like to state that I do not hate myself, I do not hate my race."
Katrina also celebrates her history of hairstyle options, which have ranged
from short-dos to up-dos to Afros. Moreover, she asserts that her commitment to the African American community cannot be reduced to hairstyle
choices alone, and she argues that her commitment to her race is most evident through her actions. Njeri, a strict "natural" hair-care enthusiast, clearly
disagrees, stating that Katrina's use of chemicals to straighten her hair represents an oppressive action that reflects negatively on her expressed racial
consciousness. Njeri does this by exploiting shared cultural knowledge of the
hazards associated with Black hair-straightening procedures. Specifically, in
lines 35–39, she signifies on hair-straightening procedures that often cause
African American women to suffer burns or scalp abrasions, stating, "When
I think back to my childhood I think about the 'burning' question on my mind
every time my mother or grandmother straightened my hair: 'If they love me,
why are they hurting me?' 'Am I so ugly that I am not acceptable as I am?' "
Njeri's testimony instantiates her firsthand experience with "pressing hair,"
the thermal hair-straightening procedure that was also parodied by comic
Robin Harris in chapter 4. Her personal narrative of her childhood vulnerability is thus designed to engender empathy for her rigid stance against hair
straightening. Njeri's bracketing of the term *burning* in quotation marks further accentuates her cultural knowledge of Black hair-straightening procedures, which, as Sinbad's comedy in chapter 4 artfully shows, also include
chemical processes. Her language play exploits a plausible sign (i.e., burning) as a fitting descriptor of the risks entailed in hair straightening. Moreover, her clever dual use of *burning* to characterize both her question and the
procedure of pressing hair invokes literal as well as decidedly cultural interpretations of the term (see Morgan 1998). Njeri's use of *burning* to describe
her own experience of a home perm indirectly targets Katrina's chemically

straightened hairstyle, a perm, and conceivably other hair-straightening procedures, deeming them risky endeavors in more ways than one.

Lexis, in-group referents, and specialized acronyms

The exchanges above also illustrate how cultural hair terms like *nappy* and in-group referents like *sistah* (i.e., Black woman; Smitherman 1994) act as membership categorization devices (Sacks 1992a; 1992b) within the AFROAM-L hair debate. Participants employ these in-group terms to locate themselves racially and ideologically within African American communities. They also deploy terms such as *sister* (see Njeri's remark in example 3, line 18) to smooth over interactional tensions. By using cultural hair terms and in-group references, subscribers evidence their cultural knowledge of African American discourse conventions and hair-care procedures; in doing so, they underwrite their right to speak (see also Burkhalter 1999; McIlvenny 1996).

    List subscribers also key their ethnic (and sometimes gender) identities and ideological alignments explicitly through acronyms such as *ASAB* (*AS A Brother*) and email addresses like *nattyreb@_* that include hair terms. (*Natty* is an adjective that describes matted dreadlocks and is also a corporeal and political signifier in the Rastafarian movement.) In example 4, the acronym *ASAB* indexes race, and Blackness in particular, as a basis for participation in this highly charged discussion—even as it reveals the writer's gender identity and hence his more marginal status within the discussion:

(4) ASAB (As a Brother)

> ASAB(as a brother), I think sisters have been hiding behind the euphemism of "easier to manage" as a reason for the continued use of hair straighteners, etc. . . .

Here, the speaker hedges his opinion by means of the qualifier *I think*. Additionally, his use of the term *sisters* marks his racial kinship with African American women, while also locating the issue of hair straightening as one that only women confront.

Signatures

Finally, signature files are another means through which AFROAM-L subscribers represent their race and gender online (see also Hall 1996; Kollock and Smith 1996). Many participants automatically append to their posts signature files that feature Afrocentric quotations and graphics. These signatures act as ethnic and political cues to the subscriber's identity. For example, Njeri's signature during the "Black Hair" thread graphically affirmed her support for "natural" hairstyles (see fig. 5.1). Her signature depicts a face with visibly short and curly hair, which seems to be a representation of herself. Alongside this graphic are the slogans "Evoke beauty, truth, light and love . . . peace!" and "be careful what you wish for . . . you might get it!," under which she specifies

```
??????   "evoke beauty, truth, light and love . . . peace!"
@ @      & "be careful what you wish for . . . you might get it!"
  ~      [Njeri's email and web address here]
 <>      [Njeri's fax number and real name here] [B.S.C.E. = 8<D]
==================================================
```

Figure 5.1. Njeri's signature file.

her contact information and professional title (B.S.C.E.—Bachelor of Science, Civil Engineering) and adds a final emoticon.

The marginalization of men in the hair thread

As shown above, participants in the AFROAM-L hair debate employed a range of African American discourse features to construct their gender and ethnic identity and cultural consciousness. In establishing their identity and knowledge through CMC, participants symbolically transcended the physical constraints of the electronic medium. In describing their hair textures with in-group hair terms such as *nappy,* for instance, participants alluded to their identities as African Americans and further legitimated their right to speak. Additionally, various participants employed indirectness to assess other participants' presumed racial authenticity and credibility and, as I learned personally, to monitor access to the hair discussion itself. Subscribers also used signifying to reprimand others for hair stances thought to be Eurocentric.

African American women's use of such discourse strategies relied on their shared knowledge of the norms governing the use and interpretation of indirect face-to-face speech styles in African American speech communities. In the exchanges above, members demonstrated this cultural knowledge in their use and interpretation of indirect discourse styles—examples include Njeri's use of *burning* to reference the risks associated with thermal and chemical hair straightening and Katrina's rejoinder to those who would parody her chemically straightened hair as "fried hair."

Additionally, women used narratives to detail their personal experiences with Black hair and hence underwrite their legitimacy in the forum. By exploiting ways of speaking through the communicative devices available to them on the Internet and in their local speech communities, female subscribers not only created a highly gendered and culture-specific space within AFROAM-L, but also boldly marked their co-membership in this electronic speech community (see also Anthias and Yuval-Davis 1992; Hall 1996; Wellman and Gulia 1999).

Conversely, Black women actively policed the tenor of the hair debate, sometimes admonishing Black men who expressed weariness of the subject or threatened to derail the discussion. In example 5, Claire chides Melvin for his careful critique of the debate by framing it as relevant to women and hence legitimate.

(5) Admonishing a Male Subscriber

1   Maybe this issue comes up so often because it is one that strikes so close
2   to home for so many people. Also, it is an issue, the triviality or
3   significance of which is ususally [sic] the very focus of the debate. That
4 · is to say, for some it is just a "hair" issue . . . for others, it is symptomatic
5   of much more. I think that's why you see it come up so frequently. And
6   it will probably come up again. At least at this point, if you don't want to
7   read the discussion, you have an obvious topic header to warn you!
8
9   *On Mon, 1 May 1995, Melvin wrote:*
10 *>Personally,*
11 *>I'm curious as to how this topic arose again, since there was*
12 *>cumbersome (e-mail wise) debate not too long ago. Blacks and blondes,*
13 *>remember! It's my opinion of course, but I think superficial topics such*
14 *>as these can overwhelm the list. I mean hair is hair is hair.*
15
16 *>And while I even rebutted a fellow who made a similar complaint about*
17 *>the listserv's content, just maybe he's got a point.*
18 *>But don't mind me, I'm just crying cuz my mail will triple for the*
19 *>duration of this subject and I have to do wholesale deletions!*
20
21 *>One more point, it also seems that topics such as this current one (HAIR)*
22 *>ellicits [sic] a greater amount of debate than many other important*
23 *>issues which can fade rapidly!*
24
25 *>Take this for what it's worth*

Shortly after Claire and Melvin's exchange, another female subscriber,
Natalie, questioned men's right to participate in the hair debate at all:

Questioning male participation

Y'know I truly believe that a woman has the right to wear her hair anyway that
she likes. We make hair such a big deal. It is about the society that we live in.
America has a large hair industry and women AND men depend upon it. I've
known brothers get upset because their woman has cut her hair, colored her hair
or braided her hair. Why are men concerned? Please!! Men are one of the reasons
that women dress the way they do, talk the way they do and style their hair the
way they do. [If] that wasn't part of the reason then we wouldn't have soooooo
many hair commercials with men running therr [sic] doggone fingers through some
woman's hair. YUCK!! . . .

In contrast to studies that find men silencing women in online discussions
(Herring et al. 1995), responses such as Natalie's boldly problematize Black

men's right to speak about Black women's hairstyle politics; they also challenge descriptions of (mostly White) women's online discourse as polite and non-adversarial (e.g., Herring 1993, 1994). In the AFROAM-L hair debate, Black women's discourse and interactional styles exemplify more direct and strategically indirect discourse styles, which are also apparent in prior studies of Black girls' and women's speech (Goodwin 1990; Jacobs-Huey 2001; Mitchell-Kernan 1972; Morgan 1993, 1994a, 1996a, 1999) and further demonstrate how "doing gender" online is racially mediated by personal narrative and discourse styles.

Conclusion

This chapter builds upon previous studies of how participants use textual, graphic, and other cultural communicative devices to produce locality and sustain identities in the expansive terrain of cyberspace (Kirshenblatt-Gimblett 1996). By illustrating how speakers' gender and racial identities are constituted in and through textual representations, the "Black Hair" discussion thread on AFROAM-L challenges previous research that emphasizes speaker anonymity as an intrinsic feature of CMC (Haraway 1985). Moreover, African American women emerge as significant players in these computer-mediated discussions, determining who can speak on the subject of hair through a range of discursive strategies that construct their racial, gendered, and cultural haircare experience and hence legitimacy in the hair discussion. Their role in AFROAM-L problematizes earlier research suggesting that women are disproportionately silenced (by men) and polite (in relation to men) during Internet dialogues. Lastly, the focus on AFROAM-L members' discursive and interactional construction of an electronic speech community extends prior descriptions of online groups as virtual communities (Rheingold 1993) or reimagined communities (Morley and Robins 1995) that exhibit group-like dynamics (Korenman and Wyatt 1996) by further delineating the manner in which cultural ways of speaking establish racial identity and a sense of community in computer-mediated communication.

   Black men were not the only group excluded in Black women's computer-mediated deliberations about the politics of their hair. Several White women were also excluded, despite their attempts to empathize and align with Black women on hair matters. In the following chapter, I examine several instances wherein European American and African American women disagree on when exactly "hair is just hair" and when "hair is not just hair." Drawing on data from the AFROAM-L hair debate, a Black hair-weaving demonstration, and a cosmetology school field trip, I ask: Why do Black and White women's attempts to reach a consensus fail? What is it about their conversational stances that engender harmony or discord? As exemplified in the AFROAM-L hair debate, answers to these questions can be found in women's narratives, particularly their memories of race and hair care as constitutive of their past and present becomings.

6

Constructing and Contesting Knowledge in Women's Cross-cultural Hair Testimonies

I n 1998, a controversy erupted when a first-year Brooklyn school-teacher, Ruth Sherman, used African American author Carolivia Herron's (1997) acclaimed children's book *Nappy Hair* to teach her ethnically diverse class of third-graders about self-acceptance and tolerance for racial differences. In this colorful tale, an African American man named Uncle Mordecai narrates a story about Brenda, a dark-skinned Black girl with the "kinkiest, nappiest, fuzziest, . . . screwed up, squeezed up, knotted up, tangled up, twisted up" hair. His story is subversively celebratory. Uncle Mordecai describes Brenda's tenaciously curly hair through a litany of metaphors that resembles playing the dozens—only his words are not ritual insults, but a tribute laced with adoration. He tells readers, for example, that combing Brenda's hair is like "scrunching through the New Mexico desert in brogans in the heat of summer," but lovingly adds that one lock of her hair symbolizes "the only perfect circle in nature." In reading the book to her class, Ms. Sherman, who is White, breathed life into Uncle Mordecai by way of a spirited southern delivery, much to the delight of her African American and Latino students. When several expressed a desire for copies of the book, Ms. Sherman happily obliged.

Trouble erupted, however, when the mother of one of the children discovered photocopied pages of the book in her child's folder. The woman duplicated the pages and included them in a packet that lambasted the "White teacher" who had been teaching demeaning racist stereotypes to Black and Hispanic kids. She and other parents distributed this packet throughout the neighborhood, garnering support from families who did not have children in Ms. Sherman's class.

The conflict soon came to a head, first in Ms. Sherman's classroom and later in the school auditorium. According to the *Washington Post*, one disgruntled parent who visited Ms. Sherman's class after school expressed surprise that there was no white hood on her desk, in a not-so-veiled reference to the Ku Klux Klan. Days later, in a hasty meeting with parents in the school auditorium, Ms. Sherman was called a "cracker" (a derogatory term for Whites) and physically threatened. She eventually had to be escorted from the room. Days later, despite appeals from school administrators, Ms. Sherman resigned.

When news of this controversy emerged, I mined all the reports I could find for details of Ms. Sherman's encounter with parents. I was looking for insights into language and interaction. In short, I wanted to know how things went down that day. I found clues in Lynette Clemetson's (1998: 38) highly descriptive article in *Newsweek*:

> Nothing prepared her [Ms. Sherman] for the storm that erupted around the book. She started using "Nappy Hair" in September. It was one in a series of multicultural books intended to get kids interested in reading. The principal had encouraged teachers to be creative—so Sherman didn't think twice about bringing in books from her own collection. But on the Monday before Thanksgiving the rookie teacher—in the middle of a math lesson—got an urgent call from the principal, ordering her to come to the auditorium. Some parents, she was told, were upset about "Nappy Hair." Sherman told her kids she'd be back in 10 minutes. That was the last time they saw her. Hearing the commotion from the hall as she approached the auditorium, Sherman ducked into the principal's office and called her fiancé. "I think something bad is happening," she whispered. "Please come get me." The minute she walked into the auditorium, all hell broke loose. "It was an ambush," says [Principal Felicita] Santiago. "They turned into a lynch mob."
>
> People yelled out racial epithets like "cracker" and shouted threats. "You'd better watch out," one warned. Anxious, Sherman smiled, a nervous habit. Her grin fueled the crowd's anger. When she rolled her eyes at the gathering, a woman in the front row lunged toward the stage. The principal and the school security guard intervened, and Sherman was rushed out of the hall. By the time it was all over, television crews were outside (parents had alerted the local media before the meeting started) and Sherman was in hysterics, waiting for someone to escort her out of the neighborhood.

Clemetson also suggested that the dark photocopied pages from *Nappy Hair* compelled one parent to organize the protest: "The photocopies just made matters worse. Reduced to flat black-and-white images, the book's illustrations of a girl with a wiry shock of hair became caricatures easy to misconstrue" (1998: 39). I would argue, in addition, that the book's prose relies on a nuanced appreciation of African American signifying practices. As Uncle Mordecai speaks of Brenda's "nappy" hair from his rocking chair, he brings to mind a long tradition of "telling lies" or colorful storytelling in African American culture. As famed ethnographer Zora Neale Hurston (1990 [1935]) explains, when African Americans "tell lies," they often exaggerate commonly held truths and stereotypes about Blacks, Whites, or other groups, to the amusement of Black audiences who are well aware of the storyteller's playful, even counter-hegemonic, intentions. Likewise, in *Nappy Hair*, Uncle Mordecai embraces the derogatory connotations of the term *nappy* in order to supplant them with equally enthusiastic quips about the glory of Brenda's hair. His words exemplify signifying at its best; the author assumes readers of varied backgrounds will understand and appreciate the cultural nuances embedded in Uncle Mordecai's narrative style and content. For me, these details make all the difference in whether we understand the controversy as an exemplar of the follies of "political correctness" or a complicated instance of cultural miscommunication. Both descriptors, I think, are applicable.

Ms. Sherman was most certainly caught in the crosshairs of a situation that was blown out of proportion. And, as Clemetson sadly notes, the real losers in this controversy are her former students. I have little doubt that parents' misunderstandings were heavily rooted in the fact that Ms. Sherman is White, despite some parents' claims that they would resent a teacher of any race bringing up such a sensitive issue in class. Yet I am equally convinced that the root of this controversy is grounded, too, in Ms. Sherman's naiveté concerning the historical politics surrounding the use of the term *nappy*.

Defined neutrally, *nappy* is a decidedly in-group descriptor of tightly curled hair. Its most prevalent connotation in African American culture is disparaging of kinky, curly, and essentially "bad" hair. As an insult, its sting is sufficient to warrant its designation as "the other N-word" (Jones 2003). It is precisely this sting that the book's African American author sought to abolish when she envisioned a self-confident child whose "willful intentional naps" epitomize a deliberate "act of God."

More recently, *nappy* has enjoyed symbolic currency as a counter-hegemonic signifier that embraces and celebrates all that it once disparaged (Jones 2003). Still, its use and interpretation are fundamentally volatile. Context remains essential to understanding when *nappy* is being levied lovingly, negatively, or subversively. Further, given its history, there remain constraints on who can use the word and in what contexts.

Yet Ms. Sherman was not fully aware of the potentially explosive nature of the term. Nor was she privy to the fact that only those who have so-called "nappy hair" have the cultural right to use and discuss the term—and even they are subject to contestation. Had she known, she most certainly would have understood how her smile (which she and others describe as a "nervous response/tic"; Clemetson 1998: 39; Leyden 1998: A3), and subsequent eye roll would more than likely be read as flippant and blatantly disrespectful to parents who felt that their children (and conceivably they themselves) were being insulted. Ms. Sherman's ignorance of these matters, together with her nonverbal communication in the auditorium, much like the parents' hasty judgments and racial accusations, fueled an unfortunate drama and fundamental misunderstanding around which sort of *nappy* was at play here.

I find the controversy compelling because it exemplifies dynamics I observed in my own research. Ms. Sherman's attempts to align with minority students succeeded in the classroom, but ultimately failed when parents (many of whom did not have children in Ms. Sherman's class) misread both the intentions behind her use of the term *nappy* and the darkened photocopies of the book's central character. Similarly, I observed several instances wherein White women have run into trouble discussing hair with Black women, despite clear attempts to align with them on the basis of gender and feminism. I revisit these conversations here, mining them for insights at the level of talk in order to illuminate what went wrong (or right) to engender women's agreement or disagreement about hair across racial lines.

Counterdiscourses of race and gender

African American and European American women face a fundamental difficulty in coming to agreement about the symbolic meaning of hair: European American women often take the position of dominant cultural perspectives on Black hair, while African American women tend to represent a counter-hegemonic point of view. These opposing perspectives emerge in discourse through such devices as intertextual narratives, descriptions, and epistemic stances.

Chatterjee (1993), for example, notes that narratives may constitute forms of resistance to "master" or hegemonic storylines. Such counterdiscourses derive political force as oppositional responses to grand historical narratives. Counterdiscourses also debunk "official" narratives of everyday life, or what Peters and Lankshear (1996: 2) describe as "legitimating stories . . . which herald a national set of common cultural ideals." For example, Baquedano-López's (1998, 2001) ethnographic study of a predominantly Latino Catholic parish in Los Angeles demonstrates how instructors teach cultural narratives in Spanish despite administrative pressures to adopt a mainstream Eurocentric curriculum and standard language in classroom instruction. These counterdiscourses celebrate Latino students' culture and language in the face of encroaching English-only legislation at both the local and statewide level. Morgan (1993, 1995) similarly uses the concept of "camouflaged" narratives to describe the means by which older southern African Americans opposed implicit rules governing language that dictated that they veil public and private descriptions of racial oppression. Through the use of indirectness and other forms of linguistic camouflage, these narratives served to deconstruct and interrogate life under hegemony. And like counterdiscourses, these camouflaged narratives acted as veiled contestations of past and present experiences. Like race and ethnicity, gender may give rise to counterhegemonic discourse. Gal (1995) suggests that aspects of women's everyday talk can be understood as strategic responses, often resistance, to dominant cultural forms. In this sense, women's talk can reflect the political essence of counterdiscourse.

My analysis in this chapter is concerned with African American women's use of counterdiscourse to debunk privileged ideologies around hair and beauty practices that are directly and indirectly invoked by European American women.

I focus on three interactions that feature African American and European American women in the process of producing and sharing subjective knowledge. The first takes place at a hair show in Los Angeles, the second at a beauty salon in South Carolina, and the third in the online hair debate on AFROAM-L analyzed in depth in the previous chapter. In their dialogues, African American women collaborate in a series of counterdiscourses that critique mainstream representations of Black hair and simultaneously marginalize the status of their European American conversationalists. African American women's counterdiscourse can be thematically represented by two dichotomous epistemic stances: *Hair is (just) hair* and *Hair is not just hair.* While these claims may appear contradictory, they both serve to oppose mainstream liberal feminist stances that often naively celebrate "choice" in hairstyle without understanding how privilege and exclusion are intricately intertwined in dominant ideologies about women's hair care and hairstyle choices. In the excerpts below, the stance *[Black] hair is (just) hair* seeks to relativize Black hair in relation to straight hair textures (which are often privileged as "mainstream"). The stance *[Black] hair is (not) just hair* is used by Black women to insist that Black hair must be understood in light of myriad political, cultural, spiritual, scientific, comedic, and other factors such as those considered in previous chapters. In each case discussed below, African American women offer these stances as critical responses to White women for comments perceived to be culturally insensitive.

Episode 1: Hair is just hair

In the first interaction I consider, African American women who are involved with Black hair care in various ways adopt the stance "Hair is (just) hair" to problematize a White cosmetology student's professed ignorance of Black hair. This exchange, depicted sequentially in examples 1 through 3, was recorded during an early-morning hair-weaving demonstration at a Los Angeles hair show and involved four African American women and one European American woman. Each of the four African American women—Linda, May, Kesha, and Kamela—and the European American woman, Carla, are affiliated with the beauty industry. May is a licensed stylist who specializes in braiding and weaving. In the interaction, she is using a loom to demonstrate how to create a weft for hair weaving. Kesha, who is standing next to Carla, markets Black hair-care seminars and publications. Linda and Kamela, on the other side of the loom, are both young licensed stylists. Carla is a cosmetology student at a local community college (see figure 6.1).

The interaction begins when May acquaints herself with each of the women who visited her booth and attempts to recruit them as members of a statewide network of licensed braiders. She first asks Kamela how long she has been braiding. May then directs her attention to Carla and asks her about her specialization as a stylist. Carla responds by expressing a desire to learn how to "work with Black hair," which May reframes as a desire to become a Black hair specialist. Carla also laments the fact that many White stylists lack the desire

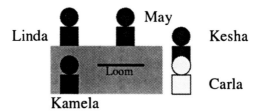

Figure 6.1. Spatial arrangement of participants in example 1

to learn how to "mess with Black folks' hair." When May asks her to speculate on why this is so and offers a hypothesis (i.e., doing Black hair may be a challenge for White students), Carla responds, "I don't know if it's much of a challenge. I have a lot of Black friends OKAY." Carla's latter response appears to offend the African American women, who exchange puzzled looks and orient physically away from Carla. I later learned that they perceived her comment as reflecting the naiveté of one who claims to understand the complex plight of Black people by arguing, "Some of my best friends are Black." Although Carla does not engage in such grand presumptions here, her response is deemed defensive and without merit and thus as worthy of the same scorn that this comment typically elicits.

Carla's controversial proclamation, however, does not deter May's line of inquiry or her conversational fervor. While the other African American women temporarily orient their attention to passersby, magazines, or one another, Carla and May criticize White students who shy away from both instruction in Black hair-care techniques and practice of such techniques on Black patrons. Perhaps conscious of the other women's momentary disregard for their conversation, May again voices Carla's preceding responses to the entire group to encourage ongoing dialogue, stating, "So what she's [Carla] saying yeah that she'd like to learn more and so I guess it's a challenge you know [she] wants to learn more about it." In this way, May favorably characterizes Carla's desire to learn more about Black hair care. She also asserts her implicit claim that learning to do Black hair may in fact be considered a challenge by Carla and other White cosmetology students.

When we examine the African American women's ensuing discourse, particularly how they privilege their own cultural understandings of Black hair over hegemonic views, we see evidence of counterdiscourse at work. African American women share a series of turns that both celebrate the versatility of Black hair and critique White stylists who avoid Black hair care. Taken together, these critiques serve to indict mainstream ideologies and practices within the wider cosmetology profession, which privilege European hair textures and styles. These ideologies and practices allow Carla and other non-Black stylists to become licensed without developing skills in styling African American hair textures and require Black stylists to learn how to style European American hair textures in order to be licensed.

As explained above, Carla has already collaborated with May in the critique against White stylists who are allegedly afraid to work on Black hair. However, Carla's positionality as a collaborator in this stance is marginalized, and at times even ignored, because the African American women's counter-discourse is co-constructed around experiences and physical attributes (i.e., Black hair) to which Carla has little or no access. This, along with their use of cultural speaking styles, serves to limit the extent to which Carla can speak on these topics, thus relegating her to the margins of the discussion. We see this happening in example 1 when, after several uncomfortable moments, Kamela decides to speak.

(1) It's a Myth That . . . [Black Hair Is a Difficult to Work With]

1	Kamela:	It's a it's a myth that um
2	May:	Go ahead
3	Kamela:	that there be hhh that people just get caught in
4		sometimes you know
5		We know as as now that I hear you say the word
6		I can say that I'm a Black hair specialist
7		because I don't do naturally straight hair
8		but what I find
9		is that by going to other hair color companies
10		because I learn how to do all that
11		so I can color that hair right for weaving
12		and I end up being the only Black stylist there
13		so I *do* understand that
14		but what I try to do is um is just let them know
15		that I have the *same* uh inhibitions sometimes
16		so we can get together
17		we can trade information
18		they can call me
19		I can talk to them
20		you know and go back and forth
21		and that'll help eliminate some of that fear
22		because the fear just come from not knowing
23		without the truth
24		I know the truth
25		- we know that our hair is very easy to work with
26		and uh [very nice to work with
27	May:	[It's so it's so versatile
28	Kamela:	yes
29	May:	Black hair is so versatile
30	Kamela:	yes
31	May:	that's what it is
32		We can do so much with it
33	Kamela:	yeah

34	May:	We can make it look like cotton in one week
35	Kamela:	that's right
36	May:	and the next week, turn around, *it's silky!*
37	Kamela:	bone straight
38		that's right
39	Kesha:	mm hmm (.) mm hmm
40	May:	ha ha so our hair is interesting

Kamela's discourse is multilayered. She initially debunks what she calls a "myth" (line 1), itself a politically laden framing of the belief that Black hair is a difficult medium. May both anticipates and ratifies Kamela's description, offering the continuer (Goffman 1974) "Go ahead" in line 2. Then, using a first-person account, Kamela affirms herself as a "Black hair specialist" (line 6), a term first introduced by May in response to Carla's professed interest in Black hair care. Here, Kamela and May are in explicit intertextual dialogue. Kamela then sets up an affiliative frame with non-Black stylists she has encountered who are allegedly ambivalent toward Black hair. She invokes her own experience as the only Black stylist in hair-coloring seminars and expresses her understanding of the "inhibitions" (line 15) of non-Black stylists. Although Kamela understands these inhibitions, she does not excuse them. Rather, in lines 9–22, she proposes a strategy of information sharing to debunk the "myth" (line 1), alleviate the "fear" (line 22), and eventually uncover the "truth" (line 22) about Black hair. This is a vivid prelude to an alternative ideology about Black hair, one that is explicitly constructed against widespread "myths" that stigmatize Black hair. How this construction takes place is of particular interest, for Kamela invokes shifting participant frameworks (Goodwin 1990) throughout the course of her talk.

Disclosing the "truth" about Black hair is actually a collaborative undertaking by May and Kamela. Beginning in line 25, Kamela constructs a framework for participation that, by the referential nature of her commentary, restricts participation in the sequence to the African American women present. This restriction of participant frameworks is indexically realized through her use of the pronouns *we* and *our* to describe both those present who have Black hair (i.e., African American women) and those who have skills in Black hair care. Significantly, May not only corroborates Kamela's positive description of Black hair by participating in the cultural discourse style of call and response (Collins 1990; Morgan 1998; Smitherman 1977), she also assumes the role of primary speaker in line 27. In their reversal of roles, Kamela now collaborates in May's description of Black hair through call-and-response back-channeling cues (*that's right*, line 35; *bone straight, that's right*, lines 37–38). Kesha also participates in the co-construction of Black hair as versatile and interesting. At line 39, she endorses the discourse collaboration in progress with the agreement marker *mm hmm (.) mm hmm*. Despite Carla's previous alignment with African American women's stance toward Black hair care, she has fewer rights to speak in this sequence given that she is not a part of the "we" group who knows that "our hair" (i.e., Black hair) is an easy medium with which to work.

In setting up a contrastive frame between "truth" and "myth," Kamela disrupts official ideologies that marginalize Black hair, problematizes White stylists who are fearful of Black hair care, and ignites a discursive celebration of the versatility of Black hair. Kamela and May's call-and-response sequence affirming the versatility of Black hair may, in fact, be an extended attempt to articulate the fact that while Black hair is different, it is in no way inferior. In these ways, Kamela's talk conveys the illocutionary and pragmatic force of her discourse. While Carla is thus far a marginal participant, she later resurfaces in the dialogue's progression. In the next sequence of talk, presented in example 2, Carla re-enters the conversation and attempts to insert the ideology that race is not a factor in White stylists' inhibitions so much as their lack of familiarity with curly hair textures.

(2) Some White People Are Afraid of Working with Curly Hair Textures

41	Carla:	There are some White people with overly kinky you know
42		curly hair =
43	Kesha:	Oh yeah
44	Carla:	= and the White students don't want to work on them either
45		because they're scared
46		I don't know what they're scared of
47	Kesha:	But see our culture is changing *so much*
48		you have all these interracial couples and all, things like that
49		<u>You</u> <u>Don't</u> <u>Know</u> *what* is coming up you know
50		and so you have to be able to be versatile as a hair stylist
51		to work with all kind of hair textures you know
52		[*((looks pointedly at Carla))*
53		[**>Black White< (.) that's not even an issue**
54		[*((points toward Carla))*
55		[**It's *hair***

Carla's second verbal contribution to the discussion occurs at line 41. Here, she explicitly introduces Whiteness into the discourse by broadening her description of the inhibitions of (White) cosmetology students. She suggests that White students are hesitant to service not only Black patrons, but also White clients who have "overly kinky" or "curly" hair textures. While Carla is representative of the generic group of White cosmetology students she critiques, she distances herself from those who are "scared" to style naturally curly hair by stating, **"I don't know what they're scared of"** (line 46, my emphasis). Through this stance, Carla ideologically aligns with Kesha, May, and Kamela, who have critiqued both cosmetology students who are reportedly fearful of doing Black hair and the myths that ground such students' perspectives.

Implicit in Carla's comments, however, are several potentially offensive characterizations that I believe compel Kesha to use counterdiscourse to reprove her. Carla initially describes curly hair as "overly kinky" (line 41), which carries with it the controversial insinuation that it is possible for hair to be too kinky. Within African American communities, the term *kinky* is also an in-group characterization of a very curly texture of Black hair (see Smitherman 1994). Since this term often carries a negative connotation, its use by Carla could be deemed offensive. Carla's commentary thus far presumes that only some Whites, but all Blacks, have "overly kinky" hair. Kesha takes issue with this implicit assumption in lines 47–55. Because there are biracial couples who presumably have children with an even broader range of hair textures, Kesha suggests that all hairstylists must be versatile enough to service whoever enters their salon. It is striking to observe the way Kesha ends her commentary (figure 6.2). She looks pointedly at Carla and states, "Black White that's not even an issue." Then, while pointing toward Carla, she adds, "It's *hair!*" This epistemic stance toward Black hair as "(just) hair" problematizes symbolic distinctions between hair textures, particularly those that are value-laden (e.g., *overly kinky*) and race-specific. As a modestly veiled reproof of Carla's position, Kesha's rebuttal acts pragmatically as counterdiscourse. Her counterdiscourse also continues the work of co-constructing with Kamela and May an ideology that is celebratory of Black hair and critical of Eurocentric practices in the wider hair-care field.

Another discourse shift occurs when the fourth African American woman present, Linda, who has thus far been largely silent, begins a personal narrative about dolls. Her narrative is nostalgic, recalling a time during her childhood when a Barbie doll (i.e., the quintessential representation of White femininity) was the only doll she owned (see Chin 2001; Handler 2000; Rogers 1999 for additional analyses of Barbie's social impact). Her narrative, presented

Figure 6.2. Kesha and Carla confer at a hair-weaving demonstration.

in example 3, celebrates the advent of the Black Crissy doll in 1969 as an empowering alternative to Barbie (fig. 6.3).

(3) I Always Had to Work with Barbie

56	Linda:	*((speaks softly))* It's not that they don't know how to do that
57		It's just that [they're not familiar
58	Kesha:	[They don't know how
59	May:	OKa:y
60	Linda:	I would say that
61		ever since I um grew up
62		I've always had to work with Barbie
63		*((looks toward Carla and Kesha))*
64		So I kind of like had a wider range [because working with *her*
65	Kesha:	[Go ahead
66	Linda:	that was basically the texture of a Caucasian person's *hair*
67	May:	Yes [Yes Yes
68	Linda:	[However
69		I *learned* how to work with that hair
70		and style it with water and grease
71		and make it pretty hhh
72		which I wanted my doll TO BE
73		because that's all I had
74		However, once my mom got me a Crissy doll
75		I was able to get [BAsically
76	Kesha:	[All right Crissy!
77		[*((claps hands, looks at Linda))*
78		[Remember the Crissy?! heh heh
79	Carla:	[heh heh heh [heh heh
80	Kesha:	[GIRL WE'RE [GOING BACK! heh heh heh
81	Kamela:	[Right down to Crissy Okay hh heh
82	Linda:	[*((smiling hesitantly, clasps hands, awaits lull in laughter))*
83		[the same the same thing
84		but then a little more on the [line of our hair
85		[*((looks toward Carla and Kesha))*
86		but [*Not*
87		[*((horizontal nod, gestures "no" with hands))*
88		it at all
89		but then I had to learn . . . on my own
90		so I did get a range to deal in kind of like different styles
91	→	[*((looks at Carla))*
92		[but I don't think that for one reason that our hair is any different
93	Kesha:	[Right
94	Linda:	[other than the fact that it is of [just a different texture
95		[*((vertical nod))*
96		and that is all

Linda initially frames her narrative to refute Kesha's prior claim that White
stylists simply do not know how to do Black hair. She suggests that many White
stylists' alleged ignorance is instead a result of their limited exposure to Black
hair, both as children and, as we will later see, as professionals. To contextualize
this argument, Linda discloses her early impressionable experiences with Crissy,
one of the first Black dolls on which she practiced hair grooming as a child.
While her turn is launched as a personal narrative (i.e., *I would say that ever
since I um grew up*, lines 60–61), it eventually becomes a collaborative narrative event, indeed an occasion for co-remembering between Linda and her
African American peers. May, Kamela, and Kesha employ call and response,
in-group referents such as *girl* (e.g., *GIRL WE'RE GOING BACK!* line 80),
various continuers (e.g., *Go ahead,* line 65), as well as lengthier and more
emphatic turns, to co-construct Linda's narrative-in-progress. The women re-
ciprocally use eye gaze to organize their orientation to and participation in the
narrative. The narrative thus emerges as a collective and nostalgic account of
their initial hair-grooming practices. It is also a means through which Black
women discursively co-affiliate with one another by virtue of shared cultural
experiences and discourse practices.

As a thinly veiled description of African American women's marginalization, Linda's Crissy narrative is imbued with the subversive force of camouflaged narratives (Morgan 1993). These African Americans' testimony
critiques and explains their past as children for whom there were very few
Black dolls on which to practice hair care. This is the pragmatic force of
several narrative tropes of marginalization and triumph that appear throughout Linda's narrative:

Figure 6.3. Black and White Crissy dolls (© Ideal Corporation)

- *I would say that ever since I um grew up I've always had to work with Barbie* (lines 60–62) denotes Linda's marginalization as a child for whom there were few Black dolls.
- *However I learned how to work with that hair and style it with water and grease and make it pretty hhh which I wanted my doll TO BE* (lines 68–72) inscribes a tale of overcoming despite limitations posed by the lack of Black dolls.
- *Because that's all I had* (line 71) reinforces Linda's marginalized status while rationalizing her need to "make do" with Barbie.
- *So I did get a range to deal in kind of like different styles* (line 90) recounts a triumphant tale of surmounting constraints (i.e., a lack of dolls with Black hair textures) that could have rendered her solely proficient in styling European American hair textures.

The Crissy narrative also functions as a counternarrative by exposing the privilege of other White stylists like Carla who have the option to choose whether or not they wish to develop proficiency in Black hair care. For the African American women, the decision to become proficient in styling European American hair textures was not an option so much as a prerequisite. Thus, while Kamela says that she does not "do naturally straight hair" (example 1, line 7), she is nevertheless trained to do it. Similarly, as shown in example 4 below, while Linda's formal education in cosmetology also did not offer much instruction in Black hair care, she nevertheless sought out opportunities to learn. Moreover, this counterdiscourse appears to be explicitly directed at Carla in particular, such as when in lines 92, and 94–96, Linda tells Carla, "But I don't think that for one reason that our hair is any different other than the fact that it is of just a different texture and that is all." While Carla lacks direct culpability for the stance for which she is reproved, she nevertheless appears to be the central target of this counterdiscourse.

In the final sequence (example 4), Kamela suggests additional factors that may color the current state of affairs within the beauty profession. Her personal narrative exposes her position of relative privilege among her African American peers. Linda responds to Kamela with a counterdiscourse that is a literal and symbolic extension of the Crissy narrative. As in examples 1 and 3, Carla's verbal contribution remains notably absent during this exchange.

(4) See You Were Blessed

97	Kamela:	I went to a community college cosmetology school
98		and so my instructors were versed in all of it
99		and so I was the one who got to pick
100		. . . what I wanted to excel in while I was there
101		. . . and and a lot of the White students
102		that got a chance to choose
103		if they wanted to excel in Black hair
104		. . . so we got a chance
105		to choose what we want(ed)

106	Linda:	See you were blessed
107		because most instructors
108		and usually when you go-
109		I know for a long time
110		it was hard to find a doll with even kinky hair
111		so if it wasn't out there for you to work
112		and learn
113		and be educated on
114		then how were you supposed to learn in these schools?
115		So now if they would put
116	May:	Yes!
117	Linda:	different textures
118		ALL different textures
119		and make every student learn from all different textures
120	Kamela:	that's (right)
121	Linda:	then they those students as well can learn on all different
122		textures
123		they won't be intimidated by it
124		because if you just only get one side - type of model
125		then that's all they're gonna work - want to work on

Narratives not only serve to engender unity among participants, but, as Baquedano-López (1998) notes, they also organize diversity within a collective. This point is underscored in example 4, where Kamela's personal narrative serves to differentiate her experiences from those of her African American peers. Following Linda's account of her belated exposure to Black dolls as a child, Kamela describes her own experiences as a cosmetology student. Her narrative implicates the curriculum and instructors in cosmetology schools in whether students develop an apprehensive or welcoming disposition toward Black hair care. Kamela's narrative also exposes her relative privilege as an African American student who was able to decide which hair textures she was exposed to in cosmetology school.

Kamela's narrative captures the attention of Linda, who characterizes Kamela's experience in spiritual terms as a blessing (line 106). Kamela's story is a catalyst for a second tale which, strikingly enough, resembles the Crissy narrative. As with Black girls who struggled to find dolls with features similar to their own, Linda asserts that many African American students face the challenge of "find[ing] a doll with even kinky hair" (line 110)—here, doll refers to a plastic mannequin, an essential professional tool in cosmetology school. To address this problem, Linda suggests that both curly haired and straight-haired mannequins be introduced in cosmetology schools to promote more equitable exposure to Black hair textures within the wider beauty profession. Linda's suggestion finds resonance at "natural" hair-care seminars I attended in College Park, Georgia, as well as the cosmetology school in Charleston, South Carolina, where I conducted fieldwork. In both sites, I observed students and seminar participants struggle to make the hair on black mannequins conform to more "kinky" hair textures. Fortunately, "natural" hair-care specialists such as Taliah Waajid have attempted to redress this imbalance by selling manne- quins with both straight and kinky hair (fig. 6.4). Following Linda's sugges- tion, May's ensuing turn, which is not represented in the above transcript, enlists the women's support in a national campaign to make cosmetology board re- quirements for African American braiders more relevant to their craft. Her commentary extends the political subtext of Linda's suggestion: she indicts the larger beauty industry that marginalizes Afrocentric hair-care practices and hairstyles.

Linda's and May's respective contributions are both charged with the oppositional undercurrent of the counterdiscourse previously discussed in ex- amples 1 through 3. It is telling to examine how the other women, particularly Carla and Kamela, participate in this exchange. Carla remains a silent periph- eral participant. However, whereas in prior sequences her gaze was directed at the women speaking, throughout most of this exchange it is directed toward the floor. Kamela, whose relative privilege might seem to align her more closely with Carla (and the other White stylists previously discussed), nevertheless maintains an affinity with May and Linda by conveying a supportive stance for the strategies they propose. Kamela's affiliative stance is conveyed through such means as back-channeling cues (e.g., *that's [right],* line 120) and an at- tentive gaze. Kesha, though silent, also signals her participation in ongoing dis- course through an attentive gaze. The differences between the African American

Figure 6.4. Straight-haired and kinky-haired Black mannequins distributed by Taliah Waajid

women thus appear to be minimized as they coalesce around strategies to de-bunk myths and allay stylists' fear toward Black hair care within the wider hair-care profession.

Episode 2: Racial asymmetries in hair-care knowledge

In the second interaction I examine in this chapter, African American students at a cosmetology school in South Carolina embrace concerns similar to those previously discussed regarding race and hair. In particular, they challenge a White stylist's professed ambivalence about her ignorance of Black hair and condemn larger Eurocentric ideologies and practices around hair in the field of cosmetology. Students also affirm their own identities as extremely versatile and much sought-after stylists. In example 5, two of the students, Katcha and Theresa, and their instructor, Mrs. Collins, are interviewing two White stylists during a fieldtrip to a local salon, as several of their classmates listen nearby.

(5) Y'all Don't Know How to Do That?

1	Katcha:	Do you train your staff?
2	Stylist 1:	They just have to be (trained)/(learned) in school
3		I mean heh heh I'm not trying to be smart
4		but I mean uh you *are* qualified heh heh
5		**We really do need an African American stylist in here**
6		***badly***
7	Stylist 2:	We do!
8	Katcha:	Why?
9	Stylist 1:	Because we don't have one . . . I'm serious!
10		Heh heh
11	Mrs. Collins:	Do you have a lot of um African Americans coming in?
12	Stylist 1:	We have a lot of people
13		that walk in here wanting relaxers
14		and want lots of things
15	Katcha:	**Y'all don't know how to do that?**
16	Stylist 1:	I know how but I don't know feel comfortable like I know
17		enough
18	Katcha:	***You didn't learn that in school?***
19	Stylist 1:	They didn't do a whole lot of that stuff when I went to
20		school
21	Students:	mmmmm
22	Stylist 1:	They didn't
23		Now they've started with more African American styling
24		and relaxers and more classes
25		because our class fussed so much
26		because we're like, "How can you expect us to do it?"
27	Mrs. Collins:	So what school did you go to?

28	Stylist 1:	I went to X Beauty College
29	Mrs. Collins:	X Beauty College
30	Stylist 1:	Now they are pretty good about having the classes
31		because my friend . . . worked there
32		. . . She said she learned all of it
33		She does African ethnic hair . . .

We have already seen how African American women adopt the epistemic stance that "hair is (just) hair" to co-construct counterdiscourse that opposes Eurocentric epistemologies and practices in cosmetology schools. It is also important to consider the contexts under which such stances can shift. In this and the prior episode, White women's attempts to align with Black women act as catalysts for Black women's oppositional responses. For example, Carla's attempts to reach common ground and align with the other women are thwarted by her comment "I have a lot of Black friends OKAY" and her potentially offensive reference to Black hair as "overly kinky." Because these comments are perceived as racial slights by several of the African American women present, Carla is unable to establish her alignment with them in later conversation. In fact, despite her professed desire to learn to do Black hair, she becomes the indirect and, at times, more explicit target of a series of counterdiscursive turns that critique White stylists who are ignorant of how to style Black hair.

A similar instance takes place in episode 2. When Katcha asks one of the European American stylists whether or not they train their staff, the stylist responds by expressing her expectation that students be appropriately trained in cosmetology school prior to seeking employment. While conceding that her answer may sound "smart" (i.e., flippant), she also assures the students that they are being appropriately prepared. This stylist's subsequent disclosure of the salon's need for Black stylists, however, is troublesome and prompts Katcha to inquire about her interlocutor's own prior training (line 8). Moreover, when the stylist reports having clients who request relaxers, a chemical hair-straightening procedure used by many Black women, Katcha asks, "Y'all don't know how to do that?" (line 15). The stylist confesses her lack of confidence in her own abilities, but Katcha is apparently unsatisfied with her answer, adding, more poignantly, *"You didn't learn that in school?"* (line 18). Katcha's question may be an indirect strategy for exposing the stylist's racial privilege in that she has not been required to learn to style Black hair, while Black stylists must be able to work with White hair textures. Moreover, the stylist assumes that the African American cosmetology students are being appropriately prepared to handle Black clients, although she is ill prepared to service her own Black patrons.

The stylist's attribution of her ignorance to improper training does very little to deter Katcha's and other students' criticism. After the interview, several of the students indicated that it was unfair for them to be expected to master different types of hair while their White counterparts at other schools gained experience in only one hair type. Their complaints are similar to Carla and Kesha's critique of White stylists who, because of their ignorance, must turn away African American clientele. Further similarities between the epistemic stances conveyed by the African American women in episodes 1 and 2 become all the more vivid when another student, Theresa, probes into the practical implications of the stylist's reported ignorance of Black hair care.

(6) Most Black Hairstylists Have a Lot of Clientele Because . . . It's More Complicated

34	Theresa:	Question! Being that . . . how many average a week
35		<how many people with ethnic - Black people
36		did you turn away a week because you don't have a Black
37		stylist?
38	Stylist 1:	A lot a lot
39	Stylist 2:	A lot
40	Stylist 1:	Way too many
41	Theresa:	Give me a number - something. Twenty? Thirty?
42	Receptionist:	Around yeah . . . I would say fifteen to twenty, up in there
43	Stylist 2:	Our problem is that we had one very good Black stylist
44		who worked with us
45		She's booth renting now
46		She built up her clientele that big ((*makes a wide gesture*))
47		We just haven't been able to find one that will stay put
48		you know
49	Stylist 1:	They get them [clientele] and then they leave
50	Theresa:	**Most most Black hairstylists have a lot of clientele**
51		**because there's just so much versatility with the hair**
52	Stylist 1:	Yeah exactly. And there is I mean, there is . . .
53	Theresa:	**And we would probably make more money than you all**
54		**because we do . . .**
55	Stylist 1:	Yeah heh heh it is the truth
56	Stylist 2:	It's true it's very true!
57	Theresa:	- It is! We do the tracks
58	Katcha:	**- It's it's more complicated**
59	Theresa:	We do this and (we're)/(they're) going to whip that out
60	Stylist 1:	So you can charge more for it
61		and I'm telling you being an um African American stylist
62		it won't take you anything to build up to a master stylist
63	Stylist 2:	Because the clientele is here

Upon learning that many Black clients are turned away, Theresa describes the relative advantage of Black stylists since they serve patrons with extremely versatile hair (line 51). It is interesting to see Katcha co-construct this view by describing Black hair as "more complicated" (line 58). Katcha and Theresa's co-assessment bears a close resemblance to Kamela and May's call-and-response sequence in example 1 about the versatility of Black hair. In my discussion with the students after the interview, I learned that their commentary was, in part, an attempt to educate White stylists that Black hair was a versatile medium and hence not to be feared. Although the stylists agree with Theresa's and Katcha's assessments and make other attempts to align with the students (as they simultaneously attempt to recruit them), it is ultimately their own ignorance of Black hairstyling procedures that constrains their ability to develop a rapport with the students.

Episode 3: Hair is not just hair

In the final interaction to be analyzed in this chapter, African American women invoke the epistemic stance that "hair is not just hair" to censure a White woman's claim that hair is independent of cultural symbolism or sociopolitical implications. In doing so, the African American women collaborate in the production of a counterdiscourse that invokes their shared marginalization as Black women who are, for the most part, rendered either invisible or exotic in hegemonic representations of beauty.

The interactions in examples 7 and 8 occurred during the highly charged discussion of the politics of hair and identity on AFROAM-L, which I examined in detail in the previous chapter. Prior to the interactions below, list members had debated such topics as whether Black women's hairstyles were true reflections of their racial consciousness (see chapter 5). Other discussions centered on the social, economic, and political factors at play in Black women's hairstyle decisions. The interactions I discuss here involve two sequences that commence when Loni, a self-identified non-Black woman, responds critically to subscribers who advocate "natural" (non-chemically treated or straightened) hairstyles for Black women. Loni espouses a liberal feminist ideology that celebrates all women's right to style their hair without social repercussions. Subsequently, she is confronted by Njeri and Marla, both African American women, who deem Loni's position culturally insensitive. In example 7, Njeri provides the first response to Loni's post. (Loni's original post is quoted in Njeri's message and is preceded by the > symbols.)

(7) I Have Straight Hair . . . So I Get a Perm

1   Dear Loni,
2   Thank-you for continuing this discussion from the perspective of a
3   non-Black woman. I will comment.
4   *At 06:31 PM 5/8/95 -0700, Loni wrote:*
5   *>I guess I qualify as one of the non-Black people on the list, I don't*
6   *>know if what I do to my hair merits any discussion, but here it is . . .*
7   *>I have straight hair that does nothing, I mean absolutely nothing.*
8   *>So, I get a perm, I mean, I always have a perm. I do this because*
9   *>when I look in the mirror, I like what I see. It doesn't matter what*
10   *>anyone else thinks, it matters what I think and I think the perm looks*
11   *>better. I really believe that most women do their hair for themselves,*
12   *>not for other people. I'm the one that looks in the mirror in the morning*

13 >*and I'm the one that has to live with my hair through the day, so it should*
14 >*be up to me to do what I want to it.*
15 OK, but you are not Black and therefore you don't appear to be able to
16 relate to the issues presented heretofore. I am assuming that you are a
17 European American, Loni. I submit to you, that IF it is true that White
18 people have the power in America, then it really doesn't matter what you
19 do to your hair because you are a member of the power clan. Your people
20 made the rules. They made the rules for beauty, throughout the world,
21 which a majority of non-White people were forced to live under.

Loni's feminist stance is articulated clearly (though not under that name) in lines 5 through 14 where she celebrates her own hair options and affirms other women's right to wear their hair in any way that pleases them. Njeri's response in lines 15 through 21, however, directly challenges Loni's cultural authority in the larger discussion. Loni's self-identified identity as non-Black (and perhaps her self-described "straight hair" in line 7) leads Njeri to assume that Loni is European American and hence unable to relate to the role of hair as an ethnic signifier for African American women. Thus, although Loni's self-effacing remark about having "straight hair" that "does . . . absolutely nothing" (line 7) depoliticizes women's hair-care practices in general, Njeri instead scolds Loni for failing to acknowledge her power privilege as a White woman in dictating the standards of beauty in America. In this way, Njeri's post constitutes a counterdiscourse that, while exposing the privilege implicit in Loni's epistemic stance that "hair is (just) hair," also impedes Loni's bid for ongoing dialogue around the idea that women should be able to choose their hairstyles without regard to sociopolitical implications.

Soon after Njeri's posting, Loni is confronted again, this time through a call-and-response sequence between Njeri and another African American woman named Marla. Interestingly, while Marla's comments appear to predominate in the message below, it is actually Njeri who is the editor, as it were, of this intertextual post. Njeri's comments are appended to quoted excerpts from Marla's prior post to Loni. (As before, the quoted message is preceded by the > symbols.) Her comments act as affirming response cries (Goffman 1974), which sporadically ratify Marla's remarks. In this sense, Njeri's response cries serve to co-construct Marla's critique of Loni's post.

(8) Hair for Non-Blacks Does Not Have the Same . . . Consequences as It Does Us

1 Thanks for helping me out, here Marla!
2 At 04:34 AM 5/9/95 -0700, Marla wrote:
3 >*To: Loni (a non-Black woman)*
4 >*Please understand that our discussion on "hair" may seem like an*
5 >*infringement of certain inalienable rights from your perspective as hair*
6 >*for non-Blacks does not hold the same political, social and emotional*
7 >*consequences as it does for us, from childhood thru present. Some of my*
8 >*(and perhaps others) childhood recollections include:*

   9   >* *Sitting in a hard chair for long hours as an elementary school-aged*
   10 >*child suffering the grueling process of "straightening" (hot comb on*
   11 >*stove), hair grease sizzling, ears and neck burning - worrying*
   12 >*endlessly about the enemy of water in all forms – "sweating*
   13 >*it back", rain, swimming, showering/bathing;*
   14 >* *Using a little White girl's brush to brush my beloved "bangs"*
   15 >*at an elementary school age and having the teacher send the*
   16 >*girl to the nurse's office with her brush to have it soaked in rubbing*
   17 >*alcohol and hot water;*
   18 Yes, break it down, Sister.
   19 >* *The imagery that any truly sexy woman will "let her hair down"*
   20 >*before becoming intimate; I could go on but won't cuz this is too*
   21 >*long already. Suffice it to say that our natural texture of hair was*
   22 >*and sadly still is taught to many of us at our earliest recollections*
   23 >*to be inferior and in constant need of being corrected to be socially*
   24 >*acceptable.*
   25 Amen!
   26 >*. . . We mistakenly apply the mythology of White feminism in the form of*
   27 >*its many "rights" to ourselves . . . this is not to say that the "right" to*
   28 >*wear our hear [hair] however we want to does not exist for Black*
   29 >*women and that any one's personal choices makes them inferior to those*
   30 >*who make other choices, but that our discussion cannot be limited to*
   31 >*political correctness and catch phrases and must delve deeper into our*
   32 >*longstanding practices of self-hatred and self-abuse to be an honest*
   33 >*discussion.*
   34 >*You as a non-Black woman MUST respect and try to understand that the*
   35 >*sentiments being expressed by some of us are based on our own*
   36 >*experiences in a racist and ignorant society that even today frowns*
   37 >*heavily upon our natural attributes.*
   38 >*Marla.*
   39 Well said.
   40 Asante sana.

Marla, who has emerged previously in the online debate as having a personal preference for "natural" hairstyles, begins her post with an appeal: she encourages Loni to try to understand the cultural significance of hair among Black women, who, unlike White women, face a separate set of economic, political, and social consequences for their hairstyle choices. Additionally, the form of Marla's appeal in lines 4 through 8 again exposes Loni's privilege as non-Black. Marla first states, "Please understand that our discussion on 'hair' may seem like an infringement of certain inalienable rights from your perspective" and then provides an expansive bulleted list of her own and other African American women's painful childhood and adulthood experiences of being marginalized due to the texture and length of their hair. When read in succession, Marla's (already compelling) bulleted items have the expressive force of call and response in a religious sermon, and indeed Njeri employs several religious and cultural response cries to affirm Marla's post (*Yes, break it down, Sister,* line 19; *Amen!,* line 25; *Well said,* line 39; and *Asante sana* [Swahili for "Thank you"] in line 40). Moreover, in line 1, Njeri thanks Marla for helping her redirect Loni's interpretation of the hair discussion. At a larger level, Marla and Njeri's critique of Loni for failing to understand the significance of hair for Black women parallels criticisms made of White liberal feminism by women of color (see Carby 1996; Crenshaw 1992; Giddings 1984). In fact, lines 26 through 33 of Marla's post to Loni explicitly critiques "White feminism" for wrongly assuming that all women share the same rights and positionalities in American society. Marla culminates her post with an appeal to Loni to expand her framework for understanding the politics of hair and identity for Black women.

Discussion

The cross-racial conversations about hair in this chapter offer a portrait of how women of diverse racial and ethnic backgrounds negotiate between various knowledges and their own experience to construct individual and collective stances about hair. African American women in particular employ such cultural discourse styles as call and response and indirectness in their counterdiscourse to align with one another and to critique hegemonic ideologies about Black hair. European American women's unwitting expression of such ideologies of their own racialized privilege are the catalysts for African American women's expression of two complementary epistemic stances that emerge under specific interactional conditions: "Hair is (just) hair" and "Hair is not (just) hair." A close investigation of these seemingly polar views, when they are employed, and toward what ends reveals congruence in their political efficacy. Namely, Black women co-construct these stances to refute Eurocentric ways of understanding racialized and gendered bodies that are directly or indirectly invoked by White women. Black women's claims that "Hair is (just) hair" and alternatively "Hair is not (just) hair" can also be understood in light of larger debates about race. Arguments favoring a universal perspective posit that African Americans are most fundamentally Americans and hence subject to the same rights and responsibilities as other citizens. In contrast, particularistic claims employ race-specific rhetorical strategies to explain how African Americans are different from other groups of Americans. People of color may deploy these different subject positions and ideologies for strategic purposes (see Moore 1994) and may negotiate their various meanings and sociopolitical implications not simply in grand political debates about civil rights but also in everyday interactions (see also Jones and Shorter-Gooden 2003).

Sandoval (1991: 15) argues that "weaving between and among such differing oppositional ideologies is, in fact, a common practice for U.S. Third World women whose struggles against not only sexism, but also race, class, and cultural hierarchies have necessitated a break with hegemonic feminist

ideology in favor of a 'differential mode of consciousness and activity.'"
She adds, "This differential mode of consciousness depends upon an ability
to read the current situation of power and of self-consciously choosing and
adopting the ideological form best suited to push against its configurations,
a survival skill well known to oppressed peoples." Sandoval asserts that the
potential for shifting and differential counterhegemonic discourses has historically served to mystify and confuse White feminists who have (mis)interpreted
the political movement of women of color as a sign of disloyalty, betrayal,
or divisiveness (see also Anzaldúa 1987, 1990; Christian 1985; Hurtado 1989;
Lorde 1981). In this context, African American women's shifting and seemingly polar epistemic stances regarding hair constitute what Sandoval (1991:
14) calls "ideological and tactical weaponry" for confronting shifting cur-
rents of power.

Conclusion

In her book *Nappyisms: Affirmations for Nappy-headed People and Wannabes!*,
Linda Jones (2003) recounts yet another "nappy" hair controversy, though on
a rather smaller scale than the hubbub over Ms. Sherman's reading of *Nappy
Hair* to her third-grade class. This instance involves Barbara, a proud member
of Jones's "natural" hair support group, and Barbara's friend, a White woman.
As Jones tells it, Barbara's friend had heard nothing but good things about nappy
hair. One day, while working as a barber in a Dallas soup kitchen, Barbara's
friend noticed a cute little Black boy waiting in line for a haircut. In the presence of several Black women, she called the boy over using words she thought
were complimentary. Her summons was something akin to "Come on over here
with your nappy-headed self!" (Jones 2003: 63) Suffice it to say that Barbara's
friend later called her wailing, "Why didn't you teellll meeee? I didn't know
what I was saying!" (64). As Barbara tried to explain, her distraught friend
interjected, "But you're always saying *nappy*. You're even in a nappy club!
What did I say wrong?" (64)
    Jones (2003: 64) evaluates this faux pas as follows:

> Now you know the type of trouble White folk find themselves in when they na-
> ively make the mistake of calling a Black person by the other "n-word" because
> their silly Black friends convinced them that it's a term of endearment. Well, that's
> the predicament Barbara's friend found herself in when she thought she was giv-
> ing the little boy his props! . . . She did not know that some of us believe there is
> something utterly profane about calling it what it is: Nappy.

In short, many African Americans would rather not hear "the other n-word"
slip from the lips of even the most empathetic White person, whether in a soup
kitchen or a classroom.
    At the time of this writing, schoolteacher Ruth Sherman and author
Carolivia Herron have teamed up to create a reading guide for *Nappy Hair*. I

am encouraged by their collaboration and hope their efforts will engender a
better understanding of how race, language, and context matter in conversations about "nappy" hair. I also hope that their effort will not reduce the *Nappy
Hair* debate to a case of political correctness gone amok. As the cases analyzed
in this chapter suggest, there was much more going on in the controversy that
begs further consideration. In particular, the cautions conveyed by the African
American parents and hairstylists in the three episodes analyzed here offer
important insights. While some may disagree with their perspectives and strategies, the counterdiscourses of these speakers demonstrate the politics of hair
and language in Black women's being and becoming. We gain, from their dialogues, a greater appreciation for *nappy* as a controversial and complex signifier. Further, we can better understand some of the motivations behind Black
women's attempts to police the use of this word, even among their most
empathetic White compatriots.

Insofar as the dialogues among African American women in this chapter leave little room for White women at the table, however, they also illustrate what happens when race, unspoken privilege, and language get in the
way of feminist alliances. I do not mean to claim that Ruth Sherman, Barbara's
friend, Carla, and the two White stylists in the South Carolina salon are blame-
worthy. Rather, I wish to suggest that Black women's resistance to or out-
right rejection of these women's well-intentioned speech and action might
also be read as an explicit call to White women to interrogate where they fit
vis-à-vis Black women in the racial and cultural divide in the United States.
Ultimately, White women's failure to recognize and address this call helped
to determine their fate in the above conversations with Black women about
hair. And Black women's resistance and, in some cases, obstinacy reflect the
extent to which racialized experiences of both Blacks and Whites can obstruct
efforts at cross-cultural and cross-racial understanding. These issues warrant
consideration when discussing the politics of hair and language in Black
women's being and becoming as children, women, cosmetology students, and
hair-care professionals.

In the final chapter, I offer a capstone of sorts to this multisited journey by
looking within and beyond my attempts to observe and write about this intimately personal, volatile, and much-parodied subject. My hope is that this reflection will further clarify these themes, particularly as they relate to my own
and other scholars' "becomings" as "native" anthropologists who, in discovering the unfamiliar in the familiar, also reveal the promise of ethnography in
language and gender studies.

7

Critical Reflections on Language, Gender, and "Native" Anthropology

My overarching goals for this book were to present situated and "lived" accounts of the role of hair and language in the formation of Black women's identities. In each of the preceding chapters, I likewise sought to illuminate how, when, and why hair matters in African American women's day-to-day experiences and how it is they work out, either by themselves or with others, when exactly "hair is just hair" and, alternatively, "hair is not just hair." We have journeyed far in pursuit of answers to these questions. We have seen cosmetology students become stylists through specialized language use and hair-care skill. We have also seen licensed stylists achieve higher levels of expertise and clout by likening themselves to "hair doctors" and even divinely gifted professionals. Clients also strived toward new aesthetic becomings by lobbying for hairstyles that they and their loved ones could enjoy.

Narratives about hair and hair-care practices have been central to these processes. Black women reflected on their experiences as children who faced a limited selection of Black dolls and years later, as cosmetologists who had little or no access to Black mannequins. Their shared memories united them, sometimes in opposition to empathetic Black men and White women who wished to share their own opinions about Black hair on the Internet, in the classroom, or in salons. Narratives also permeate the cultural space of African American comedy clubs, allowing comics and predominantly Black audiences to reflect on their beings and becomings as girls, women, men, and spouses vis-à-vis shared hair-care experiences and terminology and further clarify why sometimes "hair is just hair" and at other times "hair is not just hair" for Black women and men.

Still, there is much else to be said about the intersubjective processes whereby these discoveries were made. Hence, in this final chapter, I look within and beyond this work to broader transitions taking place within the wider social sciences (Marcus and Fischer 1986) that crosscut anthropology, African American studies, and language and gender studies and speak to "where and when" I entered this work (Giddings 1984) as a "native" anthropologist. To operationalize this concept further, I ask, following Narayan (1993), "How 'native' is a native anthropologist?" and synthesize commentary by several "native" scholars that interrogates the degree to which their gender and indigenous background authorizes carte blanche status in the field. Their arguments expose the fallacy of presuming commonalities with research participants based on shared ethnic, gendered, and class backgrounds, since all scholars, particularly "native" ones, must diligently strive to negotiate legitimacy in the field.

I also explore the centrality of linguistic and discursive knowledge for native scholars who conduct fieldwork in communities they consider to be "home." "Knowing the language(s)" of a research population is a mantra to which all ethnographers are socialized before conducting fieldwork. For native scholars of language like me, an awareness of cultural rules for verbal and nonverbal engagement can be essential to negotiating cultural legitimacy and trust; further, communicative missteps by native researchers can serve to impede research efforts. For example, verbal blunders committed by African American researchers during the initial stages of their fieldwork invoked distrust and disdain among their research participants and made researchers vulnerable to the classification of "educated fools" (Baugh 1983; Gwaltney 1993; Naylor 1988).

A third theme I shall explore concerns native and feminist scholars' confessions of "failure" in the field and dilemmas of translation of academic writing for nonacademic audiences beyond the field. To the extent that wisdom is gained from failure, scholars' reported shortcomings tell us much about the representational politics that emerge across engagements in "native" fields. Dilemmas of translation characterizing "native" scholarship further underscore the representational politics that color native researchers' experiences within and beyond the field.

Finally, I consider the political stakes inherent in native scholars' research in places that they in some way consider to be "home." Native researchers, perhaps more than others, often experience pressures to "translate" their work so that it is accessible to both lay/communal and academic audiences. This task, however, can be difficult for native ethnographers to reconcile since each constituency has multiple and often contradictory standards governing how to ask and how (and what) to say in published reports.

Throughout this discussion, I invoke insights gleaned from this multisited study. Several experiences associated with "making it to the kitchen" are offered to augment and extend discussion about the centrality of language in negotiating identity and legitimacy in and beyond the field. Recall that the "kitchen" is both an intimate space wherein girls' socialization into cultural hair-related practices often originates, as well as an in-group Black term characterizing the typically more curly hair at the nape of the neck. As discussed in the introduction, the intimate and provocative nature of both hair-related sites has increasingly sensitized me to the implications of "airing dirty laundry" about the politics of Black women's hairstyle choices. I therefore discuss how my necessary negotiation of hair-related politics evidences some of the complexities of translation and representation in "native" scholarship, particularly the dilemma of reconciling accountabilities to different audiences by gender, race, discipline, and other variables.

I offer this discussion to demonstrate how dilemmas of ethnography arise in and inform the study of language and gender. Following a number of other researchers, I want to suggest ethnography as a powerful means of exploring issues that lie at the heart of language and gender studies. These issues include women's talk within the contexts of their own speech communities; women as social actors who do "being" Black, women, professionals, and other positionalities in and through language; women who assert new ways of being and thinking through counterdiscourse, humor, and other ideological stances within formerly male-dominated stages (e.g., humor, the Internet); and, finally, women who are active participants in their own and others' becomings through specialized talk and everyday interactions. As Mary Bucholtz (1999a) notes, a "transgressive" language and gender research paradigm seeks to address such issues by taking a critical look back at the field's early theoretical assumptions and methodological practices in order to imagine more productive ways of exploring the complexity of gendered discourse and practice. This closing chapter draws inspiration from her bid for a disciplinary reflexivity and suggests several theoretically "transgressive" insights from "native" ethnography as one of many critical pathways with which to pursue "transgressive" and translatable scholarship in language and gender studies.

An experimental moment

The last three decades have witnessed a critical evaluation of dominant ideas within the social sciences. Within anthropology, this "experimental moment" (Marcus and Fischer 1986) extends beyond a single moment and has, as Rosaldo (1989: 13) notes, been driven by "enduring, not transitory, ethical and analytical issues." The ongoing reconfiguration of social thought (Geertz 1983; Tedlock 1991) within anthropology is reflected in the interrogation, evolution, and even wholesale abandonment of concepts previously considered to be central to the discipline. Fundamental concepts such as "native," "culture," and "the field" have been reframed by some scholars to represent the constructed and dynamic nature of notions such as identity, culture, and place (Appadurai 1988; Casey 1996; D'Amico-Samuels 1997; Narayan 1993).

Looking inward: A reflexive anthropology

Additionally, though certainly not without critique (see discussion by James et al. 1997; Washburn 1998), researchers are increasingly practicing gradations of a "reflexive" anthropology" (Hymes 1999 [1969]; Myerhoff and Ruby 1982). This approach is rooted in the premise that ethnographic fieldwork is an inter-subjective process that entails an interaction of various subjectivities (J. Briggs 1970; Geertz 1971; Rabinow 1977). These subjectivities include those of the researcher, the theoretical perspectives of her or his discipline, and the perspectives and representations of study participants (Srinivas 1966, 1979). Being reflexive enables a researcher to critically consider her or his own cultural biases and negotiate various ways of seeing while investigating and "translating" culture(s) (Geertz 1971). A reflexive perspective is also particularly sensitive to the socially constructed nature of knowledge production.

The practice of reflexivity and reevaluation of major tenets in anthropology has been welcomed by many scholars as a means of confronting the historical role that the discipline has played in Western colonialism and its creation of "Third World" territories (Foucault 1980; Harrison 1997a; Said 1989; Trinh 1989; Ulin 1991). A critically reflexive approach has contributed to descriptions of peoples as belonging to "imagined" (Anderson 1991) or socially constructed communities. This approach has also highlighted the fact that research participants have always acted individually and communally, traveled (Appadurai 1991; Clifford 1992; Kaplan 1996; Olwig 1997), and theorized about their own cultural identities and ideologies (Gwaltney 1993; Harrison and Harrison 1999; Kenyatta 1965; Rosaldo 1989).

Notable changes can also be observed in the ways in which researchers conduct fieldwork and present their findings. Scholars today have largely shunned the term *natives* as one that connotes a monolithic group of peoples confined to a distant exotic space (see Appadurai 1990; Clifford 1988; Gupta and Ferguson 1992, 1997; Olwig 1997). Researchers are increasingly expected to account for how their own positionalities (Kondo 1990, Narayan 1993), and ways of asking (Briggs 1994; Page 1988), seeing/interpreting (Dwyer 1982), and speaking (Whitehead 1986; Woof and Wiegman 1995) influence their production of "partial" representations of their engagements in the field (see also Abu-Lughod 1991; Clifford 1986; Haraway 1988; Okely and Callaway 1992). Anthropologists are also devoting considerable attention to the varied influences that their presence and scholarship may have on the peoples whom they study (M. Jackson 1989; Marcus and Fischer 1986). More broadly, the "field" has also been reconfigured as inclusive of such modern settings as the urban village (Passaro 1997), media (Appadurai 1990; Marcus 1996), fashion and theater (Kondo 1997), and global villages in cyberspace (Herring 1996; Morley and Robins 1995; Weston 1997). Anthropologists and other social scientists are increasingly conducting fieldwork in unprecedented places (Clifford 1997a; Garber et al. 1996; Powdermaker 1966), including their own communities.

The changing face of academia

The move by some anthropologists to conduct fieldwork at "home" is a funda-mental break from the classic tradition of what Rosaldo (1989) characterizes as the "Lone Ethnographer" riding off into the sunset in search of the native. But for the last three decades and beyond, so-called "Natives/Others" have been gazing and talking back as researchers, students, and lay critics of academic presentations and published scholarship (Caulfield 1979; Gullahorn-Holecek 1983; hooks 1989; Paredes 1984; Tedlock 1991).

Much of this scholarship has been produced by anthropologists working within their own non-Western village, or within ethnic minority communities in the United States (e.g., Aguilar 1981; Altorki and El-Solh 1988; Gordon 1998; Fahim and Helmer 1980; Haniff 1985; Hurston 1979; Messerschmidt 1981a, 1981b; Paredes 1984; R. Rosaldo 1985). While this scholarship reveals variation among "native" and "indigenous" scholars concerning their positionalities as cultural "insiders" and the reflexive nature of their scholarship, a great majority of these researchers coalesce around the goal of decolonizing Western anthropology through more reflexive modes of representation and critique (Basso 1984; D'Amico-Samuels 1997; Harrison and Harrison 1999; Trinh 1989).

Several themes that typify this "corrective" agenda (Gwaltney 1993) include examining the historical legacy of anthropologists' role in the subjugation, exploitation, and exoticization of people of color throughout the world (Amory 1997; Willis 1999 [1969]), incorporating the experiences and voices of research participants in ethnographic and other texts (Christian 1990; Collins 1990; Smith 1999), and returning something of value to the researcher's host communities (Alvarez 1996; Fahim 1979; Whitehead 1992; Williams 1996; Zavella 1996). For many scholars working in their "own" or diasporic communities, this has necessitated abandoning academic jargon (Mihesauh 1988) and various research methods that might be alienating and intrusive to participants (Hennigh 1981; Medicine 2001; Mufwene 1993), such as the use of I.Q. tests (Baugh 1983), tape recorders (Harrison 1997b; Page 1988), written surveys (Gwaltney 1993), or specific sampling techniques (Paredes 1984; see also Labov 1998). In such ways, anthropologists working "at home" embrace some of the major tenets of postcolonial and postmodern scholarship.

This, however, is not to suggest that all (or only) native researchers practice a politically engaged anthropology (Tedlock 1991), nor is it meant to imply that anthropologists who self-identify as working within their "own" societies have not deconstructed their identities as native scholars—trained in the West— or their host sites as "home" sites (e.g., Abu-Lughod 1988; Chow 1993; Jones 1970; Kashoki 1982; Kondo 1990; Mihesauh 1988; Rosaldo 1985; Srinivas 1966; Trinh 1989; Zavella 1996; Zentella 1997).

Interrogating the "native" in native anthropologist

For example, in her influential article, "How Native is a 'Native' Anthropologist?," Narayan (1993) notes that accounts by native anthropologists that solely celebrate the privileges associated with being an "insider" fail to expose the negotiation of identity and legitimacy that is necessary for all anthropologists, including those working within their own cultural communities (see also Ong 1995; Trouillot 1991). Similarly, Nelson (1996: 184) argues that native anthropologists are seldom considered insiders by default; instead, they experience various "gradations of endogeny" throughout the course of their fieldwork.

Further, Narayan exposes the complexity of assigning "native" status to scholars who, like her, are of multiple cultural backgrounds and work within communities which they consider to be "home" (see also Abu-Lughod 1988, 1991; Kondo 1986, 1990; Limón 1991). Drawing from her fieldwork in India and the Himalayas, she highlights the important role played by research participants in the choreography of ethnographic inquiry. Research participants affect the people and places to which ethnographers have access during fieldwork, thus influencing their research in substantial ways (e.g., Mohanty 1989). Research participants' self-concept may also be influenced through their interaction with researchers (e.g., Williams 1996). Moreover, study participants may ascribe to researchers particular identities and cultural roles based upon their gender, caste/class, educational status, age, family relations, sexual orientation, marital status, and so on (e.g., Harrison 1997b; Kulick and Willson 1995; Lewin and Leap 1996; Smith 1999; Whitehead 1986). In such cases, native scholars may face various challenges in negotiating their dual identities as community members and researchers.

The complexities of negotiating identity in the field are highlighted in accounts by other native scholars who, for various reasons, were ascribed such social roles as "dutiful" (Abu-Lughod 1988) and "prodigal" daughters (Kondo 1986), honored guests (Fahim 1979; Shahrani 1994), "skinfolk" and not "kinfolk" (Williams 1996), and "friends" (Kumar 1992). The task of negotiating one's identity is further complicated by the fact that participants may attribute certain identities and roles to researchers for strategic purposes. Brackette Williams's (1996) description of her fieldwork in two contrasting Afro-Guyanese communities, for example, reveals the competing loyalties and expectations of the lower-class to working-class individuals with whom she interacted from the "backdam" and her middle-class hostess from the "riverdam." Although initially unbeknownst to Williams, her own social position as an educated African American scholar served to bolster her hostess's affluence and self-ascribed elite status. Williams's frequent treks to the backdam to interact with Afro-Guyanese of lower class backgrounds symbolized a public threat to her hostess's self-concept and public image. Yet Williams's visits also worked to her own advantage by mitigating backdam residents' suspicions that she was snobbish. Williams's hostess protested her excursions to the backdam in overt and subtle ways throughout her fieldwork, forcing her to constantly negotiate her time and loyalties between the two communities.

As a "partial" native anthropologist in the African diaspora (see also Mufwene 1993), Williams's status as a college-educated African American woman served to promote as well as threaten her hostess's social face (Goffman 1959). Her affiliation with a woman whose social class positioning had diminished in recent years became a way for the hostess to reestablish herself as a member of the upper class. Hence, Williams was pressured to restrict her movement to the "riverdam." The process whereby "native" scholars are attributed particular social roles—along with their subsequent attempts to comply with and/or contest these positionalities—illuminates how "native/insider" is an insufficient descriptor for the manner in which scholars negotiate multiple identities in the field (Rosaldo 1989; Narayan 1993).

Language as a means of establishing legitimacy at "home"

The tenuousness of "native" status is also foregrounded in accounts by "native" scholars concerning linguistic and discursive knowledge as a central means of negotiating their identities in the field. As with perhaps all researchers, a native scholar's degree of communicative competence (Duranti 1994; Hymes 1972)—the ability to use and interpret "home" speech varieties appropriately across various cultural contexts—plays a significant role in her or his ability to enter a community and develop a rapport with research participants (Bernard 1994; Paredes 1984). For native scholars, fluency in "home" speech varieties and discourse styles is particularly important given the role of language as a mediator of a speaker's cultural identity (see Basso 1979, 1996; Gumperz and Cook-Gumperz 1982; Ochs 1992) and cultural "authenticity" in the eyes of discriminating research participants. For example, accounts by various native scholars indicate that their display of communicative competence can sanction their identity as both a researcher and a community member (Baugh 1983; Zentella 1997), whereas ignorance can subvert research efforts by marking researchers as culturally challenged or detached (Foster 1996; Rickford 1986).

In researching linguistic and cultural practices around Black hair, I learned that while my status as a native anthropologist can serve to my advantage, it by no means guarantees my acceptance as a trustworthy researcher in African American communities. Moreover, my demonstrated knowledge and use of African American discourse styles such as indirectness and signifying (Gates 1989; Mitchell-Kernan 1972, 1973; Morgan 1991, 1996a) were critical in gaining the trust of prospective research participants.

To negotiate my access into highly intimate cultural spaces, for example, I relied on an assortment of verbal and nonverbal strategies. In face-to-face conversations with women in beauty salons, I strategically employed African American Vernacular English (AAVE) and cultural discourse styles during intimate conversations wherein such styles were already in use and/or would be appropriate. In email conversations, I disclosed my racial identity to unseen prospective participants who appeared to be ambivalent about my background and intentions. I also revealed other strategic information, such as my own hairstyle and the fact that my mother is a hairstylist. In all these contexts, I also found it necessary to pay particular attention to participants' responses or "refusals to speak" (Visweswaran 1994) when I asked questions about hair or other sensitive matters.

In my research on AFROAM-L, for example, when I asked Njeri by way of email for access to previous computer-mediated discussions about Black hair, she asked me several questions prior to consenting. As I discussed in chapter 5, one of these questions, "BTW [by the way], how do YOU wear your hair?"

was crucial both as an attempt to control access to the discussion and as an indirect means of ascertaining my racial identity and presumably my cultural footing. Moreover, my imputed degree of cultural consciousness and, indeed, my success in gaining access to the posts preceding the computer-mediated hair debate rested in my ability to properly interpret her question, which was cloaked within a discourse style frequently used by African Americans to test and challenge the addressee's social face and expressed intentions (see also Morgan 1994b).

Displaying competence in the use and interpretation of African American speech varieties has been central for many native ethnographers in earning the trust and cooperation of their African American research participants (e.g., Gwaltney 1993; Mitchell-Kernan 1971; Williams 1996). As Morgan (1994b) argues, language is a form of symbolic capital (Bourdieu 1991) within African American speech communities through which speakers of diverse class backgrounds construct their racial consciousness. An ethnographer's ability to use and understand AAVE and cultural discourse styles can thus significantly affect her or his ability to establish a rapport with AAVE speakers (Baugh 1983; Mitchell-Kernan 1971; Nelson 1996).

The ability of native scholars to demonstrate communicative competence in African American speech varieties can also assuage widespread concerns among African Americans about "being studied" (see Jones 1970). In Gwaltney's collection of ethnographic interviews with African Americans, one participant told him, "I think this anthropology is another way to call me a nigger" (1993: xix). Another participant cautioned Gwaltney, "I'll talk to you all day long, Lankee, but don't interview me" (1993: xxiv). Despite such concerns, many African Americans were persuaded to participate in Gwaltney's research for several reasons. These reasons included his avoidance of "talking like a man with a paper in his hand" and participants' desire to support a fellow African American's career aspirations.

African American scholars who only speak mainstream varieties of English may be at a disadvantage in their attempts to develop a rapport with their research participants (Williams 1996). African American scholars have observed that failure to display communicative competence in African American speech varieties may mark one as an "educated fool"—one whose affiliation and/or identification with African American culture has, by virtue of her or his education, class positioning, or posturing, become suspect (see also Page 1988). Foster's (1996) research on African American ideologies concerning effective educators illuminates several social consequences that may result from a researcher's failure to display competence in African American speech varieties. Foster reports that several participants voiced concerns about talking to her because they believed that she did not "sound Black" over the phone. Additionally, some of the participants who were notably skeptical of her "insiderness" resolved this issue by having Foster stay at their homes for closer observation. Given participant responses to her speech and urban background, Foster reports feeling variously like an "insider" and an "outsider" at different stages of her research.

Communicative competence not only entails facility in the multiple speech varieties that characterize a particular speech community, but also an awareness of the rules governing the proper and contextual interpretation of cultural discourse styles. Nelson (1996) underscores the importance of discourse knowledge in establishing trust among her African American research participants. Nelson employed call and response to align with a consultant who was also her childhood friend. Nelson views her own and her interlocutor's use of this cultural discourse style as marking their solidarity as oppressed minorities. On the broader subject of shared culture and communicative codes, she states:

> Although the native and the researcher look alike, *speak the same language, and share many of the same beliefs and customs,* the researcher still approaches the natives to observe them. . . . The ease of access and the quality of rapport are constantly negotiated as the researcher and informant construct their identities in this intrinsically hierarchical relationship. (1996: 194, my emphasis)

For Nelson, the salient differences between "indigenous" researchers and their consultants seem to lie not at the level of language or cultural beliefs, but rather in the power differentials that exist between the "observed" and the "observer" (see also D'Amico-Samuels 1997). Foster's field experiences, described above, suggest that native anthropologists are not always equally sensitive to context-dependent discourse protocols and that this can seriously affect their success in the field. Nelson further suggests that the native anthropologist brings to her or his work a significant characteristic that exogenous investigators do not:

> When she turns off the recorder and removes the cloak of the investigator, she goes home to a community she forever shares with natives. Their fundamental beliefs, as well as their struggles and triumphs, are deeply woven into the fabric of her own existence. This profound reality acts as a relentless urging, provoking her continuous attempt to liberate the fact from romanticization. Ironically, she cannot hope to accomplish this . . . unless she is willing to closely examine the community as a system of shared values and beliefs, as well as to examine the subtle but significant distinctions among its members. (1996: 198, my emphasis)

Nelson's rendering of a native anthropologist symbolically shedding her researcher identity on the trek back home cautions against romanticization, but fails to expose "home" as a socially and culturally constructed (Lemelle and Kelley 1994), imagined (Anderson 1991), and desired concept (Kaplan 1996; Martin and Mohanty 1986). Nelson's description of the native scholar's transformation also belies attempts by native researchers to reconcile multiple allegiances and accountabilities to their ethnic and academic communities. Rather than bifurcating their identities as researchers and members of the communities they study, native and reflexive scholars have, as Nelson acknowledges, increasingly grappled with what it means to reconstitute themselves from former subjects of anthropological investigation to native researchers working in the present (Kondo 1990; Narayan 1993). Reports of failure by several native researchers critically address this and related questions, illuminating the many ways scholars negotiate their place and purpose across lay and scientific communities (see also DeVita 1990, 1992).

Confessions of "failure" in the field

Nelson divulges her own failed attempt at establishing a rapport with Mrs. Jones, an African American participant in her study. Upon greeting Mrs. Jones at her home, Nelson remarked of her rural surroundings, "How nice it is back here" (1996: 189). When Mrs. Jones retorted, "What do you mean by *back* here?" (1996: 189; my emphasis), Nelson realized that she had unwittingly offended her host. More specifically, Mrs. Jones apparently interpreted Nelson's remark as an act of signifying wherein the seemingly innocuous reference to "back here" was actually a veiled satirical critique of Mrs. Jones's rural surroundings. Nelson's subsequent efforts to repair the unintended slight were for the most part futile and resulted in her undergoing a notable shift in her established identity. Whereas Mrs. Jones had initially introduced Nelson to other prospective participants as a "friend," she later described her in less familiar terms, as a "teacher friend." Nelson is acutely aware of her shifting status and the cultural implications thereof. She observes that the foregrounding of her educated status risks associating her with "educated fools." Nelson's misstep demonstrates the intricacies and importance of language as a means of constructing legitimacy and cultural authenticity among native anthropologists, as well as the complexity of notions of home and speech community membership. Her conversational "failure" with Mrs. Jones also recalls testimonies by other native researchers whose language facility, especially adherence to discourse rules, marked them as outsiders during fieldwork at "home" (see also Kondo 1990; Rickford 1986).

Moments of discursive awkwardness experienced by Nelson and Foster elucidate some of the challenges faced by native anthropologists in negotiating their cultural integrity in the field. Failure among "indigenous" researchers to establish legitimacy among participants can be particularly unsettling, suggesting that they are "one of them but not of them" (Obeyesekere 1981). Since the researcher-participant relationship is reciprocal to some degree, with both parties fulfilling a variety of social needs and roles for the other (Narayan 1993), either the realization or the apparent erasure of difference between the observer and the observed can entail a range of emotional consequences for both groups.

For example, during her fieldwork in Japan, Kondo (1986, 1990) observed that her participants placed her in a number of meaningful cultural roles, including daughter, student, guest, young woman, and prodigal Japanese. Many of Kondo's cultural mentors became quite invested in the task of enculturating Kondo into a Japanese lifestyle that, in their eyes, befitted her gender, educational level, youth, and shared heritage. Initially, Kondo perceived her hostesses and friends as impatient of her social, linguistic, and cultural inadequacies. Later, to Kondo's pleasure, they became more approving of her progress in several domains of Japanese culture. Kondo embraced and at times contested her various ascribed identities and social roles to the point of exhaustion. Ultimately, she became so steeped in the cultural graces of Japanese working women that one day she could not differentiate her own reflection (in a butcher's display case) from that of the young Japanese housewives whom she had frequently observed. Troubled that she had been complicit in her own apparent "collapse of identity" (1990: 17), Kondo returned to the United States for a month to reground her identity as an American researcher.

Similarly, in his reflection on the study of one's own community, Ohnuki-Tierney (1984a, 1984b) confesses that he felt himself crossing a boundary that separated him from his ethnic "kin" in Kobe, Japan. As with Kondo, Ohnuki-Tierney's subsequent return to the United States enabled him to regain his perspective as a researcher. Ohnuki-Tierney is nevertheless optimistic about the practice of "native" anthropology. He suggests that research by native anthropologists is indeed possible, although the researcher may occasionally require moments of solitude and critical reflection.

Interestingly, Ohnuki-Tierney further suggests that native anthropologists might be even more effective researchers than outsiders are since they do not have participants perform for them when they first arrive in the field (see also Paredes 1984). As a result, he asserts that the ethnographic observations of non-native scholars, unlike those of native scholars, tend to become a negotiated reality between the participants and the anthropologist. Yet others have shown that native researchers also, (and necessarily [see Geertz 1971]) produce negotiated realities during and after their fieldwork (Page 1988; Tedlock 1991; Visweswaran 1994). Ethnographers' confessions of isolation and failure during fieldwork underscore this point by illuminating the gradations of endogeny that arise from their degree of linguistic and cultural competence (Mufwene 1993; Rickford 1986). Moreover, the experiences of Kondo and others emphasize how participants and researchers co-construct the native researcher's identity, role, and research agenda in overt and subtle ways (see also Dua 1979; Narayan 1995; Rabinow 1977; Whitehead 1986).

"Failures" in the field can also have significant implications beyond the field—that is, for how native scholars envision the broader anthropological enterprise. Visweswaran's (1994) *Fictions of Feminist Ethnography* recounts various moments of "failure" in her fieldwork in which her line of inquiry was rejected by several research participants. Fashioned in the form of a play, her book contains three acts portraying her interviews with two women, Uma and Janaki. Her theatrically structured narrative is radical as it illuminates how participants' gendered identities and personal accounts are constructed and partial and how agency can be performed through such means as silence.

Visweswaran's ethnographic fieldwork entailed collecting life histories from Indian women imprisoned during the Indian nationalist movement in addition to gleaning information from historical documents. In one of her initial interviews, Visweswaran learned that Uma, one of her participants, had been married only once. Yet Uma's friend Janaki later exposed Uma's "lie" by noting that Uma had been married twice and widowed in a prior arranged marriage in her youth.

Janaki's stories to Visweswaran, however, also had discrepancies. Janaki reported that when she was younger, she used to pretend that she was married, but Visweswaran later discovered in archives that as a child, Janaki's family had arranged for her to marry a man of a non-Brahmin regional caste. Strikingly, Janaki's "secret" was revealed in the presence of Visweswaran, in large part, by a mutual friend, Tangam, who tried unsuccessfully to compel Janaki to tell the "truth" while vouching for Visweswaran's loyal motives as a researcher. At one point, Janaki asked Tangam abruptly, "Why does she want to know these things?" (p. 46) and then withdrew her gaze and became silent. The emotional toll experienced by Janaki in the pursuit of these "hidden facts" (p. 47) led Visweswaran to reflect more deeply on the nature of disciplinary knowledge and relations of power between the observer and the observed.

Visweswaran argued that such instances of "lies, secrets, and silence" (Rich 1995 [1979]) bring to the fore the inevitability of failures in a feminist ethnography that presumes commonalities between all women, including her as observer and Uma and Janaki as the observed. The series of betrayals, first Janaki's and later Tangam's (albeit unwittingly staged by Visweswaran), expose the unequal power relations characterizing the process of ethnographic inquiry and the production of knowledge (see also Hale 1991; Nelson 1996). Viewing such betrayals as an allegory for the practice of feminist ethnography, Visweswaran envisions Janaki's refusal to be subject(ed) to her inquiries as a struggle to reclaim the integrity of her personal and familial secrets.

Visweswaran's fieldwork compelled her to ask, *What are the tactics a feminist ethnographer can deploy to develop a different type of ethnography?* A new ethnography, Visweswaran asserts, can be actualized by ethnographers' increased consideration of their own or others' shifting identities, interpretations, and silences over time. As Visweswaran further explains, the process of ethnographic inquiry is dialogic and complex. So, too, are the positionalities of researchers and participants, which are themselves multiple and situation-specific (Rosaldo 1986). Knowledge produced in the process of ethnographic inquiry is also situational and hence temporal and provisional (Cohen 1992). In grasping "partial" truths (Abu-Lughod 1991; Clifford 1986; Haraway 1988; Rosaldo 1989) scholars must avoid superimposing collective narratives—including gender narratives—on individual narratives as the sole means of explaining subject positioning (Chow 1993; Limón 1991). Ethnographers must also look for agency and resistance in participants' silence or "refusals to speak" (see also Page 1988; Trinh 1990). A feminist ethnography and, arguably, "native" anthropology (Gwaltney 1993) should listen to and measure such silence in order to understand the multiple messages that may be conveyed therein (Basso 1970).

Dilemmas of translation beyond the field

Kamala Visweswaren's use of failure to interrogate her presumptions of feminist ethnography is similar to Behar's (1995) poignant discussion of the politics of representation and accountability. Behar discloses the pain, betrayal, and failure that she and her parents feel after her publication of an autobiographical piece about herself and her research participant, Esperanza. In the piece, Behar shared information that some members of her family considered to be secret. These "secrets" evoked criticism from friends and empathetic readers of the way her father expressed his anger toward Behar when she was a child. Her father resented having been included in her reflexive manuscript (see also Page 1988). He asked Behar why he was not consulted about his inclusion in her autobiographical publication, raising larger questions about one's "right" to represent one's "skinfolk and kinfolk" and the nature of that representation. Behar's narrative highlights the sorrow and guilt that is experienced when one's work is undesirable to one's "kinfolk" and research participants.

Behar's predicament also illustrates the dilemmas of translation that "native" scholars may experience while negotiating accountability to multiple audiences—which often include both the academy and the communities in which they work (see Christian 1990; Nakhleh 1979). Decisions about representation, including which voices to incorporate in published reports, entail cultural brokering—that is, reconciling disparate views about how and to whom one should represent the intricacies of everyday life among individuals within a community. While this is a challenge that is to some extent shared by all social scientists (see D'Amico-Samuels 1997; Duranti 1997), managing the politics of representation may entail additional challenges for native scholars. For example, native researchers must be especially sensitive to the dangers of disclosing cultural secrets or airing what community members may consider to be "dirty laundry" (Whitehead 1986, 1992; Visweswaran 1994; Behar 1993, 1995). Given the native scholar's presumed communal ties, negative perceptions of and consequences of such admissions may be more acutely felt by the native researcher and her or his participants; further, missteps may make it more difficult to return "home." Native scholars who accommodate publication or manuscript requests by their study participants must also be mindful of the accessibility of their rhetorical strategies—if published reports are so technical as to be impenetrable, lay readers may suspect the ethnographer of being evasive or elitist. Ironically, attempts by native scholars to "translate" their research so that it is accessible to lay audiences and incorporates naturally spoken language from "home" communities may similarly be viewed as suspect by research participants.

The latter has been true in my own attempts to translate my research on Black hair in both a culturally sensitive and methodologically sound way. Since hair and language are controversial signifiers of identity and cultural consciousness in African American speech communities, my observations and analysis of Black women's everyday talk about hair aroused both suspicion and concern among African American respondents. As I noted earlier, some African American respondents were skeptical of my presenting such intimate information for the scrutiny of predominantly White academic audiences. Other African American women, within and outside the academy, appealed to me to use my research to critique Black women's hair-straightening practices, which they viewed as indicative of self-hatred or as an unhealthy reification of Eurocentric standards of beauty. Understanding the personal hair-care experiences that compelled such perspectives, I nevertheless explained that my ethnographic observations of African American women's hair-care beliefs and practices rendered such generalized interpretations inconclusive; Black women who straighten their hair do so for a range of economic, social, and personal reasons (Banks 2000; Boyd 1993; Mercer 1994; Rooks 1996). Furthermore, many straightened hairstyles worn by African American women evoke an urban flair and sensibility which, when appropriately contextualized, have very little to do with a reification of White standards of beauty (figure 7.1). Responses of this sort, however, did not always appease my largely female African American respondents. Indifferent to the disciplinary guidelines framing my study, these reviewers often had different views about the ideal format and objectives of my work.

Several respondents also questioned how published transcripts depicting their speech during hair-related conversations might be interpreted by academics (see also Bucholtz 2000; Page 1988). More specifically, some readers were concerned that transcribed excerpts of their speech would become fodder for derogatory assessments of AAVE and of themselves as AAVE speakers. In several cases, these fears were likely exacerbated by controversial national debates about "Ebonics" in early 1997 (see Lanehart 2002; Rickford 1996, 1999), and the stigma attached to AAVE in educational and professional contexts.

My response to these understandable concerns entailed describing the critical and objective way scholars of language try to evaluate naturally spoken discourse; the focus of linguistic anthropologists, I argued, is not on minority

Figure 7.1. Black women on Easter Sunday in Baltimore, Maryland, 1995 (© Bill Gaskins 1997)

languages as substandard or stigmatized as much as it is on the complexity of language and its relationship to speakers' identities. This explanation reassured some lay readers. At other times, however, my response only managed to trigger African American respondents' concerns about my own naiveté as a native scholar. The Tuskegee Syphilis Study (1932–1972), wherein 399 African American males were deceived by U.S. Public Health Service officials and denied treatment for syphilis, has generated skepticism among African American communities about the intentions of scientists (Freimuth et al. 2001).

My own challenges with translation reflect seemingly indelible incongruities between lay and academic research agendas. These agendas often pose conflicting standards for ways of asking and of representing findings. At times, these agendas also place differential value on research for the pursuit of knowledge and community uplift. While these dual goals need not be considered mutually exclusive, pursuing them may nevertheless be difficult for native ethnographers to reconcile. Scholars who conduct research for the sake of the betterment of "home" communities, for example, must first decide what the "betterment of the community" means and to whom. This goal can impose constraints on the practice of native ethnography, particularly in communities wherein the acquisition of "new" knowledge, in and of itself, is deemed insufficient. Research that complies with the political agendas of a community may also require native researchers to ask loaded questions and pursue them in ways that are at odds with their disciplinary training.

"Native" and "indigenous" scholars report a range of conceptual and practical strategies for resolving dilemmas of translation. Kondo (1997) observes that some scholars working at "home" envision ethnography as a means of unsettling the boundaries between scholarship and minority discourse, using their texts as a means of writing their individual and communal identities. In the quest for accessibility and accountability to the communities in which they work, other scholars advocate an "indigenous" or explicitly non-Western methodology that preserves "native" ideologies and cultural traditions (e.g., Medicine 2001; Smith 1999). "Indigenous" methods and interpretive frameworks also seek to minimize differentials of power among the observer and the observed, yet defining the terms of this postcolonial research agenda has at times entailed gross and idealistic generalizations about what *indigenous* means or should mean.

Chow (1993) poignantly argues in this regard that "native" scholars who feel obliged to engage in a reflexive or corrective anthropology should write not only "against culture" (Abu-Lughod 1991) but also against the "lures of Diaspora" (p. 99). Understanding that the cultural identity of "native" scholars lends a certain authenticity to their texts, Chow admonishes Western Chinese intellectuals in particular to acknowledge rather than repress the inequalities inherent in the discourse between themselves and their research subjects (see also D'Amico-Samuels 1997). Such transparency, she argues, will enable them to write against the crippling effects of both Western imperialism and Chinese paternalism. Similar admonitions against romanticizing peoples and cultures have been made by other "native" scholars (see Adorno 1994; Aguilar 1981;

Kashoki 1982; Rosaldo 1987, 1991; Smith 1999; Srinivas 1979)—each of
whom occupies a unique "native" positioning as variously indigenous, self-
trained, trained in the West, or as occupying the equally ambivalent spaces of
the border or diaspora.

Professional stakes of native anthropology

Attempts by native scholars to reconcile the politics of translation and accountability are further confounded by the need to confront the professional consequences of their "native" status and particularly their confessional accounts (see
also Tedlock 1991). Chow asserts that native research about women, especially
by Chinese anthropologists residing in the West, risks being ghettoized within
their disciplines (see also Harrison 1997a, 1997b). Native researchers who
openly grapple with their positionality or "failures" in the field, for example,
are more susceptible to being labeled navel-gazers, axe-grinders, politically
motivated, or hypersensitive (Rosaldo 1989; Smith 1999) or, ironically, not
"native" enough. Additionally, native scholars are particularly vulnerable to
accusations of having "gone native," a perception that undermines their authority and reinforces a tendency to view native scholars as novices rather than
experts (Chow 1993; Narayan 1993; Paredes 1984; Weston 1997). Likewise,
confessions of failure by native ethnographers like Kondo, Ohnuki-Tierney,
Behar and others can subvert their professional authority, placing them at further risk for marginalization within their academic communities.

      Ironically, native researchers' discussions of the intersubjective nature of
their fieldwork may in fact constitute a tactic for circumventing such stigmatiz-
ing characterizations. Insofar as the discussion of one's positioning in the field
engages key anthropological questions around the dialectics of fieldwork,
native scholars situate themselves and their work within a rigorous analytic
paradigm. Similarly, critical reflexivity in both writing and identification as
a native researcher may act to resist charges of having played the "native
card" by way of a non-critical privileging of one's "insider" status. Admittedly,
self-identification as a native/indigenous anthropologist may risk unduly
foregrounding difference to the exclusion of membership or kinship within a
broader community of anthropologists. However, it may also constitute a space
for the creation and validation of *native* as a signifier of the postcolonial reposi-
tioning of the subject, and *native anthropology* as a more general means of evoking the decolonization of anthropological thought and practice (see Mahon 2000
for a similar discussion in regard to minority art). In this sense, claiming native,
indigenous, or "halfie" status can be a tactical endeavor of critical self-positioning
against the mainstream (e.g., *native* anthropologist) and/or a normalizing
endeavor of self-positioning within the mainstream (e.g., native *anthropologist*).
Each stance provides native researchers with an empowering means of self-
identification and alignment within multiple and internally complex (lay and academic) constituencies and research paradigms. Native scholars and other
marginalized groups may deploy these different subject positions and ideologies
for strategic purposes (e.g., Clifford 1997b; Gordon 1998; Jacobs-Huey 2001;

Moore 1994; Sandoval 1991). In actual practice, native investigators also nego-tiate the various meanings and sociopolitical implications of these viewpoints—not simply in grand anthropological debates about postcolonial theory—but also in everyday interactions which pose the opportunity or need to move between inclusive and exclusive subject and ideological positionings.

Conclusion

This book is a testament to ongoing transitions taking place within anthropol-ogy and other fields wherein consultants are increasingly recognized as research participants who actively influence ethnographic texts (Page 1988) and eth-nographers are including their own voices in published reports. Amid this con-tinuing reconfiguration of social thought and practice, some native scholars have been vigorously gazing and talking back and attempting, by way of criti-cal reflexivity in writing, self-positioning, and other politically engaged orien-tations, to redress exotic representations of their communities.

Scholarship by and about "native" anthropologists has also critically ex-amined what these categories mean in theory and actual practice. Their reports illuminate the fact that native scholars negotiate and experience different positionalities in the field stemming from their ethnic, linguistic, gendered, sexual, educational, and class/caste backgrounds, as well as their degree of communicative competence. Communicative competence involves more than simply "learning the language" of one's research population. Rather, this con-cept entails fluency in the multiple languages and discourse styles characteriz-ing a speech community, as well as an ability to adhere to specific discourse rules. Linguistic proficiency and discourse knowledge are likewise important prerequisites for ethnographic fieldwork at "home" or abroad.

My own research encounters in and around the "kitchen" further suggest that while fluency in speech varieties may figure prominently as a marker of belonging for "native" scholars during fieldwork, it may also translate into a marker of exclusion depending on the context (e.g., post-fieldwork) and the presumed auditor(s). African American scholars' fluency in AAVE may be used to negotiate familiarity and legitimacy in the field. Beyond the field, however, the representation of authentic conversations may incur apprehension and overt disapproval from minority constituents whose language and cultural practices have been subject to popular disparagement. Moreover, the politics surround-ing language and translation often require native scholars to anticipate the rep-resentational contingencies of their linguistic and cultural analyses for both lay and academic audiences, each of whom manifest their own inherent diversity and complexity. When working "at home," scholars must also recognize the ways in which mainstream public sphere debates may have an impact on field-work experience—and later representations of that experience—for the com-munities in which they work.

Further insight into native anthropology as a signifier of postcolonial ideol-ogy and subject positioning can be gleaned through an analysis of researchers' rhetorical strategies throughout multiple phases of ethnography. Investigators' confessions of failures experienced during fieldwork, for example, illuminate some of the power differentials characterizing the process of ethnographic inquiry, even among researchers who share the same demographic or racial/ ethnic profile of their participants (e.g., Page 1988). Dilemmas in translation, such as the ones experienced by Behar and by me, further expose several representational challenges facing native scholars, many of whom write and speak to diverse audiences who do not always share the same standards toward how one should write against culture (Abu-Lughod 1991). Scholars who not only work within their ethnic communities, but are also critically reflexive about their positioning and positionality, must be mindful of the transparency and translatability of their published reports. In particular, researchers need to ensure that their ethnographic products do not alienate research subjects (who may be especially interested in research findings), nor alienate themselves as researchers within their specific disciplinary cohort (Behar 1996; Harrison 1997a; Mihesauh 1988; Motzafi-Haller 1997; Smith 1999; Trinh 1989); these can be difficult goals to accomplish in tandem and may require native anthropologists to adopt creative and/or non-traditional ways of envisioning themselves and their work.

As with feminist, postcolonial, or reflexive researchers, many native ethnographers have found it necessary to write against monolithic or romantic notions of culture (Abu-Lughod 1991) and in a manner cognizant of the provisional nature of interpretation (Geertz 1971; Cohen 1992; Zentella 1997). Moreover, scholars who self-identify as native ethnographers, or situate their work within a long-standing tradition of native anthropology, may do so not as a non-critical privileging endeavor. Instead, foregrounding nativeness in relation to anthropology, or oneself as a native anthropologist, can act as an empowering gesture and critique of the positioning of "natives" in the stagnant slot of the Other. It can also be a strategy for increasing the validity and reception of "native" scholarship within a broader community of scholars, with the ultimate goal of engendering more representative, translatable, and accountable research on language and gender.

This book is a passionate attempt in this regard. In my analysis of Black women's ways of being and becoming through everyday talk about and practices of hair care, I have also sought to illuminate my own becomings as a ethnographer with a deep regard for situated language use and cultural practices in African America. Namely, by learning to see African American women in the process of becoming vis-à-vis language use and hair-care practice, I also learned to see and speak as a linguistic anthropologist about the rich cultural significance of Black women's hair care and conversation.

As the prior chapters demonstrate, women "do" the work of being professional, spiritual, culturally conscious, and even political as they talk about and practice hair care. Their varied stances about the many meanings associated with hair and of themselves as "hair doctors" and divinely "gifted" stylists are vivid testaments to their complex identity work. Further, Black women's conversations in hair salons, Bible study meetings, comedy clubs, online discussions, and hair educational seminars illuminate what is precisely at stake—for them and their communities of practice—in hair-care decisions and engagements. Moreover, they teach us, in their own words and situated contexts, when, exactly, hair is hair and, alternatively, when hair is not just hair. Using ethnography and discourse analysis as a critical lens, I have learned that these perspectives are neither random nor mundane. Rather, as this journey across multiple hair contexts and conversations has made clear, these seemingly contradictory stances hint at the complexities of hair and language in shaping Black women's being and becoming throughout their lives.

Appendix

TRANSCRIPTION CONVENTIONS

[	A left-hand bracket indicates the onset of overlapping, simultaneous utterances.
(0.1)	This indicates the length of a pause within or between utterances, timed in tenths of a second.
(( ))	Double parentheses enclose nonverbal and other descriptive information.
( )	Single parentheses enclose words that are not clearly audible (i.e., best guesses).
<u>**Underline**</u>	Underlining indicates stress on a syllable or word(s).
Italics	Italics indicate talk that is in some way animated or performed (i.e. sarcasm).
Cap First Letter	Words or phrases with capitalized first letter(s) indicate talk that is carefully articulated or talk that is punctuated by a brief pause.
CAPS	Upper case indicates louder or shouted talk.
:	A colon indicates a lengthening of a sound; the more colons, the longer the sound.
°	This symbol is placed before and after words or phrases that are delivered in a soft volume.
-	Down arrow marks words or phrases delivered with a downward intonational contour.
> <	"Greater than" and "less than" symbols enclose words (and/or talk) that are compressed or rushed.
< >	"Less than" and "greater than" symbols enclose words (and/or talk) that are markedly slowed or drawn out.

<	The "less than" symbol by itself indicates that the immediately following talk is "jump-started" (i.e., sounds like it starts with a rush).
-, —	A single or double hyphens also indicate talk that is either "jump-started" (i.e., sounds like it starts with a rush) or talk that ends abruptly.
Hh(hh)	The letter *h* marks hearable aspiration; the more h's, the more aspiration. Aspiration may represent breathing, laughter, and so on. If it occurs inside the boundaries of a word, it may be enclosed in parentheses in order to set it apart from the sounds of the word.
Heh	This marks laughter.
(try 1)/(try 2)	This arrangement of words/phrases encircled by parentheses and separated by a single oblique or slash represents two alternate hearings.

NOTES

INTRODUCTION

1. All names in this book are pseudonyms.

CHAPTER 2

1. It is worth noting that to his credit, Khalif demonstrated how to "silken" or press pre-relaxed hair with an exceptionally hot metal comb without causing hair breakage, a burnt hair smell, or hair loss. I know this for a fact because I was among the more than twenty attendees who accepted his invitation to touch and smell his model's hair after he had "silkened" it. It was the first time I had ever witnessed a stylist press a client's hair after chemically straightening it without causing immediate hair damage. For me and many others, this virtuoso performance did much to augment Khalif's self-positioning as an "expert" on par with a highly trained medical doctor.

BIBLIOGRAPHY

Abrahams, Roger D. 1964. *Deep Down in the Jungle: Negro Narrative Folklore from the Streets of Philadelphia.* Chicago: Aldine.

———. 1970. *Positively Black.* Englewood Cliffs, NJ: Prentice-Hall.

Abu-Lughod, Lila. 1988. Fieldwork of a Dutiful Daughter. In *Arab Women in the Field.* S. Altorki and C. Fawzi El-Solh, eds. Pp. 139–161. Syracuse: Syracuse University Press.

———. 1991. Writing Against Culture. In *Recapturing Anthropology.* R. Fox, ed. Pp. 137–162. Santa Fe: School of American Research Press.

Adorno, Rolena. 1994. The Indigenous Ethnographer: The "indio ladino" as Historian and Cultural Mediation. In *Implicit Understandings: Observing, Reporting, and Reflecting on the Encounters Between Europeans and Other Peoples in the Early Modern Era.* S. B. Schwartz, ed. Pp. 378–402. Cambridge: Cambridge University Press.

Aguilar, John. 1981. Insider Research: An Ethnography of a Debate. In *Anthropologists at Home in North America.* D. Messerschmidt, ed. Pp. 15–26. Cambridge: Cambridge University Press.

Altorki, Soraya, and Camillia Fawzi El-Solh, eds. 1988. *Arab Women in the Field: Studying Your Own Society.* Syracuse: Syracuse University Press.

Alvarez, Celia. 1996. The Multiple and Transformatory Identities of Puerto Rican Women in the U.S.: Restructuring the Discourse on National Identity. In *Unrelated Kin: Race and Gender in Women's Personal Narratives.* G. Etter-Lewis and M. Foster, eds. Pp. 87–102. London: Routledge.

Amory, Deborah. 1997. African Studies as American Institution. In *Anthropological Locations: Boundaries and Grounds of a Field Science.* A. Gupta and J. Ferguson, eds. Pp. 102–116. Berkeley: University of California Press.

Anderson, Benedict. 1991. *Imagined Communities.* London: Verso.

Anderson, Elijah. 2003 [1976]. *A Place on the Corner*. Chicago: University of Chicago Press.

Anthias, Floya and Nira Yuval-Davis. 1992. *Racialized Boundaries: Race, Nation, Gender, Colour and Class and the Anti-racist Struggle*. London: Routledge.

Anzaldúa, Gloria. 1987. *Borderlands/La Frontera: The New Mestiza*. San Francisco: Aunt Lute.

———. 1990. *Making Face, Making Soul/Haciendo Caras: Creative and Critical Perspectives by Women of Color*. San Francisco: Aunt Lute.

Appadurai, Arjun. 1988. Putting Hierarchy in Its Place. *Cultural Anthropology* 3:36–49.

———. 1990. Disjuncture and Difference in Global Cultural Economy. *Public Culture* 2:1–24.

———. 1991. Global Ethnoscapes: Notes and Queries for a Transnational Anthropology. In *ReCapturing Anthropology*. R. Fox, ed. Pp. 191–210. Santa Fe: School of American Research Press.

Apte, Mahadev L. 1985. *Humor and Laughter: An Anthropological Approach*. Ithaca/ London: Cornell University Press.

Austin, John L. 1962. *How to Do Things with Words*. Cambridge, MA: Harvard University Press.

Avins, Mimi. 2002. Surely, She Jests. *Los Angeles Times* (March 11): E1, E4.

Bakhtin, Mikhail. 1968. *Rabelais and His World*. H. Iswolsky, trans. Cambridge, MA: MIT Press.

———. 1981. Discourse in the Novel. In *The Dialogical Imagination: Four Essays by M. Bakhtin*. M. Holquist, ed. C. Emerson and M. Holquist, trans. Pp. 259–422. Austin: University of Texas Press.

Banks, Ingrid. 2000. *Hair Matters: Beauty, Power, and Black Women's Consciousness*. New York: New York University Press.

Baquedano-López, Patricia. 1997. Creating Social Identity Through Doctrina Narratives. *Issues in Applied Linguistics* 8(1): 27–45.

———. 1998. Language, Identity, and Practice: A Study of Doctrina Classrooms at a Los Angeles Parish. Los Angeles: University of California. Unpublished dissertation.

———. 2001. Creating Social Identities Through Doctrina Narratives. In *Linguistic Anthropology: A Reader*. A. Duranti, ed. Pp. 343–358. Oxford: Blackwell.

Barreca, Regine. 1991. *"They Used to Call Me Snow White . . . But I Drifted": Women's Strategic Use of Humor*. New York: Penguin.

Basso, Keith H. 1970. To Give Up on Words: Silence in Western Apache Culture. *Southwestern Journal of Anthropology* 26(3): 213–230.

———. 1979. *Portraits of the "Whiteman": Linguistic Play and Cultural Symbols Among the Western Apache*. Cambridge: Cambridge University Press.

———. 1984. Stalking with Stories: Names, Places, and Moral Narratives Among the Western Apache. In *Text, Play and Story: The Construction of Self and Society*. Proceedings of the American Ethnological Society. E. M. Bruner, ed. Pp. 19–55. Washington, DC: American Ethnological Society.

———. 1996. *Wisdom Sits in Places: Landscape and Language Among the Western Apache*. Albuquerque: University of New Mexico Press.

Battle-Walters, Kimberly. 2004. *Sheila's Shop: Working-class African American Women Talk About Life, Love, Race, and Hair*. New York: Rowman & Littlefield.

Baugh, John. 1983. The Scholar and the Street: Collecting the Data. In *Black Street Speech: Its History, Structure, and Survival*. Pp. 36–53. Austin: University of Texas Press.

Behar, Ruth. 1993. *Crossing the Border with Esperanza's Story*. Boston: Beacon Press.

————. 1995. Writing in My Father's Name: A Diary of Translated Woman's First Year. In *Women Writing Culture*. R. Behar and D. A. Gordon, eds. Pp. 65–82. Berkeley: University of California Press.

————. 1996. *The Vulnerable Observer: Anthropology That Breaks Your Heart.* Boston: Beacon Press.

Bergant, Kathleen Ann. 1993. *Communication Skills for Cosmetologists.* Albany, NY: Milady Publishing.

Berger, Phil. 2000. And Since Then: Standup Comedy, 1975–1985. In *The Last Laugh: The World of Standup Comics.* Pp. 379–396. New York: Cooper Square Press.

Bernard, H. Russell. 1994. *Research Methods in Anthropology: Qualitative and Quantitative Approaches.* 2d ed. London: Sage.

Best of Def Comedy Jam: Set 1. 2002. Ventura Distribution. (April 23): 600 minutes.

Biber, Douglas. 1995. *Dimensions of Register Variation: A Cross-linguistic Comparison.* New York: Cambridge University Press.

Biber, Douglas, and Edward Finegan. 1994. Introduction: Situating Registers in Sociolinguistics. In *Sociolinguistic Perspectives on Register*. D. Biber and E. Finegan, eds. Pp. 3–12. New York: Oxford University Press.

Bonner, Lonnice Brittenum. 1991. *Good Hair: For Colored Girls Who've Considered Weaves When the Chemicals Became Too Rough.* New York: Crown Publishers.

————. 1996. *Plaited Glory: For Colored Girls Who've Considered Braids, Locks, and Twists.* New York: Crown.

————. 1997a. *The Kitchen Beautician.* New York: Crown.

————. 1997b. *Outlaw Beauty: A Sister to Sister Confidential.* New York: Crown.

Borker, Ruth and Daniel Maltz. 1989. Anthropological Perspectives on Gender and Language. In *Gender and Anthropology: Critical Reviews for Research and Teaching.* S. Morgen, ed. Pp. 411–437. Washington, DC: American Anthropological Association.

Bourdieu, Pierre. 1977. *Outline of a Theory of Practice.* Cambridge: Cambridge University Press.

————. 1991. *Language and Symbolic Power.* Cambridge, MA: Harvard University Press.

Boyd, Julia. 1993. *In the Company of My Sisters: Black Women and Self-esteem.* New York: Dutton.

Boyer, Horace Clarence. 1973. An Analysis of Black Church Music with Examples Drawn from Services in Rochester. New York: University of Rochester. Unpublished dissertation.

Briggs, Charles. 1994. *Learning How to Ask: A Sociolinguistic Appraisal of the Role of the Interview in Social Science Research.* Cambridge: Cambridge University Press.

————. 1996. *Disorderly Discourse: Narrative, Conflict, and Inequality.* Oxford: Oxford University Press.

Briggs, Jean. 1970. *Never in Anger: Portrait of an Eskimo Family.* Cambridge, MA: Harvard University Press.

Brown, Valerie. 1983. Mental Health Gatekeeping in Community Development: An Open or Shut Case. *Community Development Journal* 18(3): 214–221.

Bruner, Jerome. 1991. The Narrative Construction of Reality. *Critical Inquiry* 18: 1–21.

————. 1996. *The Culture of Education.* Cambridge, MA: Harvard University Press.

————. 1999a. Bad Examples: Transgression and Progress in Language and Gender Studies. In *Reinventing Identities: The Gendered Self in Discourse.* M. Bucholtz, A. C. Liang, and L. A. Sutton, eds. Oxford: Oxford University Press.

————. 1999b. You da Man: Narrating the Racial Other in the Production of White Masculinity. *Journal of Sociolinguistics* 3(4): 443–460.

————. 2000. The Politics of Transcription. *Journal of Pragmatics* 32: 1439–1465.

————. 2004. Theorizing Identity in Language and Sexuality Research. *Language in Society* 33(4): 501–547.

Bundles, A'Lelia. 2001. *On Her Own Ground: The Life and Times of Madam C. J. Walker.* New York: Pocket Books.

Burkhalter, Byron. 1999. Reading Race Online: Discovering Racial Identity in Usenet Discussions. In *Communities in Cyberspace.* M. A. Smith and P. Kollock, eds. Pp. 60–75. London: Routledge.

Butler Judith. 1990. *Gender Trouble: Feminism and the Subversion of Identity.* New York: Routledge.

Byrd, Ayana, and Lori Tharps. 2001. *Hair Story: Untangling the Roots of Black Hair in America.* New York: St. Martin's Press.

Camaroff, Jean. 1985. *Body of Power, Spirit of Resistance: The Culture and History of a South African People.* Chicago: University of Chicago Press.

Cameron, Deborah, ed. 1990. *The Feminist Critique of Language: A Reader.* 2d ed. London: Routledge.

————. 1992. "Naming of Parts": Gender, Culture and Terms for the Penis Among American College Students. *American Speech* 67(3): 364–379.

Carby, Hazel. 1996. White Women Listen! Black Women and the Boundaries of Sisterhood. In *Black British Cultural Studies: A Reader.* H. Baker, M. Diawara, and R. Lindeborg, eds. Pp. 163–172. Chicago: University of Chicago Press.

Casey, Edward. 1996. How to Get from Space to Place in a Fairly Short Stretch of Time: Phenomenological Prolegomena. In *Senses of Place.* S. Feld and K. Basso, eds. Pp. 13–52. Sante Fe: School of American Research Press.

Caulfield, Mina Davis. 1979. Participant Observation or Partisan Participation. In *The Politics of Anthropology: From Colonialism and Sexism Toward a View from Below.* G. Huizer and B. Mannheim, eds. Pp. 309–318. The Hague: Mouton.

Chatterjee, Partha. 1993. *The Nation and Its Fragments: Colonial and Postcolonial Histories.* Princeton, NJ: Princeton University Press.

Chin, Elizabeth. 2001. *Purchasing Power: Black Kids and American Consumer Culture.* Minneapolis: University of Minnesota Press.

Chow, Rey. 1993. *Writing Diaspora: Tactics of Intervention in Contemporary Cultural Studies.* Bloomington: Indiana University Press.

Christian, Barbara. 1985. Creating a Universal Literature: Afro-American Women Writers. In *Black Feminist Criticism: Perspectives on Black Women Writers.* Pp. 159–163. New York: Pergamon Press.

————. 1990. The Race for Theory. In *The Nature and Context of Minority Discourse.* R. J. Abdul and D. Lloyd, eds. Pp. 225–237. New York: Oxford University Press.

Cicourel, Aaron 1995. Medical Speech Events as Resources for Inferring Differences in Expert-Novice Diagnostic Reasoning. In *Aspects of Oral Communication.* U. M. Quasthoff, ed. Pp. 364–387. New York: Walter de Gruyter.

Clemetson, Lynette. 1998. Caught in the Cross-Fire: A Young Star Teacher Finds Herself in a Losing Battle with Parents. *Newsweek* (December 14): 38–39.

Clifford, James. 1986. Introduction: Partial Truths. In *Writing Culture: The Poetics and Politics of Ethnography.* J. Clifford and G. Marcus, eds. Pp. 1–26. Berkeley: University of California Press.

————. 1988. *The Predicament of Culture.* Cambridge, MA: Harvard University Press.

————. 1992. Traveling Cultures. In *Cultural Studies.* L. Grossberg, C. Nelson, and P. Treichler, eds. Pp. 96–112. New York: Routledge.

————. 1997a. Spatial Practices: Fieldwork, Travel and the Disciplining of Anthropology.

In *Anthropological Locations: Boundaries and Grounds of a Field Science*. A. Gupta and J. Ferguson, eds. Pp. 185–222. Los Angeles: University of California Press.

———. 1997b. Diasporas. In *Routes: Travel and Translation in the Late Twentieth Century*. Pp. 244–277. Cambridge: Harvard University Press.

Coates, Jennifer, and Deborah Cameron, eds. 1988. *Women in Their Speech Communities*. London: Longman.

Cohen, Anthony P. 1992. Post-fieldwork Fieldwork. *Journal of Anthropological Research* 48(4): 339–354.

Coleman, Larry G. 1984. Black Comic Performance in the African Diaspora: A Comparison of the Comedy of Richard Pryor and Paul Keens-Douglas. *Journal of Black Studies* 15(1): 67–78.

Collins, Patricia Hill. 1990. *Black Feminist Thought: Knowledge, Consciousness, and the Politics of Empowerment*. London: Routledge.

Connell, Robert W. 1995. *Masculinities*. Berkeley: University of California Press.

Crawford, Mary. 1989. Humor in Conversational Contexts: Beyond Biases in the Study of Gender and Humor. In *Representations: Social Constructions of Gender*. R. K. Unger, ed. Pp. 155–166. Amityville, NY: Baywood Press.

———. 1995. *Talking Difference: On Gender and Language*. London: Sage.

Crenshaw, Kimberlé. 1992. Whose Story Is It, Anyway? Feminist and Anti-racist Appropriations of Anita Hill. In *Race-ing Justice, En-gendering Power: Essays on Anita Hill, Clarence Thomas and the Construction of Social Reality*. T. Morrison, ed. Pp. 402–440. New York: Pantheon.

Cunningham, Michael, and Craig Marberry. 2000. *Crowns: Portraits of Black Women in Church Hats*. New York: Doubleday.

D'Amico-Samuels, Deborah. 1997. Undoing Fieldwork: Personal, Political, Theoretical, and Methodological Implications. In *Decolonizing Anthropology: Moving Further Toward an Anthropology for Liberation*. 2d ed. F. Harrison, ed. Pp. 68–87. Washington, DC: American Anthropological Association.

Dance, Daryl Cumber. 1998. *Honey, Hush!: An Anthology of African American Women's Humor*. New York: W.W. Norton.

Daniel, Vattal E. 1971. Ritual and Stratification in Chicago Negro Churches. In *The Black Church in America*. H. M. Nelsen, R. L. Yokley, A. K. Nelsen, eds. Pp. 119–130. New York: Basic Books.

Davis, F. James. 1991. *Who Is Black? One Nation's Definition*. University Park: Pennsylvania State University Press.

Def Comedy Jam: Best of Martin Lawrence. 2002. Ventura Distribution. (December 17): 120 minutes.

DeVita, Philip R., ed. 1990. *The Humbled Anthropologist: Tales from the Pacific*. Belmont, CA: Wadsworth.

———. 1992. *The Naked Anthropologist: Tales from Around the World*. Belmont, CA: Wadsworth.

Dresner, Zita Z. 1991. Whoopi Goldberg and Lily Tomlin: Black and White Women's Humor. In *Women's Comic Visions*. J. Sochen, ed. Pp. 179–192. Detroit: Wayne State University Press.

Drew, Paul. 1992. Contested Evidence in Courtroom Cross-examination: The Case of a Trial for Rape. In *Talk at Work: Interaction in Institutional Settings*. P. Drew and J. Heritage, eds. Pp. 470–520. Cambridge: Cambridge University Press.

Drew, Paul, and John Heritage. 1992. Analyzing Talk at Work: An Introduction. In *Talk at Work: Interaction in Institutional Settings*. P. Drew and J. Heritage, eds. Pp. 3–65. Cambridge: Cambridge University Press.

Dua, Veena. 1979. A Woman's Encounter with Arya Samaj and Untouchables. In *The Fieldworker and the Field*. M. Srinivas, A. M. Shaw, and E. A. Ramaswamy, eds. Pp. 115–126. Delhi: Oxford University Press.

Due, Tananarive. 2000. *The Black Rose*. New York: Ballantine.

Dundes, Alan, ed. 1973. *Mother Wit from the Laughing Barrel: Readings in the Interpretation of Afro-American Folklore*. Englewood Cliffs, NJ: Prentice-Hall.

Duranti, Alessandro. 1993. Intentionality and Truth: An Ethnographic Critique. *Cultural Anthropology* 8(2): 214–245.

———. 1994. *From Grammar to Politics: Linguistic Anthropology in a Western Samoan Village*. Los Angeles: University of California Press.

———. 1997. *Linguistic Anthropology*. Cambridge: Cambridge University Press.

———. 1999. Intentionality. In Language Matters in Anthropology: A Lexicon. *Journal of Linguistic Anthropology* 9(1–2): 134–136.

Duranti, Alessandro, and Donald Brenneis. 1986. The Audience as Co-author: An Introduction. Special Issue, "The Audience as Co-author." *Text* 6(3): 239–247.

Dwyer, Kevin. 1982. *Moroccan Dialogues: Anthropology in Question*. Prospect Heights, IL: Waveland Press.

Eayrs, Michele. 1993. Time, Trust, and Hazard: Hairdressers' Symbolic Roles. *Symbolic Interaction* 16(1): 19–37.

Ebong, Ima, ed. 2001. *Black Hair: Art, Style, and Culture*. New York: Universe.

Eckert, Penelope. 1996. Vowels and Nailpolish: The Emergence of Linguistic Style in the Preadolescent Heterosexual Marketplace. In *Gender and Belief Systems: Proceedings of the Fourth Berkeley Women and Language Conference*. N. Warner, J. Ahlers, L. Bilmes, M. Oliver, S. Wertheim, and M. Chen, eds. Pp. 182–190. Berkeley: Berkeley Women and Language Group.

Eckert, Penelope, and Sally McConnell-Ginet. 1992a. Think Practically and Look Locally: Language and Gender as Community-based Practice. *Annual Review of Anthropology* 21: 461–488.

———. 1992b. Communities of Practice: Where Language, Gender and Power All Live. In *Locating Power: Proceedings of the Second Berkeley Women and Language Conference*. K. Hall, M. Bucholtz and B. Moonwomon eds. Pp. 89–99. Berkeley: Berkeley Women and Language Group, 89–99.

———. 1995. Constructing Meaning, Constructing Selves. In *Gender Articulated: Language and the Socially-constructed Self*. K. Hall and M. Bucholtz, eds. Pp. 469–507. New York: Routledge.

———. 2003. *Language and Gender*. New York: Cambridge University Press.

Ervin-Tripp, Susan, and Martin D. Lampert. 1992. Gender Differences in the Construction of Humorous Talk. In *Locating Power: Proceedings of the Second Berkeley Women and Language Conference*. K. Hall, M. Bucholtz, and B. Moonwomon, eds. Pp. 105–117. Berkeley: Berkeley Women and Language Group.

Etter-Lewis, Gwen. 1991. Black Women's Life Stories: Reclaiming Self in Narrative Texts. In *Women's Words: The Feminist Practice of Oral History*. S. B. Gluck and D. Patai. Pp. 43–58. New York: Routledge.

Fahim, Hussein. 1979. Field Research in a Nubian Village: The Experience of an Egyptian Anthropologist. In *Long-term Field Research in Social Anthropology*. G. Foster et al., eds. Pp. 255–273. New York: Academic Press.

Fahim, Hussein, and Katherine Helmer. 1980. Indigenous Anthropology in Non-Western Countries: A Further Elaboration. *Current Anthropology* 21(5): 644–662.

Favor, J. Martin. 1999. *Authentic Blackness: The Folk in the New Negro Renaissance*. Durham, NC: Duke University Press.

Feagin, Joe R., and Melvin P. Sikes. 1994. *Living with Racism: The Black Middle-class Experience.* Boston: Beacon Press.

Felder, Cain Hope, ed. 1991. *Stony the Road We Trod: African American Biblical Interpretations.* Minneapolis: Fortress Press.

Fenstermaker, Sarah, and Candace West. 2002. *Doing Gender, Doing Difference: Social Inequality, Power, and Resistance.* London: Routledge.

Finnegan, Ruth. 1969. How to Do Things with Words: Performative Utterances Among the Limba of Sierra Leone. *Man* 4:537–552.

Folb, Edith. 1980. *Runnin' Down Some Lines: The Language and Culture of Black Teenagers.* Cambridge, MA: Harvard University Press.

Fordham, Signithia. 1993. "Those Loud Black Girls": (Black) Women, Silence and Gender "Passing" in the Academy. *Anthropology and Education Quarterly* 24(1): 3–32.

Foster, Michèle. 1995. Are You with Me? Power and Solidarity in the Discourse of African American Women. In *Gender Articulated: Language and the Socially Constructed Self.* K. Hall and M. Bucholtz, eds. Pp. 329–350. London: Routledge.

———. 1996. Like Us But Not One of Us: Reflections on a Life History Study of African American Teachers. In *Unrelated Kin: Race and Gender in Women's Personal Narratives.* G. Etter-Lewis and M. Foster, eds. Pp. 215–224. London: Routledge.

Foucault, Michel. 1980. *Power/Knowledge: Selected Interviews and Other Writings, 1972–77.* C. Gordon, ed., C. Gordon et al., trans. New York: Pantheon.

Freedman, Samuel G. 1993. *Upon This Rock: The Miracles of the Black Church.* New York: HarperPerennial.

Freimuth, Vicki, Sandra C. Quinn, Stephen B. Thomas, Galen Cole, Eric Zook, and Ted Duncan. 2001. African Americans' Views on Research and the Tuskegee Syphilis Study. *Social Science and Medicine* 52(5): 797–808.

Furman, Frida Kerner. 1997. *Facing the Mirror: Older Women and Beauty Shop Culture.* New York: Routledge.

Gal, Susan. 1991. Between Speech and Silence: The Problematics of Research on Language and Gender. *Pragmatics* 3(1): 1–38.

———. 1995 [1992]. Language, Gender and Power: An Anthropological Review. In *Gender Articulated: Language and the Socially Constructed Self.* K. Hall and M. Bucholtz, eds. Pp. 169–182. London: Routledge.

Garber, Marjorie, Rebecca L. Walkowitz, and Paul B. Franklin. 1996. *Fieldwork: Sites in Literary and Cultural Studies.* London: Routledge.

Garfinkel, Harold. 1967. *Studies in Ethnomethodology.* Englewood Cliffs, NJ: Prentice-Hill.

Garrett, Paul B., and Patricia Baquedano-López. 2002. Language Socialization: Reproduction and Continuity, Transformation and Change. *Annual Review of Anthropology* 31:339–361.

Gaskins, Bill. 1997. *Good and Bad Hair.* Piscataway, NJ: Rutgers University Press.

Gates, Henry Louis, Jr. 1989. *The Signifying Monkey: A Theory of African-American Literary Criticism.* New York: Oxford University Press.

———. 1994. In the Kitchen. *New Yorker* (April 18): 82–86.

Geertz, Clifford. 1971. Thick Description: Toward an Interpretive Theory of Culture. In *The Interpretation of Culture.* C. Geertz, ed. Pp. 3–30. New York: Basic Books.

———. 1983. Blurred Genres: The Refiguration of Social Thought. In *Local Knowledge: Further Essays in Interpretive Anthropology.* Pp. 19–35. New York: Basic Books.

———. 1988. *Works and Lives: The Anthropologist as Author.* Palo Alto, CA: Stanford University Press.

Getz, Greg, and Hanne Klein. 1980. *The Frosting of the American Woman: Hairdressing and the Phenomenology of Beauty*. Dallas: Southern Methodist University Press.

Gibson, Aliona. 1995. *Nappy: Growing Up Black and Female in America*. New York: Harlem River Press.

Giddings, Paula. 1994. *When and Where I Enter: The Impact of Black Women on Race and Sex in America*. New York: William Morrow.

Gilbert, Derrick I.M. 1994. *Shaping Identity at Cooke's Barbershop*. Los Angeles: University of California. Unpublished master's thesis.

Gilkes, Cheryl Townsend. 2001. *If It Wasn't for the Women . . . : Black Women's Experiences and Womanist Culture in Church and Community*. Mary Knoll, NY: Orbis.

Gimlin, Debra. 1996. Pamela's Place: Power and Negotiation in the Hair Salon. *Gender and Society* 10(5): 505–526.

Givens, Adele. 1996. *HBO ½ Comedy Special*. Home Box Entertainment.

Goffman, Erving. 1959. *The Presentation of Self in Everyday Life*. New York: Doubleday.

———. 1967. *Interaction Ritual*. New York: Pantheon.

———. 1974. *Frame Analysis: An Essay on the Organization of Experience*. New York: Harper & Row.

———. 1981. *Forms of Talk*. Philadelphia: University of Pennsylvania Press.

Goldberg, Whoopi. 1991. *Whoopi Goldberg: Live on Broadway*. Vestron Home Video (August 29): 75 minutes.

Goldstein, Tara. 1995. "Nobody Is Talking Bad": Creating Community and Claiming Power on the Production Lines. In *Gender Articulated: Language and the Socially Constructed Self*. K. Hall and M. Bucholtz, eds. Pp. 375–400. London: Routledge.

Goodwin, Charles, and Alessandro Duranti. 1992. Rethinking Context: An Introduction. In *Rethinking Context: Language as an Interactive Phenomenon*. A. Duranti and C. Goodwin, eds. Pp. 1–42. Cambridge: Cambridge University Press.

Goodwin, Marjorie. 1980. He-Said-She-Said: Formal Cultural Procedures for the Construction of a Gossip Dispute Activity. *American Ethnologist* 7:674–695.

———. 1985. The Serious Side of Jump Rope: Conversational Practices and Social Organization in the Frame of Play. *Journal of American Folklore* 98:315–330.

———. 1988. Cooperation and Competition Across Girls' Play Activities. In *Language and Gender: A Reader*. J. Coates, ed. Pp. 121–146. Oxford: Blackwell.

———. 1990. *He-Said-She-Said: Talk As Social Organization Among Black Children*. Indianapolis: Indiana University Press.

———. 1992. Orchestrating Participation in Events: Powerful Talk Among African American Girls. In *Locating Power: Proceedings of the Second Berkeley Women and Language Conference*. Kira Hall, ed. Pp. 182–196. Berkeley: Berkeley Women and Language Group.

Gordon, Edmund T. 1998. *Disparate Diasporas: Identity and Politics in an African Nicaraguan Community*. Austin: University of Texas Press.

Grice, H. P. 1957. Meaning. *Philosophical Review* 67:53–59.

Grier, William H., and Price M. Cobbs. 1968. *Black Rage*. New York: Basic Books.

Gullahorn-Holecek, Barbara. 1983. *Papua New Guinea: Anthropology on Trial*. Nova Series. Alexandria, VA: Public Broadcasting System.

Gumperz, John J., and Jenny Cook-Gumperz. 1982. Introduction: Language and Communication of Social Identity. In *Language and Social Identity*. J. J. Gumperz and J. Cook-Gumperz, eds. Pp. 1–21. New York: Cambridge.

Gunnarson, Britt-Louise, Per Linell, and Bengt Nordberg. 1997. *The Construction of Professional Discourse*. London: Longman.

BIBLIOGRAPHY 161

Gupta, Akhil, and James Ferguson. 1992. Beyond "Culture": Space, Identity and the Politics of Difference. *Cultural Anthropology* 7:6–23.

———. 1997. *Anthropological Locations: Boundaries and Grounds of a Field Science.* Los Angeles: University of California Press.

Gwaltney, John Langston. 1981. Common Sense and Science: Urban Core Black Observations. In *Anthropologists at Home in North America: Methods and Issues in the Study of One's Own Society.* D. Messerschmidt, ed. Pp. 46–61. Cambridge: Cambridge University Press.

———. 1993. *Drylongso: A Self-portrait of Black America.* New York: Vintage.

Hale, Sondra. 1991. Feminist Method, Process, and Self-criticism: Interviewing Sudanese Women. In *Women's Words: The Feminist Practice of Oral History.* S.B. Gluck and D. Patai, eds. Pp. 121–136. New York: Routledge.

Hall, Kira. 1996. Cyberfeminism. In *Computer-mediated Communication: Linguistic, Social and Cross-cultural Perspectives.* S. Herring, ed. Pp. 147–170. Philadelphia: John Benjamins.

———. 2000. Performativity. *Journal of Linguistic Anthropology* 9(1–2): 184–187.

Hall, Kira, and Mary Bucholtz, eds. 1995. *Gender Articulated: Language and the Socially Constructed Self.* New York: Routledge.

Handler, Stacey. 2000. *The Body Burden: Living in the Shadow of Barbie.* Cocoa Beach, FL: Blue Note.

Haniff, Nesha Z. 1985. Towards a Native Anthropology. *Anthropology and Humanism Quarterly* 10(4): 106–113.

Hanks, William F. 1990. *Referential Practice: Language and Lived Space Among the Maya.* Chicago: University of Chicago Press.

———. 2000. *Intertexts: Writings on Language, Utterance, and Context.* New York: Rowman & Littlefield.

Haraway, Donna. 1985. A Manifesto for Cyborgs: Science, Technology, and Socialist Feminism in the 1980s. *Socialist Review* 80:65–107.

———. 1988. Situated Knowledges: The Science Question in Feminism and the Privilege of Partial Perspective. *Feminist Studies* 14(4): 575–599.

Harper, Phillip Brian. 1996. *Are We Not Men? Masculine Anxiety and the Problem of African-American Identity.* Oxford: Oxford University Press.

Harris, Juliette, and Pamela Johnson, eds. 2001. *Tenderheaded: A Comb-bending Collection of Hair Stories.* New York: Pocket Books.

Harris, Robin. 1990. *BeBe's Kids.* Polygram Records.

Harrison, Faye V. 1997a. Anthropology as an Agent of Transformation: Introductory Comments and Queries. In *Decolonizing Anthropology: Moving Further Toward an Anthropology of Liberation.* Pp. 1–14. Washington, DC: American Anthropological Association.

———. 1997b. Ethnography as Politics. In *Decolonizing Anthropology: Moving Further Toward an Anthropology of Liberation.* Pp. 88–110. Washington, DC: American Anthropological Association.

Harrison, Ira E., and Faye V. Harrison, eds. 1999. *African American Pioneers in Anthropology.* Chicago: University of Illinois Press.

Hay, Jennifer. 2000. Functions of Humor in the Conversations of Men and Women. *Journal of Pragmatics* 32:709–742.

Henley, Nancy. 1995. Ethnicity and Gender Issues in Language. In *Bringing Cultural Diversity to Feminist Psychology: Theory, Research, and Practice.* H. Landrine, ed. Pp. 361–396. Washington, DC: American Psychological Association.

Hennigh, Lawrence. 1981. The Anthropologist as Key Informant: Inside a Rural Oregon

Town. In *Anthropologists at Home in North America: Methods and Issues in the Study of One's Own Society.* D. Messerschmidt, ed. Pp. 121–132. Cambridge: Cambridge University Press.

Herring, Susan C. 1993. Gender and Democracy in Computer-mediated Communication. *Electronic Journal of Communication* 3(2). http://ella.slis.indiana.edu/~herring/ejc.txt

———. 1994. Politeness in Computer Culture: Why Women Thank and Men Flame. In *Cultural Performances: Proceedings of the Third Berkeley Women and Language Conference.* M. Bucholtz, A.C. Liang, L. Sutton, and C. Hines, eds. Pp. 278–294. Berkeley, CA: Berkeley Women and Language Group.

———, ed. 1996. *Computer-mediated Communication: Linguistic, Social and Cross-cultural Perspectives.* Philadelphia: John Benjamins.

Herring, Susan C., Deborah Johnson, and Tamra DiBenedetto. 1995. "This discussion is going too far!": Male Resistance to Female Participation on the Internet. In *Gender Articulated: Language and the Socially Constructed Self.* K. Hall and M. Bucholtz, eds. Pp. 67–96. New York: Routledge.

Herron, Carolivia. 1997. *Nappy Hair.* New York: Alfred A. Knopf.

Holmes, Janet 1995. *Women, Men and Politeness.* London: Longman.

hooks, bell. 1981. *Ain't I a Woman: Black Women and Feminism.* Boston: South End Press.

———. 1989. *Talking Back: Thinking Feminist, Thinking Black.* Boston: South End Press.

———. 1992. *Race and Representation.* Boston: South End Press.

———. 1994. *Outlaw Culture: Resisting Representations.* New York: Routledge.

———. 1996. *Bone Black: Memories of Girlhood.* New York: Henry Holt.

Hoyt, Thomas Jr. 1991. Interpreting Biblical Scholarship for the Black Church Tradition. In *Stony the Road We Trod: African American Biblical Interpretations.* C. H. Felder, ed. Pp. 17–39. Minneapolis: Fortress Press.

Hudson, Barbara Hill. 2001. African American Female Speech Communities: Varieties of Talk: Westport, CT: Bergin & Garvey.

Hunkele, Michele, and Karen Cornwell. 1997. The Cyberspace Curtain: Hidden Gender Issues. In *Voices in the Street: Explorations in Gender, Media and Public Space.* S. Drucker and G. Gumpert, eds. Pp. 281–293. Cresskill, NJ: Hampton Press.

Hurston, Zora Neale. 1979. *I Love Myself When I'm Laughing.* A. Walker, ed. New York: Feminist Press.

———. 1990 [1935]. *Mules and Men.* New York: HarperCollins.

Hurtado, Aída. 1989. Relating to Privilege: Seduction and Rejection in the Subordination of White Women and Women of Color. *Signs* 14:833–855.

Hymes, Dell. 1972. On Communicative Competence. In *Sociolinguistics.* J.B. Pride and J. Holmes, eds. Pp. 269–285. Harmondsworth, Middlesex: Penguin.

———, ed. 1999 [1972]. *Reinventing Anthropology.* Ann Arbor: University of Michigan Press.

Ilyin, Natalia. 2000. *Blonde Like Me: The Roots of the Blonde Myth in Our Culture.* New York: Touchstone.

Ivanov, Vyacheslav. 2000. Heteroglossia. *Journal of Linguistic Anthropology* 9(1–2): 100–102.

Jackson, John L. 2001. *Harlemworld: Doing Race and Class in Contemporary Black America.* Chicago: Chicago University Press.

Jackson, Michael. 1989. *Paths Towards a Clearing: Radical Empiricism and Ethnographic Inquiry.* Bloomington: Indiana University Press.

Jacobs-Huey, Lanita. 1996a. Negotiating Price in an African American Beauty Salon. *Issues in Applied Linguistics* 7(1): 45–59.

―――. 1996b. Negotiating Social Identity in an African American Beauty Salon. In *Gender and Belief Systems: Proceedings of the Fourth Berkeley Women in Language Conference*. N. Warner et al., eds. Pp. 331–343. Berkeley: Berkeley Women and Language Group.

―――. 1998. We Are Just Like Doctors, We Heal Sick Hair: Cultural and Professional Discourses of Hair and Identity in a Black Hair Care Seminar. In *SALSA V: Proceedings of the 5th Annual Symposium About Language and Society-Austin, Texas Linguistics Forum 39*. M. Chalasani, J. Grocer, and P. Haney, eds. Pp. 213–223. Austin: Texas Linguistics Forum.

―――. 1999. Becoming Cosmetologists: Language Socialization in an African American Beauty College. Los Angeles: University of California. Unpublished dissertation.

―――. 2001. Epistemological Deliberations: Constructing and Contesting Knowledge in Women's Cross-cultural Hair Testimonies. In *EnGendering Rationalities*. N. Tuana and S. Morgen, eds. Pp. 335–359. Albany: SUNY Press.

―――. 2002. The Natives Are Gazing and Talking Back: Reviewing the Problematics of Positionality, Voice, and Accountability Among "Native" Anthropologists. *American Anthropologist* 104(3): 791–804.

―――. 2003a. Black/"Urban" Standup Comedy: A Performance by Brandon Bowlin. *Theatre Journal* 55(3): 539–541 (October).

―――. 2003b. "Ladies Are Seen, Not Heard": Language Socialization in a Southern African American Cosmetology School. *Anthropology and Education Quarterly* 34(3): 277–299.

―――. 2004. Remembering Chrissy: enGendering Knowledge, Difference, and Power in Women's Hair Care Narratives. *Transforming Anthropology* 11(2): 30–42.

―――. Forthcoming. *BTW, How Do YOU Wear Your Hair?: Establishing Racial Identity, Consciousness, and Community in an African American Listserv Group*. Computer-mediated Conversation. S. Herring, ed. Cresskill, NJ: Hampton Press.

Jacoby, Sally. 1998. Science as Performance: Socializing Scientific Discourse Through the Conference Talk Rehearsal. Los Angeles: University of California. Unpublished dissertation.

Jacoby, Sally, and Patrick Gonzales. 1991. The Constitution of Expert-novice in Scientific Discourse. *Issues in Applied Linguistics* 2(2): 149–182.

James, Allison, Jenny Hockey, and Andrew Dawson. 1997. *After Writing Culture: Epistemology and Praxis in Contemporary Anthropology*. London: Routledge.

Johnstone, Barbara. 1997. Southern Speech and Self-expression in an African American Woman's Story. In *Language Variety in the South Revisited*. C. Bernstein, T. Nunnally, R. Sabino, eds. Pp. 87–97. Tuscaloosa: University of Alabama Press.

Jones, Charisse, and Kumea Shorter-Gooden. 2003. *Shifting: The Double Lives of Black Women in America*. New York: HarperCollins.

Jones, Delmos J. 1970. Toward a Native Anthropology. *Human Organization* 29:251–259.

Jones, Linda L. 2003. *Nappyisms: Affirmations for Nappy-headed People and Wannabes!* Dallas, TX: Manelock Communications.

Jones, Lisa. 1994. *Bulletproof Diva: Tales of Race, Sex and Hair*. New York: Doubleday.

Kaplan, Caren. 1996. *Questions of Travel: Postmodern Discourses of Displacement*. Durham, NC: Duke University Press.

Kashoki, Mubanga E. 1982. Indigenous Scholarship in African Universities: The Human Factor. In *Indigenous Anthropology in Non-Western Countries: Proceedings of a Burg Wartenstein Symposium*. H. Fahim, ed. Pp. 35–51. Durham, NC: Carolina Academic Press.

Kendall, Shari, and Deborah Tannen. 1997. Gender and Language in the Workplace. In *Gender and Discourse*. R. Wodak, ed. Pp. 81–105. London: Sage.

Kennedy, Randall. 2002. *Nigger: The Strange Career of a Troublesome Word*. New York: Pantheon.

Kenyatta, Jomo. 1965 [1959]. *Facing Mount Kenya: The Tribal Life of the Gikuyu*. New York: Vintage Books.

Kirshenblatt-Gimblett, Barbara. 1996. The Electronic Vernacular. In *Connected: Engagements with Media*. G. Marcus, ed. Pp. 21–65. Chicago: University of Chicago Press.

Kochman, Thomas, ed. 1972. *Rappin' and Stylin' Out: Communication in Urban Black America*. Urbana: University of Illinois Press.

Kochman, Thomas. 1981. *Black and White Styles in Conflict*. Chicago: University of Chicago Press.

Kolko, Beth, Lisa Nakamura, and Gilbert Rodman. 2000. *Race in Cyberspace*. London: Routledge.

Kollock, Peter, and Mark Smith. 1996. Managing the Virtual Commons: Cooperation and Conflict in Computer Communities. In *Computer-mediated Communication: Linguistic, Social and Cross-cultural Perspectives*. S. Herring, ed. Pp. 109–128. Philadelphia: John Benjamins.

Kondo, Dorinne K. 1986. Dissolution and Reconstitution of the Self: Implications for Anthropological Epistemology. *Cultural Anthropology* 1:74–96.

———. 1990. *Crafting Selves: Power, Gender and Discourses of Identity in a Japanese Workplace*. Chicago: University of Chicago Press.

———. 1997. *About Face: Performing Race in Fashion and Theater*. New York: Routledge.

Korenman, Joan, and Nancy Wyatt. 1996. Group Dynamics in an E-Mail Forum. In *Computer-mediated Communication: Linguistic, Social and Cross-cultural Perspectives*. S. Herring, ed. Pp. 225–242. Philadelphia: John Benjamins.

Kostarelos, Frances. 1995. *Feeling the Spirit: Faith and Hope in an Evangelical Black Storefront Church*. Columbia: University of South Carolina Press.

Kotthoff, Helga. 2000. Gender and Joking: On the Complexities of Women's Image Politics in Humorous Narratives. *Journal of Pragmatics* 32:55–80.

Kroskrity, Paul. 1993. *Language, History and Identity: Ethnolinguistic Studies of the Arizona Tewa*. Tucson: University of Arizona Press.

———. 2000a. Identity. *Journal of Linguistic Anthropology* 9(1–2): 111–114.

———, ed. 2000b. *Regimes of Language: Ideologies, Politics, and Identities*. Santa Fe, NM: School of American Research Press.

Kulick, Don, and Margaret Willson, eds. 1995. *Taboo: Sex, Identity, and Erotic Subjectivity in Anthropological Fieldwork*. London: Routledge.

Kumar, Nita. 1992. *Friends, Brothers, and Informants: Fieldwork Memoirs of Banaras*. Berkeley: University of California Press.

Labov, William. 1998. Co-existent Systems in African American Vernacular English. In *African American English: Structure, History, and Use*. S. Mufwene, J. Rickford, G. Bailey, and J. Baugh, eds. Pp. 110–53. London: Routledge.

Lake, Obiagele. 2003. *Blue Veins and Kinky Hair: Naming and Color Consciousness in African America*. New York: Praeger.

Lakoff, Robin. 1975. *Language and Woman's Place*. New York: Harper & Row. (Reprinted in 1989).

———. 2004. *Language and Woman's Place; Text and Commentaries*. M. Bucholtz, ed. Oxford: Oxford University Press.

Lanehart, Sonja L. 2002. *Sista Speak! Black Women Kinfolk Talk About Language and Literacy*. Austin: University of Texas Press.

Lave, Jean, and Etienne Wenger. 1991. *Situated Learning: Legitimate Peripheral Partici-pation.* Cambridge: Cambridge University Press.

Lawrence, Martin. 1994. *You So Crazy.* HBO Studios. (November 9): 84 minutes.

Lemelle, Sidney, and Robin Kelley. 1994. *Imagining Home: Class, Culture, and Nationalism in the African Diaspora.* London: Verso.

Lerner, Gene H. 1996. On The "Semi-permeable" Character of Grammatical Units in Conversation: Conditional Entry into the Turn Space of Another Speaker. In *Inter-action and Grammar.* E. Ochs, E. Schegloff, and S.A. Thompson, eds. Pp. 238–276. Cambridge: Cambridge University Press.

Levine, Lawrence W. 1977. Black Laughter. In *Black Culture and Black Consciousness.* Pp. 298–366. London: Oxford University Press.

Lewin, Ellen, and William L. Leap, eds. 1996. *Out in the Field: Reflections of Lesbian and Gay Anthropologists.* Urbana: University of Illinois Press.

Leyden, Liz. 1998. N.Y. Teacher Runs into a Racial Divide. *Washington Post* (December 3): A3.

Limon, José. 1991. Representation, Ethnicity, and Precursory Ethnography: Notes of a Native Anthropologist. In *Recapturing Anthropology: Working in the Present.* R. Fox, ed. Pp. 115–135. Santa Fe, NM: School of American Research Press.

Litt, Jacquelyn S. 2000. *Medicalized Motherhood: Perspectives from the Lives of African-American and Jewish Women.* New Brunswick, NJ: Rutgers University Press.

Lock, Margaret. 1993. Cultivating the Body: Anthropology and Epistemologies of Bodily Practice and Knowledge. *Annual Review of Anthropology* 22:133–155.

Lommel, Cookie. 1993. *Madame C. J. Walker: Entrepreneur.* Los Angeles: Melrose Square.

Lorde, Audre. 1981. The Master's Tools Will Never Dismantle the Master's House. In *This Bridge Called My Back: Writings by Radical Women of Color.* C. Moraga and G. Anzaldúa, eds. Pp. 98–101. Watertown, MA: Persephone Press.

Mahon, Maureen E. 2000. The Visible Evidence of Cultural Producers. *Annual Review of Anthropology* 29:467–492.

Majors, Yolanda. 2001. Passing Mirrors: Subjectivity in a Mid-Western Hair Salon. *Anthropology and Education Quarterly* 32(1): 116–130.

———. 2003. Shoptalk: Teaching and Learning in an African American Hair Salon. *Mind, Culture and Activity* 10(4): 289–310.

———. 2004. "I Wasn't Scared of Them, They Were Scared of Me": Constructions of Self/Other in a Midwestern Hair Salon. *Anthropology and Education Quarterly* 35(2): 167–188.

Marberry, Craig. 2005. *Cuttin' Up: Wit and Wisdom from Black Barber Shops.* New York: Doubleday.

Marcus, George E. 1995. Ethnography in/of the World System: The Emergence of Multi-sited Ethnography. *Annual Review of Anthropology* 24:95–117.

———, ed. 1996. *Connected: Engagements with Media.* Chicago: University of Chicago Press.

———. 1998. *Ethnography Through Thick and Thin.* Princeton, NJ: Princeton University Press.

Marcus, George E., and Michael Fischer. 1986. *Anthropology as Cultural Critique: An Experimental Moment in the Human Sciences.* Chicago: University of Chicago Press.

Martin, Biddy, and Chandra T. Mohanty. 1986. Feminist Politics: What's Home Got to Do with It? In *Feminist Studies/Critical Studies.* T. de Lauretis, ed. Pp. 191–211. Bloomington: Indiana University Press.

Mastalia, Francesco, Alfonse Pagano, and Alice Walker. 1999. *Dreads.* New York: Workman.

McCracken, Grant. 1995. *Big Hair: A Journey into the Transformation of Self.* New York: Overlook Press.

McElhinny, Bonnie. 1995. Challenging Hegemonic Masculinities: Female and Male Police Officers Handling Domestic Violence. In *Gender Articulated: Language and the Socially Constructed Self.* K. Hall and M. Bucholtz, eds. Pp. 217–244. New York: Routledge.

McGee, Gloria, and Leola Johnson, with Peter Bell. 1985. *Beautiful and Recovering.* Center City, MN: Hazeldon Foundation.

McIlvenny, Paul. 1996. Popular Public Discourse at Speakers' Corner: Negotiating Cultural Identities in Interaction. *Discourse and Society* 7(1): 7–37.

Medicine, Beatrice. 2001. *Learning to Be an Anthropologist and Remaining "Native."* Chicago: University of Illinois Press.

Meehan, Eugene. 1981. *Reasoned Argument in Social Science: Linking Research to Policy.* Westport, CN: Greenwood Press.

Mendoza-Denton, Norma. 1996. "Muy Macha": Gender and Ideology in Gang Girls' Discourse About Makeup. *Ethnos* 6(91/92): 47–63.

———. 1999. Fighting Words: Latina Girls, Gangs, and Language Attitudes. In *Speaking Chicana: Voice, Power, and Identity.* D. L. Galindo and M. D. Gonzalez, eds. Pp. 39–56. Tucson: University of Arizona Press.

Mercer, Kobena. 1994. Black Hair/Style Politics. In *Welcome to the Jungle: New Positions in Black Cultural Studies.* Pp. 97–138. Cambridge, MA: MIT Press.

Mertz, Elizabeth. 1992. Linguistic Ideology and Praxis in U.S. Law School Classrooms. *Pragmatics* 2(3): 325–334.

Messerschmidt, Donald. 1981a. On Anthropology "at Home". In *Anthropologists at Home in North America: Methods and Issues in the Study of One's Own Society.* Pp. 1–14. Cambridge: Cambridge University Press.

———, ed. 1981b. *Anthropologists at Home in North America: Methods and Issues in the Study of One's Own Society.* Cambridge: Cambridge University Press.

Mihesauh, Devon A., ed. 1988. *Natives and Academics: Researching and Writing About American Indians.* Lincoln: University of Nebraska Press.

Mills, Sara. 1994. Knowledge, Gender, and Empire. In *Writing Women and Space: Colonial and Postcolonial Geographies.* A. Blunt and G. Rose, eds. Pp. 29–53. London: Guilford Press.

Minh-ha, Trinh T. 1989. *Women, Native, Other.* Bloomington: Indiana University Press.

———. 1990. Critical Reflections. *Artforum* 28(10): 132 (2 pages).

Mitchell-Kernan, Claudia. 1971. *Language Behavior in a Black Urban Community.* Monograph, Language Behavior Lab Oratory, No. 2. University California, Berkeley.

———. 1972. Signifying, Loud Talking, and Marking. In *Rappin' and Stylin' Out: Communication in Black America.* T. Kochman, ed. Pp. 315–335. Chicago: University of Illinois Press.

———. 1973. Signifying. In *Mother Wit from the Laughing Barrel.* A. Dundes, ed. Pp. 310–328. New York: Garland.

Mohanty, S. P. 1989. *Us and Them.* New Formations 8:55–80.

Moore, Henrietta L. 1994. *A Passion for Difference.* Bloomington: Indiana University Press.

Morgan, Marcyliena. 1991. Indirectness and Interpretation in African American Women's Discourse. *Pragmatics* 1(4): 421–451.

———. 1993. The Africanness of Counterlanguage Among Afro-Americans. In *Africanisms in Afro-American Language Varieties.* S. Mufwene, ed. Pp. 423–435. Athens: University of Georgia Press.

———. 1994a. No Woman No Cry: The Linguistic Representation of African American

Women. In *Cultural Performances: Proceedings of the Third Berkeley Women and Language Conference*. M. Bucholtz, A. C. Liang, L. Sutton, and C. Hines, eds. Pp. 525–541. Berkeley: Berkeley Women and Language Group.

———. 1994b. The African American Speech Community: Reality and Sociolinguistics. In *The Social Construction of Reality in Creole Situations*. M. Morgan, ed. Pp. 121–150. Los Angeles: Center for African American Studies.

———. 1995. *Just to Have Something: Camouflaged Narratives of African American Life*. Unpublished manuscript. UCLA.

———. 1996a. Conversational Signifying: Grammar and Indirectness Among African American Women. In *Interaction and Grammar*. E. Ochs, E. Schegloff, and S. Thompson, eds. Pp. 405–434. Cambridge: Cambridge University Press.

———. 1996b. Redefining Language in the Inner City: Adolescents, Media and Urban Space. In *Proceedings of the 4ᵗʰ Annual Symposium About Language and Society-Austin*. A. Chu, A-M. Guerra, and C. Tetreault, eds. Pp. 13–25. Austin: University of Texas, Department of Linguistics.

———. 1998. More Than a Mood or an Attitude: Discourse and Verbal Genres in African American Culture. In *African American English: Structure, History, and Use*. S. Mufwene, J. Rickford, G. Bailey, and J. Baugh, eds. Pp. 251–281. London: Routledge.

———. 1999. "No Woman No Cry": Claiming African American Women's Place. In *Reinventing Identities: Category to Practice in Language and Gender*. M. Bucholtz, A. C. Liang, L. A. Sutton, eds. Pp. 27–45. Oxford: Oxford University Press.

———. 2002. *Language, Discourse, and Power in African American Culture*. Cambridge: Cambridge University Press.

———. 2004. "I'm Every Woman": Black Women's (Dis)placement in Women's Language Study. In *Language and Woman's Place: Text and Commentaries*. R. T. Lakoff, M. Bucholtz, eds. Pp. 252–259. Oxford: Oxford University Press.

Morley, David, and Kevin Robins, eds. 1995. *Spaces of Identity: Global Media, Electronic Landscapes, and Cultural Boundaries*. London: Routledge.

Morrison, Toni. 1995. *The Nobel Lecture in Literature: 1993*. New York: Knopf.

———. 2000 [1970]. *The Bluest Eye*. New York: Knopf.

Motzafi-Haller, Pnina. 1997. Writing Birthright: On Native Anthropologists and the Politics of Representation. In *Auto/Ethnography: Rewriting the Self and the Social*. D. Reed-Danahay, ed. Pp. 195–222. Oxford: Berg.

Mufwene, Salikoko. 1993. Investigating Gullah: Difficulties in Ensuring "Authenticity." In *Language Variation in North American English: Research and Teaching*. A. Glowka and D. Lance, eds. Pp. 178–190. New York: Modern Language Association of America.

Myerhoff, Barbara, and Jay Ruby. 1982. Introduction. In *A Crack in the Mirror*. J. Ruby, ed. Pp. 1–35. Philadelphia: University of Pennsylvania Press.

Myers, William H. 1991. The Hermeneutical Dilemma of the African American Biblical Student. In *Stony the Road We Trod: African American Biblical Interpretations*. C. H. Felder, ed. Pp. 40–56. Minneapolis: Fortress Press.

Myers-Scotton, Carol, ed. 1998. *Codes and Consequences: Choosing Linguistic Variables*. Oxford: Oxford University Press.

Nakhleh, Khalil. 1979. On Being a Native Anthropologist. In *The Politics of Anthropology: From Colonialism and Sexism to the View from Below*. G. Huizer and B. Mannheim, eds. Pp. 343–352. The Hague: Mouton.

Narayan, Kirin. 1993. How Native Is a "Native" Anthropologist? *American Anthropologist* 95:671–685.

———. 1995. Participant Observation. In *Women Writing Culture*. R. Behar and D. A. Gordon, eds. Pp. 33–48. Berkeley: University of California Press.

168

Naylor, Gloria. 1988. *Mama Day.* New York: Vintage.

Nelson, Linda Williamson. 1990. Code-switching in the Oral Life Narratives of African American Women: Challenges to Linguistic Hegemony. *Journal of Education* 172(3): 142–55.

———. 1996. Hands in the Chit'lins: Notes on Native Anthropological Research Among African American Women. In *Unrelated Kin: Race and Gender in Women's Personal Narratives.* G. Etter-Lewis and M. Foster, eds. Pp. 183–199. London: Routledge.

Nelson, Hart M., Raytha L. Yokley, and Anne K. Nelsen, eds. 1971. *The Black Church in America.* New York: Basic Books.

Nichols, Patricia C. 1978. "Black Women in the Rural South: Conservative and Innovative." *International Journal of the Sociology of Language* 17: 45–54.

———. 1980. Women in Their Speech Communities. In *Women and Language in Literature and Society.* S. McConnell-Ginet, R. Borker, and N. Furman, eds. Pp. 140–149. New York: Praeger.

———. 1983. Linguistic Options and Choices for Black Women in the Rural South. In *Language, Gender, and Society.* B. Thorne, C. Kramerae, and N. Henley, eds. Pp. 54–68. Rowley, MA: Newbury House.

Obeyesekere, Gananath. 1981. *Medusa's Hair: An Essay on Personal Symbols and Religious Experience.* Chicago: University of Chicago Press.

Ochs, Elinor. 1992. Indexing Gender. In *Rethinking Context: Language as an Interactive Phenomenon.* A. Duranti and C. Goodwin, eds. Pp. 336–358. Cambridge: Cambridge University Press.

———. 1994. Stories That Step into the Future. In *Perspectives on Register: Situating Register Variation Within Sociolinguistics.* D. Biber and E. Finegan, eds. Pp. 106–135. Oxford: Oxford University Press.

Ochs, Elinor, and Lisa Capps. 1996. Narrating the Self. *Annual Review of Anthropology* 25:19–43.

Ochs, Elinor, and Bambi B. Schieffelin. 1984. Language Acquisition and Socialization: Three Developmental Stories. In *Culture Theory: Essays on Mind, Self, and Emotion.* R. Shweder and R. LeVine, eds. Pp. 276–320. New York: Cambridge University Press.

Ochs, Elinor, and Carolyn Taylor. 1995. The "Father Knows Best Dynamic" in Dinnertime Narratives. In *Gender Articulated: Language and the Socially Constructed Self.* K. Hall and M. Bucholtz, eds. Pp. 97–120. New York: Routledge.

Ochs, Elinor, Emanuel Schegloff, and Sandra Thompson, eds. 1996. *Interaction and Grammar.* Cambridge: Cambridge University Press.

Ohnuki-Tierney, Emiko. 1984a. *Illness and Culture in Contemporary Japan: An Anthropological View.* Cambridge: Cambridge University Press.

———. 1984b. "Native" Anthropologists. *American Ethnologist* 11:584–586.

Okely, Judith. 1996. *Own or Other Culture.* London: Routledge.

Okely, Judith, and Helen Callaway, eds. 1992. *Anthropology and Autobiography.* London: Routledge.

Olwig, Karen Fog. 1997. Cultural Sites: Sustaining Home in a Deterritorialized World. In *Siting Culture: The Shifting Anthropological Object.* K. Olwig and K. Hastrup, eds. Pp. 17–38. London: Routledge.

Ong, Aihwa. 1995. Women Out of China: Traveling Tales and Traveling Theories in Postcolonial Feminism. In *Women Writing Culture.* R. Behar and D. Gordon, eds. Pp. 350–372. Berkeley: University of California Press.

Page, Helán E. 1988. Dialogic Principles of Interactive Learning in the Ethnographic Relationship. *Journal of Anthropological Research* 44(2): 163–181.

Paredes, Américo. 1984. On Ethnographic Work Among Minority Groups. In *New*

Directions in Chicano Scholarship. R. Romo and R. Paredes, eds. Pp. 1–32. Santa Barbara, CA: University of California Center for Chicano Studies.

Passaro, Joanne. 1997. "You Can't Take the Subway to the Field!": "Village" Epistemologies in the Global Village. In *Anthropological Locations: Boundaries and Grounds of a Field Science.* A. Gupta and J. Ferguson, eds. Pp. 147–162. Los Angeles: University of California Press.

Peiss, Kathy Lee. 1998. *Hope in a Jar: The Making of America's Beauty Culture.* New York: Metropolitan.

Peters, Michael, and Colin Lankshear. 1996. Postmodern Counternarratives. In *Counternarratives: Cultural Studies and Critical Pedagogies in Postmodern Spaces.* H. Giroux, C. Lankshear, P. McLaren, and M. Peters, eds. Pp. 1–39. New York: Routledge.

Pomerantz, Anita. 1975. Second Assessments: A Study of Some Features of Agreements/Disagreements. Irvine: University of California. Unpublished dissertation.

Powdermaker, Hortense. 1966. *Stranger and Friend: The Way of an Anthropologist.* New York: W.W. Norton.

Powlis, LaVerne. 1988. *Beauty from the Inside Out: A Guide for Black Women.* New York: Doubleday.

Queens of Comedy. 2003. Paramount Studios. (January 7): 79 minutes.

Rabinow, Paul. 1977. *Reflections on Fieldwork in Morocco.* Berkeley: University of California Press.

Rheingold, Howard. 1993. *The Virtual Community: Homesteading on the Electronic Frontier.* New York: HarperPerennial.

Rich, Adrienne. 1995 [1979]. *On Lies, Secrets and Silence: Selected Prose 1966–1978.* New York: W.W. Norton.

Rickford, John R. 1986. Riddling and Lying: Participation and Performance. In *The Fergusonian Impact.* Vol. 2. J. Fishman, ed. Pp. 89–106. New York: Mouton de Gruyter.

———. 1997. Commentary: Suite for Ebony and Phonics. *Discover* 18(12): 82–87.

———. 1999. The Ebonics Controversy in My Backyard: A Sociolinguist's Experiences and Reflections. *Journal of Sociolinguistics* 3(2): 267–275.

Rock, Chris. 1996. *Bring the Pain.* Uni/Dream Works Records.

Rogers, Mary F. 1999. *Barbie Culture.* London: Sage.

Rooks, Noliwe. 1996. *Hair Raising: Beauty, Culture, and African American Women.* New Jersey: Rutgers University Press.

Rosaldo, Michelle Z. 1982. The Things We Do with Words: Ilongot Speech Acts and Speech Act Theory in Philosophy. *Language in Society* 11:203–235.

Rosaldo, Renato. 1986. When Natives Talk Back: Chicano Anthropology Since the Late Sixties. In *The Renato Rosaldo Lectures, 1985.* Pp. 3–20. Tucson, AZ: Mexican-American Studies and Research Center.

———. 1987. Politics, Patriarchs, and Laughter. *Cultural Critique* 6:65–86.

———. 1989. *Culture and Truth: The Remaking of Social Analysis.* Boston: Beacon Press.

———. 1991. Fables of the Fallen Guy. In *Criticism in the Borderlands: Studies in Chicano Literature, Culture, and Ideology.* H. Calderón and J.D. Saldívar, eds. Pp. 84–93. Durham, NC: Duke University Press.

Rotella, Carlo. 2003. *Cut Time: An Education at the Fights.* New York: Houghton Mifflin.

Sacks, Harvey. 1992a. *Lectures on Conversation.* Vol. 1. Cambridge, MA: Blackwell.

———. 1992b. *Lectures on Conversation.* Vol. 2. Cambridge, MA: Blackwell.

Said, Edward. 1989. Representing the Colonized: Anthropology's Interlocutors. *Critical Inquiry* 15:205–225.

Sandoval, Chela. 1991. U.S. Third World Feminism: The Theory and Method of Oppositional Consciousness in the Postmodern World. *Genders* 10:1–24.

Schieffelin, Bambi B. 1990. *The Give and Take of Everyday Life: Language Socialization of Kaluli Children.* Cambridge: Cambridge University Press.

Schieffelin, Bambi B., Kathryn A. Woolard, and Paul V. Kroskrity, eds. 1998. *Language Ideologies: Practice and Theory.* Oxford: Oxford University Press.

Scranton, Philip. 2000. *Beauty and Business: Commerce, Gender, and Culture in Modern America.* New York: Routledge.

Searle, John. 1975. Indirect Speech Acts. In *Syntax and Semantics.* Vol. 3. P. Cole and J. L. Morgan, eds. Pp. 59–82. New York: Academic Press.

―――. 1983. *Intentionality: An Essay in the Philosophy of Mind.* Cambridge: Cambridge University Press.

Severn, Bill. 1971. *The Long and Short of It: Five Thousand Years of Fun and Fury Over Hair.* New York: David McKay Company, Inc.

Shahrani, M. Nazif. 1994. Honored Guest and Marginal Man: Long-term Field Research and Predicaments of a Native Anthropologist. In *Others Knowing Others: Perspectives on Ethnographic Careers.* D. Fowler and D. Hardesty, eds. Pp. 15–67. London: Smithsonian Institution Press.

Shoaps, Robin Ann. 2002. "Pray Earnestly": The Textual Construction of Personal Involve-ment in Pentecostal Prayer and Song. *Journal of Linguistic Anthropology* 12(1): 34–71.

Simon, Diane. 2000. *Hair: Public, Political, Extremely Personal.* New York: St. Martin's Press.

Sinbad. 1990. *Brain Damaged.* Polygram Records (July 24).

Sinclair, Simon. 1997. *Making Doctors: An Institutional Apprenticeship.* Oxford: Berg.

Smith, Frances Lee. 1993. The Pulpit and Woman's Place: Gender and the Framing of the "Exegetical Self" in Sermon Performances. In *Framing in Discourse.* D. Tannen, ed. Pp. 146–175. Oxford: Oxford University Press.

Smith, Jessie Carney. 1991. Annie Turnbo Malone. In *Notable Black American Women.* J. C. Smith, ed. Pp. 724–726. Farmington Hills, MI: Thomson Gale.

Smith, Linda Tuhiwai. 1999. *Decolonizing Methodologies: Research and Indigenous Peoples.* London: Zed.

Smitherman, Geneva. 1977. *Talkin and Testifyin: The Language of Black America.* Boston: Houghton Mifflin.

―――. 1994. *Black Talk: Words and Phrases from the Hood to the Amen Corner.* New York: Houghton Mifflin.

Srinivas, M. N., ed. 1966. Some Thoughts on the Study of One's Own Society. In *Social Change in Modern India.* Pp. 147–163. Berkeley: University of California.

―――. 1979. The Fieldworker and the Field: A Village in Karnataka. In *The Field-worker and the Field: Problems and Challenges in Sociological Investigation.* M. Srinivas, A. M. Shaw, E. A. Ramaswamy, eds. Pp. 19–28. Oxford: Oxford University Press.

Stanback, Marsha Houston. 1985. Language and Black Woman's Place: Evidence from the Black Middle Class. In *For Alma Mater: Theory and Practice in Feminist Scholarship.* P. A. Treichler, C. Kramarae, and B. Stafford, eds. Pp. 177–193. Chicago: University of Illinois Press.

Stotter, Ruth. 1994. *About Story: Writings on Stories and Storytelling: 1980–1994.* Stinston Beach, CA: Stotter Press.

Sunaoshi, Yukako. 1994. Mild Directives Work Effectively: Japanese Women in Command. In *Cultural Performances: Proceedings of the Third Berkeley Women and Language Conference.* M. Bucholtz, A. C. Liang, L. A. Sutton, and C. Hines, eds. Pp. 678–690. Berkeley: Berkeley Women and Language Group.

Synnott, Anthony. 1993. *The Body Social: Symbolism, Self and Society.* London: Routledge.

Talbot, Mary. 1995. A Synthetic Sisterhood: False Friends in a Teenage Magazine. In *Gender Articulated. Language and the Socially Constructed Self.* K. Hall and M. Bucholtz, eds. Pp. 143–165. London: Routledge.

Tannen, Deborah. 1994. The Sex-class-linked Framing of Talk at Work. In *Cultural Performances: Proceedings of the Third Berkeley Women and Language Conference.* M. Bucholtz, A. Liang, L. A. Sutton, and C. Caitlin Hines, eds. Pp. 712–728. Berkeley: Berkeley Women and Language Group.

———. 1995. *Gender and Discourse.* Oxford: Oxford University Press.

Taylor, Clarence. 1994. *The Black Churches of Brooklyn.* New York: Columbia University Press.

Tedlock, Dennis. 1991. From Participant Observation to the Observation of Participation: The Emergence of Narrative Ethnography. *Journal of Anthropological Research* 47(1): 69–94.

Thorne, Barrie, and Nancy Henley, eds. 1975. *Language and Sex: Difference and Dominance.* Rowley, MA: Newbury House.

Todd, Alexandra Dundas, and Sue Fisher. 1993. *The Social Organization of Doctor-patient Communication.* Norwood, NJ: Ablex Publishing Corporation.

Trouillot, Michel-Rolph. 1991. Anthropology and the Savage Slot: The Poetics and Politics of Otherness. In *Recapturing Anthropology: Working in the Present.* R. Fox, ed. Pp. 17–44. Santa Fe: School of American Research Press.

Troutman, Denise. 1999. Breaking Mythical Bonds: African American Women's Language. In *The Workings of Language: From Prescriptions to Perspectives.* R. S. Wheeler, ed. Pp. 217–232. Westport, CT: Praeger.

———. 2001. African American Women: Talking That Talk. In *Sociocultural and Historical Contexts of African American English.* S. Lanehart, ed. Pp. 211–237. Philadelphia: John Benjamins.

———. Forthcoming. "And Aren't I a Woman?": African American Women and Language. *Discourse and Society.*

Uchida, Aki. 1992. When "Difference" is "Dominance": A Critique of the "Anti-Power-Based" Cultural Approach to Sex Differences. *Language in Society* 21:547–568.

Ulin, Robert C. 1991. Critical Anthropology Twenty Years Later: Modernism and Postmodernism in Anthropology. *Critique of Anthropology* 11(1): 63–89.

Visweswaran, Kamala. 1994. *Fictions of Feminist Ethnography.* Minneapolis: University of Minnesota Press.

Wacquant, LoWc. 2004. *Body and Soul: Notebooks of an Apprentice Boxer.* Oxford: Oxford University Press.

Waitzkin, Howard. 1985. Information Giving in Medical Care. *Journal of Health and Social Behavior* 26:81–101.

Washburn, Wilcomb E. 1998. *Against the Anthropological Grain.* Somerset, NJ: Transaction.

Watkins, Mel. 1994. *On the Real Side: Laughing, Lying, and Signifying—The Underground Tradition of African American Humor That Transformed American Culture, from Slavery to Richard Pryor.* New York: Simon and Schuster.

———, ed. 2002. *African American Humor: The Best Black Comedy from Slavery to Today.* Chicago: Lawrence Hill.

Weekes, Debbie. 1997. Shades of Blackness: Young Black Female Constructions of Beauty. In *Black British Feminism.* H. S. Mirza, ed. Pp. 113–126. London: Routledge.

Weisenfeld, Alan, and Herbert Weis. 1979. Hairdressers and Helping: Influencing the Behavior of Informal Caregivers. *Professional Psychology* 10(6): 786–792.

Wellman, Barry, and Milena Gulia. 1999. Virtual Communities as Communities: Net Surfers Don't Ride Alone. In *Communities in Cyberspace*. M. A. Smith and P. Kollock, eds. Pp. 195–219. London: Routledge.

Werry, Christopher. 1996. Linguistic and Interactional Features of Internet Relay Chat. In *Computer-mediated Communication: Linguistic, Social and Cross-cultural Perspectives*. S. Herring, ed. Pp. 47–64. Philadelphia: John Benjamins.

West, Candace, and Don H. Zimmerman. 1987. Doing Gender. *Gender and Society* 1:125–151.

Weston, Kath. 1997. The Virtual Anthropologist. In *Anthropological Locations: Boundaries and Grounds of a Field Science*. A. Gupta and J. Ferguson, eds. Pp. 163–184. Los Angeles: University of California Press.

Whitehead, Tony L. 1986. Breakdown, Resolution, and Coherence: The Fieldwork Experiences of a Big, Brown, Pretty-talking Man in a West Indian Community. In *Self, Sex, and Gender in Cross-cultural Fieldwork*. T. Whitehead and M. E. Conaway, eds. Pp. 213–239.

———. 1992. Expressions of Masculinity in a Jamaican Sugartown: Implications for Family Planning Programs. In *Gender Constructs and Social Issues*. T. Whitehead and B. Reid, eds. Pp. 103–141. Chicago: University of Illinois Press.

Williams, Brackette F. 1996. Skinfolk, Not Kinfolk: Comparative Reflections on the Identity of Participant-observation in Two Field Situations. In *Feminist Dilemmas in Fieldwork*. D. Wolf, ed. Pp. 72–95. New York: Westview Press.

Williams, Demetrius K. 2004. *An End to This Strife: The Politics of Gender in African American Churches*. Minneapolis, MN: Augsburg Fortress.

Williams, Elsie A. 1995. Mabley's Persona. In *The Humor of Jackie Moms Mabley: An African American Comedic Tradition*. Pp. 69–117. New York: Garland.

Williams, John A., and Dennis A. Williams. 1993. *If I Stop, I'll Die: The Comedy and Tragedy of Richard Pryor*. New York: Thunder's Mouth Press.

Willis, William S. Jr. 1999 [1969]. Skeletons in the Anthropological Closet. In *Reinventing Anthropology*. D. Hymes, ed. Pp. 121–152. Ann Arbor: University of Michigan Press.

Woof, Judith, and Robyn Wiegman, eds. 1995. *Who Can Speak? Authority and Critical Identity*. Chicago: University of Illinois Press.

Wright, R. L. 1976. Language Standards and Communicative Style in the Black Church. Austin: University of Texas. Unpublished dissertation.

Wynter, Leon E. 1993. Braided Hair Collides with Business Norms. *Wall Street Journal* (May 3): B1.

Young, Katherine. 1993. *Bodylore*. Knoxville: The University of Tennessee Press.

Zavella, Patricia. 1996. Feminist Insider Dilemmas: Constructing Ethnic Identity with Chicana Informants. In *Feminist Dilemmas in Fieldwork*. D. Wolf, ed. Pp 138–159. New York: Westview Press.

Zentella, Ana Celia. 1997. *Growing Up Bilingual*. Oxford: Blackwell.

Zook, Krystal Brent. 1995. *Straight Expectations: Black Women and the Hair Product That Seduced and Betrayed*. Los Angeles Weekly (March 10).

INDEX

accountability, 14, 67, 131, 140, 141, 143, 144
acronyms, 100
advertisements, 3
aesthetics, 12, 18, 20, 21, 27
  hair, 17
  and spiritual becomings, 50
  stand-up comedy and, 74, 75, 76, 77, 87, 88
African American Vernacular English (AAVE), 8, 97, 135, 136, 142, 145
African diaspora, 10, 29, 31, 40, 44, 136
AFROAM-L electronic discussion list debate, 14, 89–103, 109, 135–136
  acronyms and, 100
  data, 91–93
  discourse strategies and, 94–95
  hair is not just hair and, 123–126
  indirectness on, 95–97
  in-group terms and, 100, 101
  men and, 100–103
  signature files, 100
  signifying and, 97–100
Afros, 73–74, 99

agency, 18, 19, 20, 30, 35, 61
agreement expletives, 88
agreement markers, 112
alignment, 14, 27, 31, 39–40, 68, 100, 107–108, 126
American Mainstream English, 97
anointing with oil, 52–53, 61
anthropologists, 8, 10, 14, 15, 132–133
  linguistic, 11, 142
  native, 10, 14, 130, 133–135, 137, 138, 141, 143, 145, 146
  reflexive, 143
  See also ethnographers
anthropology, 5, 9, 15, 17, 131, 136
  native, 139, 140, 144–145
  reflexive, 131–132, 143
  transitions in, 145
  See also ethnography
anticipatory completions, 38, 74, 76–77
artificial hair, 73, 74, 77–80
authenticity, 4, 14, 143
  of hair, 73, 74, 77
  importance of language for, 138
  Internet debate and, 89, 95, 101

LaVergne, TN USA
14 October 2010
200836LV00002B/18/A

9 780195 304169